USING PERFORMANCE MEASUREMENT IN LOCAL GOVERNMENT
A Guide to Improving Decisions, Performance, and Accountability

With case examples contributed by 23 government officials
from across the country

Paul D. Epstein

Van Nostrand Reinhold/Council on Municipal Performance Series

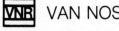 VAN NOSTRAND REINHOLD COMPANY

Copyright © 1984 by Van Nostrand Reinhold Company Inc.

Library of Congress Catalog Card Number: 84-3522
ISBN: 0-442-21603-3

Manufactured in the United States of America

Published by Van Nostrand Reinhold Company Inc.
135 West 50th Street
New York, New York 10020

Van Nostrand Reinhold Company Limited
Molly Millars Lane
Wokingham, Berkshire RG11 2PY, England

Van Nostrand Reinhold
480 Latrobe Street
Melbourne, Victoria 3000, Australia

Macmillan of Canada
Division of Gage Publishing Limited
164 Commander Boulevard
Agincourt, Ontario M1S 3C7, Canada

15 14 13 12 11 10 9 8 7 6 5 4 3 2 1

Library of Congress Cataloging in Publication Data

Epstein, Paul D.
    Using performance measurement in local government.

    Bibliography: p.
    Includes index.
    1. Local officials and employees--United States--
Rating of. 2. Local officials and employees--United
States--Rating of--Case studies. I. Title.
JS363.E67   1984   352'.005142'0973   84-3522
ISBN 0-442-21603-3

To R, H, and Z.

Series Introduction

This book is the first in a new Van Nostrand Reinhold/Council on Municipal Performance Series. We are pleased to have Paul D. Epstein as the first author in this series. His many years of experience managing performance measurement and productivity improvement programs for the Cities of New York and Detroit, and assisting local governments across the country while managing research and demonstration projects in municipal performance measurement for the U. S. Department of Housing and Urban Development, make him especially well qualified to lead off the series. Thanks are due to Van Nostrand Reinhold and to the members of the Board of Directors and supporters of the Council on Municipal Performance for their foresight in supporting this important series.

John Tepper Marlin, Series Editor
President
Council on Municipal Performance

Foreword

"Seat of the pants" management is no longer adequate for providing local government services. Severe resource constraints have made it increasingly difficult to provide responsive services and still meet public mandates. This is true not only for big cities but for local governments of all sizes across the country. In San Francisco we have built a large base of performance information on all of our city's services to help us manage our limited resources more effectively and maintain accountability to the public. Performance measurement may be a sophisticated, "modern" approach to public management, but it is rooted in common sense. As the author describes in chapter 1 of this book, "performance measurement techniques . . . allow decision makers to take a look systematically at government services and community conditions without having to be everywhere at once."

Local officials have the right to be skeptical about any book on performance measurement. We don't have time to wade through reams of data on every aspect of our communities, and it is a waste of the taxpayers' money to collect information that serves no useful purpose. Local officials must be able to use performance measurement in a practical way for it to be worth the cost and effort. That is the very practical focus of this book: how to *use* performance measurement. The author presents a variety of principles and techniques to help local officials use performance measurement to improve decision making, service performance, and public accountability. These principles and techniques are brought to life by numerous examples of the innovative use of performance measurement in large and small jurisdictions across the country. I am proud that San Francisco is one of the innovative communities featured in this book.

Our management by objectives (MBO) program is featured in chapter 4 as an example of the use of measurement and objective setting to improve performance. MBO has been a central strategy in our efforts to improve local services despite tax limitations adopted in California, federal budget cuts, and other limitations on local resources. Since we began in 1978, our MBO program has helped improve performance in a wide variety of services and, in some cases, has helped us achieve significant savings and revenue increases. A wide range of performance measures support the objectives of each department, and performance reports provide department managers and me with important information throughout the year. Just as important, we work to keep the objectives and measures relevant to changing conditions, and we have evaluated the MBO process itself and revised it as needed to make a strong program even stronger.

Since the example on our MBO program was written for this book, San Francisco's business community, in cooperation with the city and county, embarked on an important strategic planning effort to strengthen the future stability and vitality of our city. With our MBO program firmly established, we have a mechanism in place to link strategic plans to actionable projects and objectives, and to insure that today's performance improvements contribute to the strength of tomorrow's San Francisco.

When faced with tough decisions, local officials must, to a large extent, rely on their personal experience and common sense to guide their judgment. But one's good judgment or common sense becomes much more reliable when it is guided by pertinent facts about service performance. I am glad that the city has extensive quantitative performance information available on, for example, the cleanliness of our streets and condition of our parks, the response time of our protective services, the unit cost of maintenance activities, and the effectiveness of special mental health and substance abuse programs. And I am fortunate to be aided by managers who can *use* such information to help me understand the expected impact of proposed actions such as budget cuts or the purchase of new equipment. Although our MBO program doesn't necessarily make our job any easier, it does give me added confidence that we're making the best choices when the tough questions must be decided.

An important message of this book is that measurement by itself does not improve performance; any management technique requires skillful use and must be integrated with other strategies to improve operations.

This book is for local officials who want to take action informed by common sense combined with practical and reliable performance information.

DIANNE FEINSTEIN
Mayor
City and County of San Francisco

Acknowledgments

The usefulness of this book has been enhanced by the examples from actual local government experiences contributed by expert practitioners from across the country. Many of them also assisted me by reviewing various drafts and outlines. They are due special thanks. They are:

Libby Anderson, Director of Financial Management, San Diego, California

Cathie Behrend, Coordinator of Management Decentralization, Mayor's Community Assistance Unit, City of New York

Ronald M. Bergmann, Department of General Services, formerly of the Mayor's Community Assistance Unit, City of New York

Neal G. Berlin, City Manager, Iowa City, Iowa

Tom Finnie, Deputy City Manger, Charlotte, North Carolina

James R. Fountain, Jr., Assistant City Manager and former City Auditor, Dallas, Texas

William J. Grannan, Town Selectman, Arlington, Massachusetts

Paul E. Haney, City Councilman, Rochester, New York

Richard L. Hays, Assistant to the Planning Director and former Organization Effectiveness Supervisor, San Diego, California

R. Peter Henschel, Office of the Mayor, San Francisco, California

Marilyn K. James, formerly of the Chief Administrative Office, San Diego County, California

Douglas Lee, Building and Land Regulation Adminstrator, formerly of the City Administrator's Office, Washington, D.C.

Patrick Manion, Assistant to the Mayor, Phoenix, Arizona

Richard G. McGraw, Controller, Genessee County, Michigan

Arthur A. Mendonsa, City Manager, Savannah, Georgia

Serre A. Murphy, New York City Transit Authority, formerly of the Mayor's Community Assistance Unit, City of New York

Harold Nass, Deputy Director, Community Assistance Unit, City of New York

John S. Niles, Former Productivity Improvement Director, Washington, D.C.

Duncan Rose, County Administrator, Seminole County, Florida, formerly of the Office of Management Services, Dallas, Texas

David A. Rubinstein, City Manager, Walker, Michigan, formerly City Manager, Englewood, Ohio
Trudy J. Sopp, Organization Effectiveness Supervisor, San Diego, California
Pam Syfert, Director of Budget and Evaluation, Charlotte, North Carolina
Paul R. Woodie, Assistant City Manager, Dayton, Ohio

In addition, special thanks are due the following local practitioners, consultants, and researchers, who provided valuable reviews of draft chapters and manuscripts, and materials that were drawn upon for parts of the text:

Todd Areson, formerly of the National League of Cities
George Barbour, PMC Associates
Robert E. Baumgardner, Carter Associates
Beverly Beidler, Former City Councilmember, Alexandria, Virginia
J. Peter Braun, Township Manager, Randolph Township, New Jersey
Gerald Brighton, University of Illinois
Carol deProsse, Former City Councilmember, Iowa City, Iowa
Constance Quirk Dow, formerly of the Rhode Island Department of Community Affairs
Peter Gartland, Town Manager, Hanover, New Hampshire
Richard Gollub, formerly of the Urban Institute
David Grossman, Nova Institute
John Hall, United States Fire Administration
Harry Hatry, Urban Institute
Frederick O'R. Hayes, Selkirk Associates
Roger Herman, Former City Manager, Rittman, Ohio
David Knapp, Deputy City Manager, Boulder, Colorado
Fred Knight, International City Management Association
Richard Langendorf, University of Miami
Roland Malan, County Auditor, King County, Washington
John Musial, Wayne State University
Lois Parke, Former County Councilmember, New Castle County, Delaware
Christine Rapking, New Jersey Division of Motor Vehicles
Peter Rousmaniere, Former Vice President, Council on Municipal Performance
Brendan Sexton, Director, Mayor's Office of Operations, City of New York
Paul Steinbrenner, County Administrator, Jackson County, Oregon
Lawrence Susskind, Massachusetts Institute of Technology
John S. Thomas, Booz Allen Hamilton
Dean Vanderbilt, Former Director of Management Services, Dallas, Texas
Dan Whitehurst, Mayor, Fresno, California
Robert Winslow, formerly of the Office of Management Services, Dallas, Texas
Paul Yingst, Energy and Technology Director, St. Petersburg, Florida

I prepared the original manuscript and several revisions while I was a member of the Government Capacity Building Division of HUD's Office of Policy Development and Research. Through her encouragement of in-house research, Former Assistant Secretary for Policy Development and Research Donna E. Shalala (now President of Hunter College in New York City) provided an important impetus for the project which resulted in this book. Alan R. Siegel, Former Division Director, approved and helped shape the project, and, together with Hartley Fitts, current Division Director and Manager of HUD's Capacity Sharing Program, provided support and guidance in the preparation of this book.

Various sections of this book have been tested and refined for instructional purposes in classes, workshops, and seminars across the country. I am thankful to the following people for testing the material or for their assistance in making these instructional uses possible: Professors Carol Lewis and Blue Wooldridge of the University of Connecticut; Dean David Hoover of the University of Hartford; Janet Daily and Dr. F. William Heiss, formerly of the Denver Urban Observatory; Professor Steven Gold of Drake University; Donald Fisk of the U.S. Department of Labor; Professor Arthur Levine, Baruch College of the City University of New York; and Arthur Prager, formerly of the Mayor's Office of the City of New York.

The addition of new material and revisions to many sections of this book, to help make it more timely and complete for publication, were sponsored by the Council on Municipal Performance, John Tepper Marlin, President. I am especially grateful to John for his efforts to help get this book published, and for the honor of it being the first publication in COMP's new series with Van Nostrand Reinhold.

Finally, my special thanks to Mayor Dianne Feinstein of San Francisco for providing an excellent Foreword, and for proving that time spent using performance measurement is valuable even to a busy elected chief executive.

Paul D. Epstein

Contents

List of Examples

Chapter 5

Chapter 6

1
Introduction

"Do more with less" is a phrase which haunts many local officials. They know all too painfully what people mean by "less," but what do the pundits, the politicians, and most importantly, the public mean by "more"? And how do local government officials provide "more" when there always seem to be fewer resources available?

Rising labor, materials, and energy costs; higher pension and insurance costs; and higher interest rates for public borrowing have all reduced the amount of resources each local tax dollar can buy to provide needed public services. On top of that, voters have imposed many state and local tax and spending limitations, rejected numerous bond issues, and said they don't believe they receive adequate value for their tax dollars.*

Many local officials must feel they are in a tightening vise between pressure for better services and reduced ability to pay for them. They know they are not free to spend tax dollars any way they like. There are state and federal mandates to meet, and legal restrictions on the use of certain funds. They may have collective bargaining agreements to fulfill. In many older communities, there is a growing need for expensive capital investments to rebuild streets, bridges, sewers, and other components of the capital infrastructure. These investments leave fewer funds for everyday operating services. In growing communities, development not only brings an increased tax base, it brings a greater infrastructure to maintain and more people in need of basic services.

Can local officials convince a skeptical public that, given inflation and spending constraints, people are getting reasonable value for their tax dollars? Perhaps a more basic question is this: can local officials convince *themselves*? Can they know whether the community is getting a reasonable return in services that meet public needs? Put another way, can local officials find out how well their government's services are being performed? Local officials in a number of communities across the country have learned they *can* find out. They have learned to *measure the performance* of their government's services and have used this information to advantage in a variety of ways, one of which is to improve communications with the public.

---

*For example, Louis Harris found in nationwide surveys that 94 percent of Americans felt "too much money is wasted by an inefficient bureaucracy" and a nearly 2 to 1 majority of Americans felt they receive "negative value" at the local level. See Louis Harris, "Confidence in Government," in *The Bureaucrat,* Spring 1979, pp. 23-27.

Performance measurement is not the only management solution to local problems. Revenue and expenditure forecasting; improved budgeting, accounting, and auditing; and management of risks, pensions, debt, and cash are a few other good practices that can help local officials survive a fiscal squeeze. However, in a needs assessment involving over 2000 local officials from across the country, performance measurement was cited as one of the highest priority financial management needs of local governments. Local officials also cited integration of performance measurement, budgeting, and accounting as a high priority need,* indicating they see performance measurement as an important part of a community's total management system.

The idea of performance measurement in local government has been around for some time, but it is particularly important for the challenge of managing local government in the 1980s.

This book aims to help local officials understand performance measurement. Its main emphasis is on the many ways in which local officials can *use* measurement for the benefit of the government and the community. At the end of most chapters, examples are provided to illustrate uses of performance measurement and communication with the public in actual local government settings, including 19 examples contributed by local officials concerning uses in their communities. Jurisdictions covered in these examples vary in population from about 14,000 to over 7 million. Some of the performance measurement techniques described have been documented for jurisdictions with as few as 6000 people and have probably occurred in even smaller communities. The appendix provides addresses and phone numbers for organizations with experience in fostering measurement and improvement efforts in local governments.

Lengthy lists of performance measures are not provided in this book for any particular service or type of local government. Instead, different types of efficiency, effectiveness, and other measures are described, with some illustrative examples provided in chapter 2. Publications that contain lists of performance measures for various public services are included in the bibliography.

In the remainder of this chapter, questions which might interest local officials regarding performance measurement are discussed. The answers to those questions are the topics covered in the remaining chapters in this book.

What is performance measurement?

Performance measurement is a general term that covers any systematic attempt to learn how responsive a local government's services are to the needs of the community, and to the community's ability to pay. There are a variety of

*National Conference on the Financial Management Needs of Local Government: Final Conference Report, Office of Policy Development and Research, U.S. Department of Housing and Urban Development, June 1978.

measurement techniques such as citizen surveys, work measurement, and trained observers, to name but three. The terminology can be confusing because many terms are used to describe measurement efforts, including effectiveness, efficiency, workload, productivity, cost effectiveness, cost benefit analysis, and program evaluation. The simplest way to think of this topic is by analogy to the private sector: performance measurement is government's way of determining whether it is providing a quality product at a reasonable cost.

Chapter 2 describes a variety of forms of measurement, concentrating on the two most important: effectiveness and efficiency. Effectiveness measures service responsiveness to public needs and desires; service *quality* is an important effectiveness consideration. Efficiency compares the *quantity* of service provided (e.g., tons of refuse collected) to the *resources* (e.g., labor hours) used to produce it; efficiency provides a measure of how reasonable service *costs* are.

The "trained observer" method of performance measurement is a visual measurement technique. Observers literally "take a look" at community or public facility conditions and report on what they see. Because of this visual aspect, the trained observer method can provide a clear picture of performance measurement in general. The following example attempts to draw such a picture through a description of the trained observer method. The example shows that the difference between measuring performance and simply taking a look is that a performance measurement technique must be *systematic.* While not all performance measurement techniques are visual, they all allow decision makers to take a look systematically at government services and community conditions without having to be everywhere at once.

EXAMPLE 1.1 TRAINED OBSERVERS: TAKING A LOOK AT PUBLIC FACILITIES

Any performance measurement technique must be systematic. For example, suppose a citizen wants to learn how well his or her neighborhood park is maintained. The simplest way is to go out and take a look. However, if the citizen looks right after a busy holiday weekend, during which a large crowd may have overloaded the facilities and left behind a lot of garbage, the impression gained might be quite different than if a maintenance crew has just picked up the litter, mowed the grass, and cleaned the bathrooms.

If the citizen makes a series of visits to the park over a period of time, and systematically plans the visits to observe the park under a variety of conditions, some other interesting facts may be learned; for example:

- How long maintenance crews let the grass grow before moving;

- How much litter piles up before it is removed, and how long it takes for the litter to build up again;
- How long it takes before damaged facilities are repaired;
- How complete a job of routine maintenance the crews do (e.g., do they vary a lot in quality and frequency?).

The citizen may not only be interested in one neighborhood park, but may be a public official interested in the maintenance of all the parks in the community (e.g., the city manager or director of parks and recreation). This official may not have the time to visit systematically and observe the conditions in all parks over a period of time. Instead others, say, the chief of each park district or members of a citizens' park board, may be enlisted to take a look for the official, expanding coverage to all parks. For someone to understand what these observers report back, all observers must use the same criteria for what are considered "good" and "bad" conditions. This uniformity can be achieved through training and practice. Photographic references might be established to help the observers maintain consistency. Finally, the observers' "looks" can be converted into numerical ratings (e.g., excellent = 1, good = 2, fair = 3, poor = 4). The numerical ratings allow district- and jurisdictionwide averages to be calculated, as well as other statistical calculations. They make it easier to compare maintenance in one park to another, or one district to another, or in a district – or the whole jurisdiction – from one month to the next or from one year to the next. These ratings – based on the observers' direct "looks" – help decision makers learn whether their community's park maintenance is getting better or worse over time, and whether the parks in one part of the community are maintained better than those in another.

This example described the trained observer method of performance measurement. It is used in a number of jurisdictions to measure the effectiveness of various services by monitoring the conditions of parks, playgrounds, streets (both cleanliness and state of repair), and other facilities. The use of the trained observer and other effectiveness measurement techniques to measure varying needs and conditions in different neighborhoods, and to adjust resource allocations to make services more responsive to those needs, is discussed in Example 2.1 at the end of chapter 2, contributed by the city manager of Savannah, Georgia.

Does performance measurement measure productivity?

Productivity means different things to different people, especially in the public sector. Ask 10 public officials to define productivity. Ten different answers is the likely result. When the International City Management Association tested this theory, they ended up publishing 14 different definitions of productivity in the May 1980 issue of *Public Management.* Because it is often confusing, the word *productivity* is used sparingly in this book. It is not mentioned among the definitions and descriptions of forms of measurement in chapter 2. Before chapter 6, *productivity* appears only in some examples contributed by local officials, and then only when it is part of a program or report title, or part of a quote. In chapter 6, the word *productivity* is used in its strictly economic sense as the ratio of the *value* of a final product or service and the cost of the resources used to produce it. If one insists on trying to place a *dollar value* on the final product or service delivered by a government, then "performance measurement," as described in this book, does not measure productivity. However, if the value of a local service is seen as the number of units of service delivered (e.g., number of miles of streets resurfaced) then "efficiency" measurement, as defined in chapter 2, can often be used to measure productivity. Some local governments take a broader view of productivity. For example, New York's Citywide Productivity Program defines productivity as "responsiveness to the needs, desires, and pocketbooks of the community."* Such a broad definition encompasses both effectiveness and efficiency as defined in chapter 2. From this viewpoint, the different forms of performance measurement measure different components of productivity.

What are the *uses* of performance measurement?

Performance measurement of public services is not an end in itself. If local officials do not *use* the performance information they receive, it's not worth the cost to collect and report.

Local governments have found many uses for performance measurement. This book examines those uses in three ways: to improve decision making (chapter 3), to improve service performance (chapter 4), and to improve public accountability (chapter 5).

Chapter 3 examines how local officials can use measurement to improve decision making. Performance measurement by itself will not improve local government performance. *People* make *decisions* to take *actions* to improve performance. Measurement helps by providing an idea of the results of an action before it is taken, or of the results of a decision before it is made. Consider the musician who wants to buy a grand piano to play at home, but lives in a 10th floor apartment in a building with no freight elevator. The apartment does have a picture window that can be opened. Should the first step be to put down thousands of dollars for the piano, hire a crane, and shout "hoist away," or

*From materials provided to staff from all city agencies by the Mayor's Office of Operations in Productivity Planning Meetings, New York City, May 24–25, 1982.

should the first step be to measure the window to see if the piano will fit? With the complexities of modern government, making important policy and management decisions without some measurement data can be a little like shouting "hoist away" with that piano, and a lot more costly.

Chapter 3 also focuses on the people in local government who must make decisions, and how they can use performance measurement. The perspectives of elected officials, chief executives, and service managers are featured. The chapter shows how measurement helps people sharpen their decision making; measurement does *not* make decisions for them. Elected officials are particularly concerned with this point, as they insist upon maintaining their political flexibility. The different officials (elected and appointed, staff and line) involved in a measurement effort should collaborate in selecting performance measures that will be useful to them all. The three examples at the end of chapter 3 show how:

- One community uses performance measurement for basic resource allocation decisions concerning a single service (street maintenance);
- A city council uses performance measurement in a variety of ways;
- A local government uses a formal "decision framework," in which performance measurement is intertwined with essential decision making throughout the organization, from the elected officials' policy goals to service managers' operating strategies.

Chapter 4 examines how measurement can be used to improve service performance. While chapter 3 focuses on people and decisions, chapter 4 focuses on making local services more effective and efficient. Communities organize their measurement and improvement efforts in many different ways. Chapter 4 covers a variety of approaches, organized as follows:

- Performance targeting and monitoring, such as management by objectives;
- Detailed measurement for making operational and organizational improvements, including:
  - Industrial engineering and operations research approaches,
  - Organization development,
  - Performance incentives with quality controls;
- Program evaluation and performance auditing.

Chapter 4 includes 11 examples by local practitioners describing how they have improved performance in their communities with the use of measurement. The chapter not only illustrates individual measurement and improvement approaches, it shows how different approaches tend to be complementary, reinforcing each other for better results. Another important issue discussed is the selection of service programs for detailed study and improvement. Chapter 4 also shows how a performance improvement program must be dynamic. To remain useful and credible, it must change with the changing needs of the community.

Chapter 5 adds the idea of communication with the public for good public accountability. Performance measurement can be used to improve accountability to the public, as it can be used to tell citizens how well services are being performed, whether the performance is getting better or worse, whether community conditions are improving or deteriorating, and whether service costs are rising or falling. Without good communication, however, local officials cannot provide a clear picture of performance to the public. Communication can also work in the other direction and become a part of measurement, as citizens can tell the government their perceptions of community conditions, satisfaction with public services, and service improvement priorities. Chapter 5 proposes that communication is the link between performance and public accountability and that good communication can be good politics. With the aid of four examples, including two by elected officials, chapter 5 describes various levels of communication between a local government and its citizens, including:

- Government reports and presentations *to the public* to let citizens know about problems and performance and to provide publicity for performance improvement efforts;
- Government-conducted surveys in which citizens' responses are used to help direct public policy;
- Service improvement efforts that include citizen participation to help identify problems and contribute to solutions;
- Citizen involvement approaches in which citizens get to ask questions of their own and make policy recommendations early in the government decision-making process, thereby helping to ensure that their views are considered by the decision makers.

How can a local government justify the cost of a performance measurement program?

If a government makes use of its performance measures and manages itself better because of them, the measurement program will be well worth the cost and effort. To a large extent, the value of performance measurement is a subjective judgment. What is it worth to elected and appointed officials to have better information available when they make decisions? They may well feel measurement is worth its cost if they are more confident in making tough decisions. Are they more confident about those budget cuts and increases? Are they more confident that a new program — or a significant change in an old one — is really the answer to a problem? Are they more confident that a problem exists, or doesn't exist, in the first place? Do they feel they are able to discuss important issues more intelligently with other officials who claim their programs or their constituencies have special needs?

Chapter 6 discusses the value of measuring and improving local services. In particular, it discusses:

- The value of improving decision making:
- The value of improving service effectiveness;
- The value of improving service efficiency;
- The orgainzational value of measurement and improvement efforts.

Improved resource allocation decisions and improved effectiveness make services more responsive to citizens' needs, thereby increasing the value these citizens receive for their tax dollars. Although an actual dollar value can often be calculated for efficiency improvements, it can be misleading. Local officials must decide whether they want to achieve efficiency benefits in the form of increased services, budget savings, or some combination of both. The most appropriate mix of benefits for a community will not always yield the highest efficiency value. As shown by example in chapter 6, a local government can be tempted to take benefits in the form of increased services it cannot afford or does not need. Also, the value of efficiency gains is diminished if these gains occur at the cost of work quality or service effectiveness. It is valid to calculate an efficiency value of savings or increased services achieved. It must be interpreted and used with care.

While no dollar amount can be placed on the organizational benefits of measurement, these benefits may well be the most valuable of all. The learning process in establishing measurement and improvement efforts can get people to think more creatively about the service they provide. If their new perspectives can be fostered and picked up by others, the effects of measurement on the organization will be lasting. Future improvements will be easier to achieve and more readily generated from within the organization.

Is a performance measurement and improvement program difficult to implement?

A performance measurement and improvement program certainly can include its share of difficulties. Chapter 7 includes a list of thirty ways to sabotage performance measurement and improvement programs. Any attempt to achieve improvement is an attempt to achieve *change;* and change is rarely readily accepted in organizations. Care in implementing and developing a measurement program can help local officials avoid or minimize implementation and organization problems. *Chapter 7 provides pointers for implementing and developing measurement and improvement efforts.* Managers thinking of starting a new measurement program and those wishing to revitalize an existing one will be interested in the suggestions provided for creating a climate for change, planning a measurement and improvement program, and building and maintaining its credibility. Chapter 7 also includes suggestions on obtaining and using consultants to assist in starting a measurement program or to implement performance improvements.

How long can a performance measurement and improvement program last?

Many performance measurement and improvement programs do not last long in their initial forms, but if managed with care they continually evolve into more useful programs which can last many years. As described in chapter 4, Phoenix, Arizona started its program in 1970, and was still going strong in 1982, although the 1982 program was very different from the 1970 program. Chapter 7 stresses opportunism and change to encourage new uses of measurement and an evolution of the measurement program to accommodate changing community conditions, management needs, and political styles. The 19 examples in this book contributed by local officials concerning uses of performance measurement in their communities were written from 1979 to 1982. If a reader were to visit all of those communities in the mid-1980s, he or she may find two or three communities which have completely dropped their programs due to major political, administrative, or fiscal changes. However, the reader is likely to find that most communities featured in this book are still using performance measurement, though probably in somewhat different ways than described here. Those differences, representing program changes in response to changing needs, are the key to those communities' long-lasting success.

What can interested local officials do to explore the use of performance measurement in their own communities?

The first thing an interested local official should do is carefully assess the local situation for potential uses of performance information, the feasibility of various measurement and improvement approaches, and the motivations of people whose cooperation is needed to implement measurement efforts. Chapter 7 includes assessing the local situation as the first step in creating a climate for change. Every local government is different. Each must tailor its measurement and improvement efforts to meet its own special needs.

2
Effectiveness, Efficiency, and Other Forms of Measurement

"Local government is a service institution," or so reads the preamble to the Detroit City Charter. Who would disagree? While local governments are also legal and political entities that pass ordinances, codes, zoning restrictions, and the like, most funds and employees are dedicated to providing services to the public. Of all levels of government, the local level is the most direct provider of public services. These *public* services, commonly paid for by the community, should fulfill *public* purposes. In other words, they should be responsive to the needs of the community. Certainly, citizens want local services to be responsive to their needs. And since they also have to pay for them through their taxes and other fees, they do not want service costs to be excessive.

This chapter describes how local governments can measure their responsiveness to the community's needs, desires, and fiscal constraints, by measuring the effectiveness and efficiency of local services. Four categories of effectiveness measurement are discussed: measurement of community conditions, service accomplishments, citizen satisfaction and perception, and adverse impacts of a service. Sample effectiveness measures and data collection techniques are provided for each category. Some technical considerations in measuring efficiency are discussed as well as how to compare organizational or individual performance to "work standards." Effectiveness and efficiency measurement can provide both external (public) accountability and internal (management) accountability for local government performance. Several other forms of measurement that are useful for internal management purposes are described at the end of the chapter. The chapter concludes with an example contributed by the city manager of Savannah, Georgia, describing Savannah's use of effectiveness measurement to make services responsive to differing needs in different neighborhoods.

EFFECTIVENESS AND EFFICIENCY OF PUBLIC SERVICE

Everyone wants government to be "more effective and efficient." That is a common refrain heard from politicians, government managers, businesspeople, and citizens. Do the terms *effectiveness* and *efficiency,* thrown around so loosely by so many people, have any real meaning in local government? They do, whether the people who use them so liberally (or conservatively) realize it or not. Local government effectiveness and efficiency *can* be measured. Such measurements can tell you how responsive local services are to community needs or public purposes, and whether costs are reasonable in view of the services provided.

Public speakers often use the words *effectiveness* and *efficiency* interchangeably. In measurement terms, they are *not* interchangeable. They represent two distinct, complementary ideas.

Effectiveness measurement is a method for examining how well a government is meeting the public purposes it is intended to fulfill. Put another way, *effectiveness refers to the degree to which services are responsive to the needs and desires of the community.* Effectiveness encompasses both *quantity* and *quality* aspects of a service. For example, public transit effectiveness depends not only on the number of people who use it, but also upon whether these people have safe, comfortable, rapid, convenient, timely, and reliable journeys. Local officials may also be concerned with how many people would like to use public transit but do not — because it is too expensive, does not go near their destination, or is felt to be unsafe. This approach would lead to a measure of *unmet needs or desires,* or more generally unmet "demand."

Efficiency measurement is a method for examining how well a government is performing the things it is doing without regard to whether those are the right things for the government to do. Specifically, *efficiency refers to the ratio of the quantity of service provided (e.g., tons of refuse collected), to the cost, in dollars or labor, required to produce the service.* An "efficiency measure" can be either an output/input ratio, such as the number of trees trimmed per crewday or an input/output ratio, such as the dollar cost per permit application processed. Local governments regularly calculate both forms of efficiency measures. For some applications, energy can be an appropriate type of cost to use in an efficiency ratio (e.g., miles of streets mechanically swept per gallon of gasoline).

To remember the distinction between effectiveness and efficiency, it is useful to contrast them as being "outward" and "inward" looking forms of measurement:

- In measuring effectiveness, a government looks out to the public to determine the impact of services on community conditions.
- In measuring efficiency, a government looks inward to its own operations to determine whether it is producing a reasonable amount of services for each tax dollar.

EFFECTIVENESS: DIFFICULT TO CONTROL BUT IMPORTANT TO MEASURE

Local governments exist to provide services that are responsive to public needs. An effective local government provides the right kind of services in the quantity and quality needed to satisfy public needs and desires. A service can be considered effective if its unmet needs or desires are kept at a satisfactory level.

Of course, public service programs cannot control or satisfy all changes in need or demand. Unusually heavy snows will increase the need for snow removal and can make that service appear ineffective if it cannot quickly satisfy the increased need. An unusually rainy season can have the same effect on park maintenance services. On the other hand, a gas shortage can increase the demand for public transit, and by causing ridership to go up, make public transit appear *more* effective. Also, crime rates may be more sensitive to social and economic conditions than to any police programs.

Even though many changes in demand are uncontrollable, effectiveness measures are valid measures of public performance. While local officials cannot be held accountable for acts of God, the oil companies, or the national economy, they can be held accountable for anticipating some of these events and adjusting to *all* of them. After the biggest snowfall in 20 years, it may be unreasonable to expect all the roads to be open within a few hours. But can the local government respond in a rational fashion, opening important routes quickly and systematically restoring full travel in a reasonable time? Or is the response haphazard with some areas shutdown for many days? Can the public transit company meet the increased demand brought on by a gas shortage with more frequent service, and perhaps keep a good percentage of its new riders when the gas shortage abates? Or will the new riders return to their cars as soon as they can because they received slow, overcrowded, uncomfortable transit service?

While large, uncontrollable swings in demand can cause service effectiveness to suffer, it is important to know how fast a local government can adjust to change and recover its lost effectiveness. In this respect, a local government is just like a business trying to make a profit. While it cannot completely control the demand for its products and services, it must be prepared to anticipate and adjust to changes in demand in order to remain effective.

As described in the next section, some measures of effectiveness are more controllable than others. In spite of how controllable they are, effectiveness measures convey useful information. Generally a combination of "more controllable" and "less controllable" measures are needed to provide a complete picture of service effectiveness.

DIFFERENT WAYS TO MEASURE EFFECTIVENESS

To determine effectiveness measures for a public service, it is helpful to consider the public purposes that service is intended to fulfill. Some public purposes are generally accepted and require little examination. Since it is generally accepted that police and fire services are intended to control crime and fire, rates of crime and fire incidences are clearly important indicators of service effectiveness. However, these rates do not tell the whole story of crime and fire effectiveness, so it is important to look deeper and examine more specific purposes. A deeper analysis may yield effectiveness measures such as citizen perceptions of safety in their neighborhoods, or the number of schoolchildren attending fire prevention demonstration programs.

If a community has written goals and objectives for some of its services, these may help to identify measures of effectiveness. Goals stated in terms of meeting community needs can be particularly useful. For example, the goal:

Maintain a satisfactory level of cleanliness in the city's streets logically leads to defining standards of street cleanliness. Using photographs of clean and littered streets, trained observers can measure how many streets meet those cleanliness standards. New York City; Charlotte, North Carolina; and Savannah, Georgia, all use trained observers to measure street cleanliness.

Goals or objectives stated in terms of activity counts are less useful for defining effectiveness measures, although they may be very useful for other management purposes. For example, the objective:

Sweep 100 curb-miles of streets per week leads to measuring the number of curb-miles swept. This measure may be useful for supervising crews and determining sweeping efficiency, but it says nothing about how clean the streets are.

Since the idea of effectiveness — meeting public needs and desires — is so broad, there is a range of different measures of service effectiveness. These different effectiveness measures can be grouped into four general categories:

1. *Measures of community conditions* are important measures of effectiveness as they are the most explicit measures of community needs. These are generally the effectiveness measures that are least controllable by local services, so it is important to supplement them with other, more controllable measures of effectiveness.
2. *Measures of service accomplishments* can be more directly tied to a specific service program than can general community conditions.
3. *Measures of citizen or client satisfaction and perceptions* cover satisfaction with public services and perceptions of community conditions on the part of citizens in general, or specific clients or target groups of particular programs (e.g., library users, the elderly, residents of a community development neighborhood).
4. *Measures of the unintended adverse impacts* of a service on the community examine the extent to which public services create needs or problems that might not otherwise exist, or unintentionally aggravate existing problems.

Measures of community conditions

Many measures of community conditions are simply measures of undesirable conditions the community will always want to reduce, or are measures of desirable conditions the community wants to increase or maintain. Undesirable conditions can include rates of each type of crime reported, fire incidence rates, numbers of serious traffic accidents, injuries and losses of life and property due to crimes, fires, and accidents. Desirable conditions can include good air and water quality, clean streets and alleys, and stable or increasing property values.

Some measures of community conditions useful for effectiveness measurement can be anchored to a set of standards or benchmarks that are professionally determined or set by an authoritative source. Examples of measures determined in this way are:

- Measures determined by "trained observer" ratings against photographic standards, which are used by a number of communities across the country to measure visually observable physical conditions such as cleanliness or state of repair of parks, playgrounds, streets, and housing exteriors.
- Measures determined by ratings against descriptive standards or codes, such as by building or health inspectors (who are also trained observers); such effectiveness measures as "number of unsafe structures," "number of substandard housing units," or "number of restaurants operating with outstanding health code violations" may result.
- Standards set by the federal government such as family income level for low, moderate, and middle income classifications, or the Bureau of Labor Statistics method for determining the percentage of unemployment.
- Measures determined by special equipment such as air, water, and noise pollution readings; for pollution measures, such as air quality ratings, medical standards are often used to convert highly technical measures (e.g., number of parts per million of sulfur dioxide) to easily understood measures (e.g., number of days per year of "unhealthy" air quality). Other special equipment includes the "roughometer," used for measuring the roughness of road surfaces.

A community may wish to set *equity standards* when measuring community conditions and to rate each neighborhood above or below average, or above or below certain "minimally acceptable" levels for such characteristics as street, park, housing, and sewer conditions; income and unemployment levels; crime and fire rates, etc.

In measuring community conditions a local government can use its own sources as well as outside sources of data, such as census data or surveys of business conditions that may be compiled by a local chamber of commerce. It is important to be aware of the limitations of whatever data sources are used, such as their accuracy and timeliness. For example, counts of crime incidents strictly from reports made to police will not take into account unreported crimes (as much as 30–50 percent for some categories). Citizen surveys that ask questions about whether people have been victimized by crime generally provide more accurate percentages. Census data tend to underrepresent certain groups of people (e.g., urban poor, aliens), and the infrequency of the census tends to limit its usefulness. Many jurisdictions find it useful to collect additional demographic information to update or complement the census.* If business or other surveys are taken from different sources for different time periods, different businesses, or different areas, take care to make sure that time periods, definitions, and procedures are similar and reliable enough to warrant comparison.

Measures of service accomplishments

Since many community conditions are out of the immediate control of local government programs, particularly social and economic conditions, it is important to have effectiveness measures that focus on the accomplishments of the programs themselves, rather than the overall community conditions they are trying to improve. This does not mean local governments should be considered completely unaccountable for general conditions. Elected officials and top managers are responsible for long-term policies and planning to try to improve poor conditions and maintain good conditions. But measures are also needed to hold public officials accountable for shorter-range program results, and to let officials know whether programs are accomplishing what is intended, so they have a basis for increasing, reducing, or otherwise modifying each program.

Service accomplishment measures can include both quantity and quality considerations. For example, the frequency of refuse collection is an important quality consideration of that service. For a community with varying frequencies of collection, a useful measure of effectiveness can be the number (quantity) of households receiving two collections (as opposed to one) per week. For refuse disposal programs, a quality measure is the level of hazard at solid waste disposal sites (which has been measured by trained observers in Nashville), and a quantity measure is the number of usable years remaining at landfill sites (an effectiveness measure used by many communities). For a street repair program, a useful effectiveness measure can be the number (quantity) of potholes or cracks filled that do not reopen (quality) within X days after being repaired.

For programs aimed at particular target groups of people, such as many social programs, two complementary ways to measure service accomplishment are to determine:

Updating Census Information for Local Government Use: An Information Bulletin of the Community and Economic Development Task Force of the Urban Consortium, Public Technology, Inc., Washington, D.C.

- *The number of people from the target population reached* by the program to some defined, significant extent; an absolute number may be used or a percentage of the entire target population, or both;
- *The impact of the program upon the clients it reached.*

For a job training program aimed at the unemployed, data should include how many unemployed people completed job training courses. At least as important as that quantity measure is this measure of *results* or *impact:* How many, and what percentage of, unemployed training program graduates received jobs within three months of completing training. Similarly for other employment, health, or social services, both the number of clients reached and the extent of improvement in their earnings, health, and other social functioning are useful in measuring effectiveness. Generally, measures of a program's impact on its clients are considered better indicators of effectiveness than numbers of clients reached. But since impact is often difficult to control or to attribute specifically to the program, and often difficult to define (e.g., for recreational programs), the number (or percentage) of clients reached is also a useful form of effectiveness measurement.

Measures of response to citizen requests for services are often useful "accomplishment" measures of effectiveness. Policies vary among communities concerning when to provide service in response to different kinds of requests. For street repairs, some local governments attempt to fill every citizen-reported pothole as soon as possible, while others only immediately repair those considered imminent hazards and schedule the others to be repaired as part of the normal work schedule of the repair crews. For the latter case, a useful effectiveness measure can be "number of hazardous street repairs made within 24 hours of being reported." Similar effectiveness measures can be developed around response policies for dead tree removal and street tree trimming, sewer and catch basin cleaning, street and alley cleaning, animal control, and most other services for which a local government receives citizen requests.

Response time is important for emergency services (police, fire, ambulance, rescue operations). Response time to emergencies, measured in minutes, is reported by many fire departments and other emergency service units. Many communities examine not only average response times, but the distribution of the response times achieved. Some communities set an undesirable level of late response which leads to the effectiveness measure "number of responses to emergencies later than X minutes after receiving the report." For emergency services, measures of performance at the scene of an emergency — or of the results of that performance — are at least as important as how fast they get there. For example, some fire departments measure the extent of fire spread after the first fire fighting vehicle arrives. Emergency service departments often conduct prevention activities such as inspections and public classes and demonstrations. Since it is impossible to tell how many crimes, fires, or accidents have been prevented, numbers of clients reached is a useful effectiveness measure for some prevention activities. (Clients can be defined as citizens in general or special groups such as schoolchildren, elderly people, home owners, or businesspeople.)

Measures of service accomplishments complement measures of community conditions. The two types of effectiveness measures may be used jointly to good advantage. For example, if both street and alley cleaning frequency and street and alley cleanliness are reported on a neighborhood basis, it will be possible to tell whether the neighborhoods with the greatest cleanliness problems are getting the most frequent service. Those neighborhoods could also be targeted for prevention activities, such as antilitter campaigns and increased health and sanitation inspections, which may be measured by numbers of inspections, numbers of violations reported and eliminated, and numbers of residents participating in antilitter or community clean-up projects. The next step will be to see how measures of cleanliness (community conditions) have improved as a result.

As several local governments have found, targeting government activities and "accomplishments," based on needs determined by measuring community conditions, is a valuable use of effectiveness measurement.

Measures of citizen or client satisfaction and perceptions

Citizen and client satisfaction provide useful measures of service effectiveness, especially for services for which explicit measures of impact are difficult to define or collect. Even if measures of impact and community condition are available, citizen satisfaction and perceptions are important to consider. For example, even if there is very little actual crime in parks, buses, or other public facilities, if people *think* such crimes occur frequently, those facilities will be underused. Elected officials know that citizens take their *perceptions* of community conditions and not the actual conditions into the voting booth.

One way to get an indication of satisfaction with government services is to keep track of the number of complaints registered by citizens. Most local governments try to be responsive to citizen complaints. Some have organized central complaint bureaus or action centers with publicized phone numbers. The existence of a central complaint bureau makes it easy to analyze complaints geographically and by service, and to follow up with all or a sample of complainants to see how satisfied they are with the government's response. Trends in complaints can indicate problems needing special attention. However, complaints should never be used as the only measure of service effectiveness or citizen satisfaction. Complaints, of course, only represent the most vocal citizens — the squeaky wheels demanding oil. They do not tell whether most citizens are actually satisfied with the services they receive, or where the people are with even greater needs who are either too frustrated to complain or do not know how.

Surveys of citizens or service clients provide a much more representative picture of citizen satisfaction and perceptions than do compilations of complaints. A citizen survey can be thought of as a controlled way to make use of the eyes, ears, and opinions of a large number of well-placed people without having to pay them salaries. People will tell a survey interviewer if they have been the victims of crimes, if they have been awakened by noisy sanitation crews, whether they have adequate opportunities for recreation, whether they feel their neighborhoods are safe and clean, how satisfied they are with any or all services, which services they think should be increased or curtailed, and lots of other useful information.

Surveys can be aimed only at the users or clients of a particular service (e.g., public transit, libraries, social services) to learn how to improve the service. Or surveys can be aimed at the general population of a jurisdiction or a neighborhood to get a general picture of citizen satisfaction with particular services, perceptions of neighborhood conditions, and other information most accurately obtainable through surveys (e.g., victimization rates for many crime categories). General population surveys can also identify why people do not report crimes, take the bus, use the library, or go to the park. Citizens' reasons for *not* using certain services can be valuable information, particularly if they point out corrective or adaptive action the government can take that will lead to more service use (e.g., adjust the hours of operation).

Surveying citizens and service clients is by now a well-developed discipline in which many consulting firms, research organizations, and universities have expertise, as have an increasing number of local governments. The costs can vary widely depending on procedures used, sample size required, and other factors. Communities of all sizes, from Rockport, Massachusetts (population 6000), to Dallas, Texas (population over 900,000), have found surveys useful and *affordable.* Surveys not only provide useful information to local officials, they can be an important link in a chain of communication between a government and its citizens, as is discussed further in chapter 5.

Measures of unintended adverse impacts of a service on the community

One of the basic questions that effectiveness measures should answer about a service is, "How well is the service accomplishing its *intended* purpose?" While trying to answer that question, keep in mind another important question:

What problems or needs have been created, or community conditions worsened, through the provision of this service?

The second question recognizes that a service can have *unintended* negative effects upon the community, even while it achieves its intended purpose. Has a police crackdown on a particular type of crime caused an increase in legitimate citizen complaints of police harassment? Have solid waste collection crews been spilling refuse as they collect it or disturbing residents with excessive noise? Has a public transportation system, intended in part to reduce pollution by reducing private auto use, been causing air and noise pollution problems of its own?

Many measures of adverse impacts, which perhaps should be called "ineffectiveness measures," can be collected by the use of surveys, trained observers, complaint records, and other techniques. If a community uses trained observers for "quality control" purposes, these observers may not only observe these impacts but take corrective action before serious problems develop (e.g., a sanitation supervisor who sends crews back to remove spilled refuse).

USING EFFECTIVENESS MEASURES TO MAKE SERVICE RESPONSIVE TO COMMUNITY NEEDS

The picture of community needs and desires, citizen perceptions and satisfaction, and service accomplishments that a broad array of effectiveness measures can provide can be quite useful to local officials. For example, this knowledge can help local officials:

- Target programs to neighborhoods with special problems (e.g., housing deficiencies);
- Reallocate existing services according to need (e.g., sweep streets more frequently where litter collects faster; put more police on duty during the time of day when the most crime occurs);
- Learn about inexpensive changes that can make services more helpful to citizens (e.g., more or clearer signs in libraries or at bus stops);
- Learn how community conditions and perceptions change after a service delivery change has been in effect for a period of time (a service delivery change could be a service increase, reduction, redistribution, or operational improvement);
- Learn how equitably neighborhoods fare with respect to community conditions, especially before and after periods of service delivery change;
- Make future budgeting and capital improvement decisions more consistent with community needs and desires;
- Learn not only better ways to allocate general government resources (i.e., the budget), but also how best to allocate the *limited resources available to plan and implement service improvements* (i.e., staff analysts and consultants).

In short, effectiveness measures can help local officials make services more responsive to community needs and demands. As described by the city manager in Example 2.1 at the end of this chapter, Savannah, Georgia has a performance measurement program explicitly designed to improve the responsiveness of public services, particularly with respect to meeting the differing needs of different neighborhoods. The example describes how Savannah measures a variety of community conditions, and targets government activities and accomplishments based on the differing needs of each neighborhood. Several of the decision-making examples in chapter 3 also involve the use of effectiveness measurement.

MEASURING EFFICIENCY, OR WHAT DID WE GET FOR ALL THAT MONEY?

Efficiency measurement relates the *cost* of a government activity to the *quantity* of product or service produced by that activity. While it makes no reference to whether an activity (or its product or service) fulfills a community need or demand, efficiency measurement can be extremely useful to local officials.

Knowledge of the efficiency of a particular activity can tell local officials what it will cost to provide the level of service they desire or, conversely, what level of service will be received for the amount they are willing to pay. Officials considering cutting a number of positions from the budget can better understand the cost of the cut in terms of services lost for the activities reduced. Efficiency data allow them to estimate the reduction in the number of potholes repaired, acres of grass mowed (or the number of times the same acreage is mowed), number of inspections made, number of applications for public assistance processed, or other service outputs for the activities being examined.

By measuring the efficiency of an organization over a period of time, or by comparing the efficiency of different operational units in a government performing the same activities, potential operating problems and opportunities for improvement can be identified. Once these opportunities are recognized, detailed study of the selected activities can yield methods for improving operations as well as new efficiency standards the organization should be able to achieve. The result for the community is often an increase in the amount of services it receives. If the improved activity is revenue producing (e.g., collecting fines, issuing permits for fees, treasury management), increased efficiency can mean increasing revenue to the government, reducing dependence on taxes and other general revenue sources.

Why make the effort to measure regularly the efficiency of government operations? Word usually gets around when a local government activity appears grossly inefficient (e.g., the street repairers who spend most of their time leaning on their shovels waiting for the asphalt to come, the inspectors more likely to be found in the local bar than the buildings they are to inspect). Shouldn't an alert manager know what operations to improve without efficiency measurement? The answer is another question: Why wait to be embarrassed by visible problems? Why not catch them early and save valuable labor and equipment from being unproductive? Efficiency measurement will not clear up every embarrassing situation before it makes the local paper, but it may help prevent some and it will provide valuable information about an organization that becomes subject to public scrutiny and criticism, for whatever reason.

A local government should not wait for a financial crisis to begin measuring and improving efficiency. Employees are not likely to cooperate with measurement and improvement efforts if layoffs are probable because of a financial crisis. When a crisis does arise, decisions must be made too quickly to allow for adequate data collection and analysis of operational efficiency. If measurement had been going on beforehand, however, useful data would be available when the decisions must be made.

There are numerous technical considerations in measuring efficiency. A few of the more significant ones are discussed briefly below.*

To relate performance to costs, costs must be specified for each activity measured

The labor used in each government organization measured cannot be treated in a lump sum but *must be accounted for by each activity* carried out by the organization. This practice is called *cost accounting*. If efficiency is to be measured in dollars rather than just the labor time used, cost accounting is needed for other costs in addition to salaries (e.g., equipment and supplies). Depending upon the use to be made of the data, it may also be advisable to allocate some costs often considered to be "indirect" (e.g., fringe benefits, maintenance, capital expenses). Cost accounting approaches exist for governments of all sizes, interested in various levels of investment in data collection and processing. Many of the computerized integrated financial systems that cities and counties have been purchasing and developing have a built-in capability for cost accounting. It is up to the local government using the system to collect its cost data by activity. The system will calculate "total" costs per activity (including whatever indirect costs are programmed to be calculated and are recorded by the jurisdiction in the system). Some of these systems will also accept (or can be easily programmed to accept) output data, and then will calculate unit cost and/or unit labor efficiency measures. The City of Milwaukee has been using its financial management system to calculate efficiency measures in this way for many years.

Smaller communities can do cost accounting *without* a computer, at least as far as direct costs and some of the easier-to-calculate indirect costs (e.g., fringe benefits). Based on its experience assisting four small municipalities, the State of Rhode Island has prepared a manual to help smaller local governments do cost accounting by hand and to develop performance measures.** Smaller communities can also take advantage of computers by sharing large systems with other jurisdictions or investing in minicomputers. Financial systems have been designed for both. And with the rapid development and marketing of low priced microcomputers and microcomputer software, automated cost accounting and financial management are affordable to any community willing to make the data collection effort.

---

*For an in-depth discussion of these technical considerations, including an examination of efficiency measurement issues in four local government services, see Hatry et al., *Efficiency Measurement for Local Government Services: Some Initial Suggestions*, Urban Institute, Washington, D.C., 1980.

**Performance Measurement and Cost Accounting for Smaller Local Governments*, Rhode Island Department of Community Affairs, Providence, 1979.

Performance measurement should reflect the quality
as well as the quantity of output

Managers and workers who believe efficiency measures are being used as criteria to evaluate their work can react perversely by emphasizing production of a large *quantity* of the unit of service measured, while ignoring the *quality* of service provided. For example, a poorly repaired pothole that opens up again quickly and is refilled could count as two service units, while a properly filled hole that does not reopen would only count as one. The police can easily increase the number of arrests if they do not have to worry about whether successful prosecutions can be obtained. One way around this problem is *not to count a unit of work toward the total output of an activity unless it passes some kind of quality test.* For a police arrest, the quality test could be whether the arrest survives the initial judicial screening. If adequate records are accessible for each case from the criminal justice system, this can be a fairly easy approach to control for quality while measuring police apprehension efficiency. For other services, additional data collection procedures may be needed to test work quality while measuring service output. This data collection burden might be reduced by *sampling* units of work for quality, rather than by checking every single unit of service output.

Local governments that regularly and comprehensively measure the *effectiveness* of their services need not be terribly concerned about the quality/quantity problems inherent in efficiency measurement. Service quality will generally be reflected in a varied group of effectiveness measures, so governments can use their effectiveness data as an indication of whether efficiency is achieved at the expense of work quality. *The real issue is not whether a community has the most sophisticated data collection system but whether its public employees, managers, and policy makers consider service quality important.* Well-trained supervisors who routinely employ quality control procedures will do more for service quality than any measurement system. Performance measurement can let managers and policy makers know when special attention to quality control may be called for in specific services.

The "difficulty" of the incoming workload should be considered
when measuring the efficiency of a public organization

It is more difficult (and likely to be more time-consuming) to identify and apprehend offenders for crimes in which there were no witnesses than for crimes in which witnesses were present. Terrain and weather conditions affect the amount of time and effort needed to make quality street repairs. Providing quality drinking water is more difficult and costly if the source of incoming water is polluted. For many services, apparent changes in efficiency may really reflect changes in the *difficulty* of the incoming workload, rather than any operational changes.

This issue has recently been raised by research into government efficiency. Ideally, the problem would be overcome by separately calculating the efficiency for several levels of difficulty for each activity measured. Alternatively, local governments could keep track of the percentages of work that are considered to have different "degrees of difficulty" and report those percentages along with corresponding efficiency measures. Managers concerned that such procedures will add undue data collection burdens should at least be alert to the conditions that change the difficulty of incoming workload. They should then report such changes, when they occur, in supporting narratives to efficiency reports. Park managers, for example, can report that heavy rains reduced mowing opportunities or caused mowing to require greater effort. Vehicle repair managers can report that the new fleet purchased by the government required the development of new shop procedures and special training for maintenance crews, causing efficiency to drop temporarily. Managers in the public child care system can report that an unusually high number of children with severe physical or behavioral problems were referred to the system, making their rapid and efficient placement into institutions more difficult. Many communities with regular performance reports include narrative sections that give managers the opportunity for such explanations. Some local governments *require* explanations for all measures reported significantly above or below expectations.

The purpose of reporting information on workload difficulty is not to explain away all changes in efficiency but to give managers and policy makers some additional useful information when they consider which government activities may require special efforts to improve efficiency levels.

USING WORK STANDARDS TO DETERMINE SERVICE EFFICIENCY

There are some technical variations on strict input/output or output/input ratios that can indicate how efficiently an organization is performing. These involve the use of *work standards,* which are standard times that a particular activity (like mowing an acre of lawn) should take to complete, or conversely, a standard number of units of work to be completed within a standard time. Standard times are really units of labor and are expressed in terms of labor time; for example, employee-hours or crew-days. Two of the practitioner-contributed examples in chapter 4 (Example 4.3 on San Diego, California and Example 4.4 on Genesee County, Michigan) feature the use of work standards to help improve efficiency.

Sometimes local governments determine "standards" historically — using whatever number of outputs a crew or organization was able to achieve last week or last month, or during a particular test period in which output and labor time were verified. That approach, which ignores the actual procedures used by personnel to achieve a level of output, has the danger of perpetuating past inefficiencies, as the standards may be based on inefficient work methods.

A much better way to set work standards is first to examine carefully the activity in question to determine the best methods employees can use to work efficiently and safely with the equipment available without sacrificing quality. This analysis is usually done by industrial engineers or methods analysts who often seek to eliminate unnecessary time-consuming steps from a work process (work simplification) and reduce unproductive time of employees (e.g., time spent waiting for another employee to complete a step in the work process). Once the best methods, or "good practice procedures" have been established for the equipment available, work standards are determined by a systematic, objective method such as an industrial engineer's time and motion studies. These are often referred to as *engineered work standards*. Work standards should be reviewed periodically to make sure they are up to date with new equipment, procedures, or *quality* requirements that may have been introduced to a job.

Work standards are only useful for activities with standard, identifiable products (e.g., vehicle repairs completed, decayed teeth filled, acres of grass mowed) and specific, well-defined procedures that are repeated the same way each time an activity is performed. For example, work standards for making welfare eligibility determinations should be possible, but may not be appropriate for client counseling. Standard times for fingerprinting could be developed, but not for crime investigations.

There are two ways work standards are used to indicate organizational efficiency:

Comparisons of actual performance to the work standard

Two possible ratios can be calculated when comparing actual performance to a work standard. The actual time per unit of output could be calculated and compared to the standard time. A ratio of one would indicate the work standard has been achieved exactly. If the actual time per unit is smaller than the standard time (a ratio of less than one), the standard has been bettered. If the ratio is greater than one, efficiency has been worse than the standard.

Alternatively, the actual total output for a period could be compared to the amount of work that should have been completed based on the work standard and the amount of labor time available during the period. Again, a ratio of one means the standard has been exactly achieved. Using this approach, a ratio of less than one (less output than the standard amount for the labor available) means efficiency has been worse than the standard, and a ratio of more than one means the standard has been bettered. A ratio of actual output to standard output for the labor time available is often referred to as the *percentage of standard achieved*.

Calculations of "combined" efficiency measures

For many government organizations the same employee or crew participates in several different activities. It may be advantageous to calculate the *combined* efficiency of all activities done by the organization or crew, instead of, or in addition to, the efficiency of each activity. If each activity has a definable product and standard and repeatable procedures, a standard time could be calculated for each activity. Then the different standard times can be used to *weight* each activity differently when calculating combined efficiency. In other words, if the standard time to tune up a vehicle's engine is four times the standard time to change its oil, each tune-up would count four times as much as each oil change in the combined efficiency ratio. A combined efficiency measure is an output/input ratio in which the output is not uniform, but the sum of different units of work completed weighted according to the standard times for each activity. The input is the *total* labor time actually used. This approach has been used to calculate the combined efficiency of a variety of local government organizations, from vehicle repair shops to dental clinics. The technique is, however, frequently known by titles other than "combined efficiency measures." For instance, in chapter 4, Example 4.4, Genesee County, Michigan uses "manpower utilization rates" (their version of "combined efficiency measures") to help improve the efficiency of office services.

OTHER FORMS OF MEASUREMENT THAT ARE SOMETIMES USEFUL

Measures of effectiveness and efficiency can provide a comprehensive picture of the *performance* of public services. Because effectiveness and efficiency measures describe government responsiveness to the public's needs and ability to pay, they can be used to achieve *external (or public) accountability,* as well as *internal (or management) accountability* for public service performance. There are other forms of measurement, which do not represent external performance accountability, but which public officials have found useful for management purposes. Costs, for example, while not themselves measures of efficiency, must be tracked for sound financial management and *fiscal* accountability. Workload measures are also not by themselves efficiency or effectiveness measures; however, they can be useful for managing and planning services. These, and other measures public officials find helpful for internal management use, can often be collected at the same time as data for calculating efficiency and effectiveness. These other forms of measurement include:

- *Process time,* such as the time it takes to fill a purchase order or hire an employee. For equipment repair, this is often referred to as "downtime." Process times are often useful for charting out the way an organization or activity works, to identify unproductive time, and to find ways to improve procedures. Some process times, such as the response time to a fire or other emergency, are also measures of effectiveness.

- *Backlogs* often exist where there are process times. Backlogs can include, for example, the amount of forms or letters waiting to be typed, or the number of vehicles awaiting repair. Sometimes small or controlled backlogs are desirable, since they can provide a basis for evenly scheduling work and keeping all employees active, working productively. When a backlog refers to *people* on a waiting list, it may well be a measure of effectiveness.
- *Rates of unavailability or nonuse of resources, including:*
  - *lost capacity,* such as the percentage of vehicles or other equipment out of service, or the amount of water lost in a water supply system due to leakage;
  - *unused capacity,* such as load factors of public transit vehicles, or the percent of personnel time spent "unproductively" (e.g., waiting for equipment or material, taking a break).
- *Revenue* measures are important for tracking current financial conditions and forecasting future income. They include actual revenue collected from each form of tax, fee, and other source; revenues received compared to the amounts assessed, billed, or otherwise anticipated; revenues lost (e.g., due to faulty calibration of water meters).
- Various *demographic* information can help indicate demand for services without necessarily reflecting on effectiveness through good or bad community conditions. Examples are population, number of households requiring refuse collection, miles of streets and alleys.
- *Project management* measures, or measures of adherence to time and cost schedules for one-time projects. These are often not measures in the usual sense but steps in a schedule that must be completed within a certain time and cost (e.g., complete facility design, receive construction bids, begin construction). While generally applied to capital improvement and community development projects, project management measures can be applied to any project with a definable end, such as passage of an ordinance or a bond issue, or development and implementation of work standards. Project management measures can be compiled for several projects to indicate the performance of the agencies responsible (e.g., number of projects proceeding or completed on time, number of projects within cost, total cost of projects compared to planned cost). *These measures are especially useful for measuring the performance of agencies that work on a project-by-project basis, such as engineering divisions and planning departments.*

SOME "PSEUDO-MEASURES" OF SERVICE PERFORMANCE

There are three forms of measurement that are often mistakenly used to represent the effectiveness and efficiency of local government services. They are referred to here as "pseudo-measures" as a warning against misusing them to measure service performance. These three forms of measurement are resources per capita (e.g., number of library books, police on patrol, or fire trucks per capita); client-staff ratios (e.g., number of students per teacher); and per capita costs of services (sometimes measured as service costs per dollar of assessed property value).

These pseudo-measures are not entirely useless to local governments. Problems arise when they are misused to represent service effectiveness or efficiency.

Some local governments use resources per capita and client–staff ratios as guidelines for budgeting and work scheduling. They sometimes try to change these ratios in order to increase citizen or client satisfaction, or to increase client progress (e.g., improve condition of social service clients). However, these are only measures of *resources* applied. *They say nothing about the effectiveness or efficiency of a service.* When resource per capita ratios or client–staff ratios are changed, changes in effectiveness should not be assumed. Instead, attempts should be made to measure changes in effectiveness explicitly (e.g., through citizen or client surveys, or measures of client progress).

Per capita costs have been cited recently as useful indicators of the *fiscal* behavior of a community. When used in this way, costs per capita (or per dollar of assessed value) are calculated for several years, and these *trends* are viewed along with other fiscal trends to help judge the fiscal health of the community. However, service costs per capita say nothing about the actual product delivered; they say nothing about the quantity of output or quality of service. Thus *service costs per capita should never be used to represent the efficiency or effectiveness of services.*

PERFORMANCE MEASURES ARE MEANT TO BE USED

This chapter discussed effectiveness, efficiency, and other measures of local government services. These measures are not meant to be researchers' devices that are only intended to put numbers on local services. These measures are meant to be practical tools for public officials to *use* in making local services more responsive to the needs of the community, and the community's ability to pay. The next three chapters emphasize the ways in which local officials can use performance measurement to help them make decisions, improve services, and improve accountability to the public. Each of these chapters ends with examples contributed by local practitioners describing how they have used performance measurement in their own communities.

**EXAMPLE 2.1 SAVANNAH'S RESPONSIVE PUBLIC
SERVICES PROGRAM**

Arthur A. Mendonsa
City Manager
Savannah, Georgia

A ride through the neighborhoods of most urban communities would disclose marked differences in terms of physical condition and appearance. Some are clean, while others are littered with debris and trash. Some contain clean, attractive, and sound houses on well-manicured lots, while others contain dilapidated and unattractive housing on unkept lots. Some are adequately served by drainage, water, and sewer facilities, while others are not. These neighborhoods would also differ in the number of fires and crimes that occur, the adequacy of their water and sewer facilities, and the convenience and availability of recreational facilities.

The condition of different neighborhoods presents a major challenge to a responsible and responsive local government. That challenge is to insure that public services properly and adequately address the different needs of different neighborhoods. This challenge is met satisfactorily only when each public service produces a minimum acceptable result in each neighborhood, regardless of its socioeconomic and physical condition.

How can a community establish an acceptable effectiveness standard for each service in each neighborhood? Savannah's answer to this question lies in its Responsive Public Services Program, started in 1973. Its purpose was to establish a mechanism for measuring conditions in each neighborhood affected by the city's public services, in order to identify neighborhoods where services were deficient, and then design programs to reduce such deficiencies. The objective of the program was, and is, to insure that each neighborhood is served equitably by the city's public services. The guiding principle of this effort is that the citizens of each neighborhood are entitled to a minimum acceptable standard of neighborhood livability, regardless of their socioeconomic condition.

This is how Savannah's Responsive Public Services Program works: The city is first divided into study neighborhoods and the condition of each neighborhood is determined by measuring the following conditions:

1. The amount of litter in the neighborhood. A scale of 0 to 6 is used and is applied to a sample of street blocks and properties. A rating of 0 means that no litter exists. A rating of 6 means that much litter and debris exist.
2. The structural fire rate. The rate is established by calculating the number of structural fires per 1000 structures in the neighborhood.

3. The crime rate. The rate for each Part I crime (the most serious crimes) committed in each neighborhood is calculated.
4. Flooding conditions. The rate and frequency of structural and property flooding is calculated on the basis of the number of structures affected in relation to the total for the neighborhood.
5. Water and sewage sufficiency. The proportion of housing units in each neighborhood without adequate water and sewage service is calculated.
6. Condition of streets. The miles of unpaved streets and the degree of deterioration of paved streets in proportion to the total miles of streets in the neighborhood is calculated.
7. Housing conditions. The proportion of housing in each neighborhood classified as substandard is calculated.
8. Availability and adequacy of recreational facilities. The accessibility and variety of recreational opportunities in each neighborhood are measured through citizen surveys and the application of recreation facility standards.

Each condition is measured for each neighborhood in units that permit the neighborhood to be compared with each of the other neighborhoods and with the average for all neighborhoods. This comparison identifies which neighborhoods are substandard in relation to other neighborhoods, both collectively and individually. Those that fall below the average for all neighborhoods for a particular condition are classified as substandard; those that meet or exceed the average are classified as standard.

After the substandard neighborhoods for each of the conditions studied have been identified, an analysis is made to determine what changes are needed in specific service programs to bring the neighborhood closer to the city norm for a particular condition. Needed improvements in each neighborhood are then placed on a priority schedule and are carried out when funds are available.

Savannah uses the Responsive Public Services Program to establish priorities for street paving, to target fire prevention and crime control programs, to target housing assistance, to schedule the construction of water and sewer facilities, recreational facilities, and drainage facilities, and to target litter control programs.

This approach has made Savannah's public services more responsive to public needs. It has provided a mechanism which ensures that problem neighborhoods receive priority attention by serving as the basis for developing the annual community development plan and operating budget. It has also taken much of the subjectivity out of the scheduling of public improvements.

3
Using Measurement to Improve Decision Making

Measurement by itself will not improve local government performance. *People* make *decisions* to take *actions* to improve performance. Measurement helps people make better decisions. Measurement then lets them know how good those decisions were or how well they were executed.

This chapter focuses on the people in local government who must make decisions and how performance measurement can help them make those decisions. The importance of careful selection of measures through a collaborative process is emphasized, including how well-selected measures can sharpen decision making and enhance the usefulness of measurement. The chapter includes a discussion of how different measurement and decision-making approaches evolve in different communities. The practitioner-contributed examples at the end of the chapter demonstrate these differences as they vary from basic resource allocation decisions in a single service to a strategically organized decision framework in a local government that applies measurement techniques to essential decisions throughout its organization.

DECISION MAKERS AND THEIR USES OF PERFORMANCE MEASUREMENT

Anyone working in a local government can be a decision maker, and performance measurement can influence almost anyone's decisions. Even frontline personnel, such as street sweepers, might *decide* to work more quickly and carefully if the speed and quality of their performance were tied to some tangible incentive (e.g., more pay or the opportunity to go home early). Generally speaking, decision makers are thought of as people in supervisory, management, or policy-making positions.

Supervisors and middle managers in operating departments can use measurement for scheduling daily operations, for quality control decisions (e.g., which lawns to remow or streets to resweep), and employee evaluation. Senior line managers such as department heads can use measurement to justify budget requests, to change the staffing levels and organization of work groups for more efficient operations, and to do tactical planning (e.g., determine the optimal locations for fire stations).

USER	USE
Elected Body (e.g., Council or Commission)	• Strategic planning – developing community objectives • Resource allocation – Budget development – Capital planning • Communicating to the public about government performance (see chapter 5)
"Top Management" (e.g., City or County Manager, Budget or Management Director)	• Negotiate budget with departments and justify it to council • Control costs for all services • Serve as an early warning of service problems • Improve service effectiveness
Department Heads, Middle Managers, and Supervisors	• Improve service efficiency and effectiveness • Quality control • Tactical planning • Improve employee performance
Line Employees	• Improve work environment – make it possible to do a better job • Improve pay or other benefits

Figure 3-1. Users and uses of local government performance measurement. This chart provides a *conceptual* breakdown. In *practice,* the users and uses overlap, and vary for each local government. For example, everyone is involved in resource allocation at some time or other.

Top managers and staff managers, such as city managers, county executives, deputy mayors, or budget directors can use measurement to help negotiate and justify budgets, to serve as an early warning of service problems, and to analyze selected services in detail to help improve performance.

Elected officials can use performance measurement for strategic planning (e.g., which neighborhoods should receive development projects, what long-range service changes are needed in the community) and resource allocations decisions (operating and capital budgets).

Figure 3-1 summarizes information on the users of performance measurement and how they use performance measurement within a local government. As roles and responsibilities of users vary from community to community, so will their uses of measurement. Often, several levels of management and policy officials will be involved in the same decision. For example, the location of a fire station may start out as a tactical planning decision for the fire chief, but it may very well end up as a policy decision made by the elected council. Also, all managers and elected officials usually get involved at some point in the budget development process.

Example 3.1 at the end of this chapter is a dialogue excerpt from a HUD-sponsored conference on local financial management. This dialogue involves an elected county commissioner, a public works director, and a city manager, who briefly explain, in their own words, how they use performance measurement. The elected commissioner from Genesee County, Michigan emphasizes the use of measurement for resource allocation to meet citizen desires, and for labor reductions to meet a budget crisis. The public works director from Sherman, Texas describes how measurement helped him learn about his department when he first took his job, and how he has used it since to monitor the work of his department and justify proposed changes to his city manager and council. The city manager of Sherman emphasizes how measurement has given him and his staff credibility with the city council and the public.

DECISIONS THAT MAKE SERVICES MORE RESPONSIVE TO PUBLIC NEEDS

As described in chapter 2, measures of effectiveness can help determine how responsive a local government's services are to the community's needs and desires. Public officials who seriously consider these performance measures are in a good position to make decisions that make services more responsive to public needs and desires.

Two questions local decision makers constantly face are *how much* and *which*. These questions are the crux of many decisions affecting service responsiveness.

- *How much* funding should go to each service?
- *How much* of a particular service is adequate to meet community needs?
- *How much* of a service are people willing to pay for?
- *Which* neighborhoods should be targeted for special services or improvements?
- *Which* businesses should be targeted? *Which* streets? *Which* parks? *Which* people?
- *How much* can we cut back a service?
- In *which* neighborhoods can we cut back?

The list is endless.

The City of Dallas uses effectiveness measurement to help decide questions of how much and which for its street maintenance program. With their street inventory system keeping track of street conditions throughout the city, Dallas officials have a systematic way to make their street maintenance services responsive to community needs. The street inventory is an information system that stores trained observer ratings of street condition for every segment of street in Dallas. As described in Example 3.2 at the end of the chapter, an analysis of the street inventory information tells the city manager and city council what they would have to spend to bring street conditions up to specific levels of quality, helping them make the budget decision of how much to spend on street maintenance. The director of street maintenance uses the condition ratings of each street segment to decide which streets to improve. Example 3.2 also notes how street inventory information has become an aid for decisions in other programs. Dallas's experience demonstrates that once a performance measurement technique gains use and acceptance in a local government, its value as a decision-making tool can expand with the needs and creativity of the community.

SELECTING PERFORMANCE MEASURES
TO AID DECISION MAKING

The idea of "selectivity" is important for any practical performance measurement program. It costs time, money, and effort to collect and report data, so it is important to *select,* as carefully as possible, those performance measures that are expected to be useful and not to waste resources collecting and reporting data that will not be needed.

Well-selected performance measures can help
sharpen decision making

Performance measures do more than just provide decision makers with objective data to help them find the answers they need. Decision makers may learn they are asking the wrong questions or worrying about the wrong decisions. Well-selected performance measures can provide new insights into the services being examined, and, thereby, help sharpen the decision-making process by bringing into focus the most important decisions.

For example, as part of a HUD-funded demonstration, Dallas library managers decided they wanted to know why people were or were not satisfied with the Central Research Library. The managers planned to use that information in deciding how to adjust their research library services to satisfy more users. They also were hoping to learn better ways of using the interior space of a new building for the Dallas Central Research Library, which was under construction. To collect this information, a survey of library users was conducted keyed to the question, "Are you satisfied with the services provided by the Central Research Library?" The library managers were pleased to learn that most users were satisfied with the services, but surprised to learn that many people answered they were satisfied even though they failed to find the information they came to the library to find. This led the library managers to realize they were asking the wrong questions; they were concentrating on too general a level of decision making. Instead of asking about satisfaction in general, the more important question was why people could not find specific information. This information could then be used to change services so that people could find the information they wanted, and find it quickly. Consequently, another user survey, this time concentrating on library users' search procedures and factors related to successful and unsuccessful searches, was administered. The results of the later survey were used to make decisions that have led to changes in current operations and in planned floor arrangements of the new Central Research Library.

Was the Dallas library's first set of performance measures poorly selected, making the first survey a wasted effort? Actually, those measures were carefully selected based on an analysis of the decision-making process used by Dallas library managers. The results of the first survey challenged some of the basic assumptions behind those decision-making processes, including the assumption that a satisfied library user was one who usually found what he or she came for. So the first survey was a necessary step on the way to the second. Without it, library managers would not have questioned their assumptions and changed their decision emphasis. With it, they could refine their performance measures and resulting survey questions to provide useful data for a sharpened decision-making process.

A collaborative approach to selecting performance measures helps insure they will be used

Selectivity in collecting and reporting data by itself does not guarantee useful performance reports. The process used for selecting performance measures, as well as who is involved in the selection process, are also important. A *collaborative* approach among the people directing a measurement program, the people expected to use the data, and the people who must collect it can help insure that the data reported will be put to use. This collaboration will usually involve analysts from central or "staff" management (e.g., a mayor's or city manager's office, an office of management and budget), and personnel from operating or "line" service agencies (e.g., police, fire, public works). A collaboration between staff and line personnel is helpful in several ways:

- A useful mix of expertise is obtained, combining special analytic capabilities, which are usually stronger on a central management staff, with the operating personnel's practical knowledge of how a service is actually delivered, including all of the day-to-day service problems and a feeling for which measures will be major burdens to collect and which ones will not.
- Service agency managers are less likely to feel threatened by measures they helped select than by measures insisted on from above, making it easier to achieve the cooperation necessary from the service agencies to obtain accurate, timely data.
- If service agency managers collaborate in the selection of measures, they can help direct the selection to performance measures they see as useful, and they are thus more likely to use the data reported.

The Dallas library project and performance measurement programs in many other communities have used staff-line collaboration to select and analyze performance measures, with useful results. In San Francisco, for example, the development of performance measures in social services involved over 150 managers and supervisors in an agency of over 3000 employees. As discussed in chapter 4, this type of careful preparation has been vital to San Francisco's successful management by objectives program.

Elected officials can also be users of performance data. In some local governments, elected officials set broad community goals, which in turn influence the performance measures appointed officials select for collection and reporting. In these cases elected officials participate, however indirectly, in the collaborative process to select useful measures. The role of elected officials as decision makers and performance data users is integral to the remaining sections of this chapter.

ELECTED OFFICIALS AS USERS OF PERFORMANCE MEASUREMENT

An elected position on a city or county council or commission is generally a part-time position, often unpaid. People are elected because of their political positions, and their voter recognition and confidence, not because of their analytical abilities. Once in office, they have only a limited time to devote to many important policy decisions they must make for their community. Thus, elected officials are not always considered a prime audience for performance measurement, since they do not have the time or ability to analyze detailed objective performance data, and their decisions are ultimately political, anyway. However, if carefully presented to elected officials, performance reports can help them use their limited time more effectively. Performance measurement can help them identify where they can make routine decisions and where the political process is more important. It can help them get to the heart of complex issues, put their political arguments in an objective context, and sharpen their decision-making abilities. As one council member remarked on the effect of a new budget process based on performance objectives:

> "We still have long arguments over the budget, but now we argue about important things."

Elected officials have also found performance measurement to be particularly useful in helping them communicate with the public, and in helping them make use of public perceptions and opinions when setting policies. These are uses covered in detail in chapter 5.

Selectivity is especially important in reporting performance to elected officials, so they are not mired in more data than they can take the time to understand. Since the ability to understand performance reports quickly is essential to elected officials, the inclusion of supporting narratives explaining significant performance changes and other important results is particularly useful. The narrative may include operating departments' explanations for good or poor performance, as well as staff analyses of the meaning of certain data.

The acceptance of a performance measurement system by elected officials depends not only on their ability to understand the measures, but also on their feeling that the system *helps them* make decisions, rather than that it makes decisions for them. Remember, performance measures don't make decisions, *people* do. Performance measurement works for elected officials when it gives them more confidence in the decisions *they* make. The usefulness of a performance measurement system to elected officials was well described by Carol de Prosse, a former member of the Iowa City, Iowa, City Council in a symposium of the Municipal Finance Officers Association:

> Performance measurement is good for planning, budgeting, work schedules, manpower allocation and control, production planning and control, and cost accounting. The legislative body is particularly involved in the planning and budgeting aspects of performance measurement. As an elected body, our decisions are political ones — or at least perceived as political. If they also happen to be rational and logical, so much the better. . . . Any system that puts too many restrictions on the council's ability to make political decisions will be rejected. In local government, any system of performance standards and measurement must be flexible enough to produce an improvement in efficiency and effectiveness, but at the same time permit the democratic process to work.

The city council is the main audience for the performance measurement approach used in Iowa City. While all city agencies are covered, the level of detail and frequency of reporting are not particularly useful for most operating decisions of agency managers. But department heads take performance measurement seriously because they know the council does. Iowa City's performance reports are used by the council primarily for goal setting, budget development, and monitoring programs of special concern. And while not using the performance reports on a day-to-day basis, agency managers find that performance objectives help them by letting them know what is expected of them.

As described by the city manager in Example 3.3 at the end of this chapter, the council triggers Iowa City's performance measurement and budgeting efforts with an annual goal setting session. While quarterly performance reporting is the norm, more frequent special measurement and reporting techniques may be added for special council priorities, such as the Community Development Block Grant Program (CDBG). The city manager also employs a simple, inexpensive monthly survey as a community outreach tool to improve service responsiveness and to give the council a "feel" for community perceptions of city services. As the survey was not designed for statistical accuracy, it is not used for budgeting or major policy decisions. Council members feel it helps them keep their fingers on the pulse of the community.

Iowa City's experience holds an important message for smaller communities. Each measurement technique used by Iowa City is relatively simple and inexpensive, allowing the city to use a variety of techniques, providing complementary information, within limited resources.

STRATEGICALLY ORGANIZED DECISION MAKING

As the Dallas street maintenance and library examples indicate, performance measurement can be used by departmental managers to make decisions regarding their service programs. The Iowa City example shows how performance measurement can be organized to aid the decision making of an elected council. It is possible for a local government to intertwine performance measurement with essential decision making throughout its organization. Such an approach would strategically organize decisions made by elected officials, top management (or staff managers such as budget directors), and managers of operating service programs. All of their decisions would be linked by consistent policies, objectives, and performance measures.

An organizationwide strategic decision framework has evolved in the City of Dayton, Ohio. Dayton uses various performance measurement approaches to help insure that the elected city commission's policies reflect community needs and that these policies are translated into the objectives and performance of the operating service programs. Dayton's program strategies decision framework now includes a strategic planning process, a management by objectives (MBO) system, a five-year program budgeting structure, and a performance-based merit pay plan for upper and middle managers. As described in Example 3.4, Dayton's program strategies assume a continuum of decisions, actions, and measurable results operating within three strategic dimensions: policy, situation, and approach. This continuum involves several layers of decision makers, including elected city commissioners, the city manager and assistants, the director and staff of Dayton's Office of Management and Budget (OMB), and the senior and middle managers of operating programs.

In Dayton's policy dimension, the city commission decides upon broad policy goals (grand strategies) for economic vitality, neighborhood vitality, and other commission priorities. The policy goals are supported by three- to five-year action plans (strategy statements) which involve program priorities and targets to help achieve the policy goals.

The approach dimension represents Dayton's operating programs and objectives. It involves the commission and management through the budget process and involves the program managers and Dayton's OMB through the MBO system and the incentive pay plan. Program approaches, measurable managerial objectives, and day-to-day operating tactics are decided upon to support the broad policy goals and policy action plans. Various forms of measurement are used to support managerial objectives, such as effectiveness, efficiency, workload, and process time measurement. These measures are monitored quarterly, and some are audited by Dayton's OMB.

The "situation dimension" provides an essential effectiveness measurement link to complete the decision framework. A wide variety of community conditions are measured, as well as citizen perceptions of conditions and satisfaction with services. Dayton officials pay particular attention to trends in measured conditions and perceptions. The resulting picture of a changing "community situation" helps the city commission keep policy goals and plans consistent with community needs and helps management decide upon realistic program approaches, objectives, and tactics aimed at improving community conditions.

THE EVOLUTION OF IMPROVED DECISION MAKING

This chapter deals with the people who are decision makers in local government and how they can use performance measurement to help them make decisions. The next chapter concerns the many ways communities organize their performance measurement approaches to achieve improved service performance.

Whether improved decision making or improved performance is the focus of discussion, it is important to realize there is no single model, or ultimate combination of measurement approaches, to which local governments should aspire. Each community must develop measurement programs and techniques that fit its own special circumstances, abilities, and management styles. For example, while Iowa City's and Dayton's measurement programs are largely centrally managed, most of Dallas's measurement efforts are done at the discretion of the operating departments, without direct central control. The City Manager's Office provides technical assistance in measurement to some departments, such as the library, upon request. Dallas's only *regular* performance measurement program managed by the City Manager's Office is the annual citizen survey. But even the departmental performance data — such as the street inventory reports — may find their way into city council decisions.

Another important point is that performance measurement and improved decision making do not appear overnight. They take careful planning, resources, patience, and time to implement. And even the world's most careful planning will not reveal beforehand what will result several years later. Dayton's program strategies framework did not develop from a grand design that was planned beforehand. Each individual measurement approach — the surveys, MBO, the incentive pay plan, and other techniques — were added incrementally as needs and opportunities arose. It took a creative city management staff to integrate new approaches with existing ones into a unified, performance-based decision framework.

It is difficult to force improved decision making. It tends to evolve with the needs of the community and the management and personal styles of the decision makers. The important thing to remember when designing and implementing new performance measurement approaches is that *people* must be able to implement the approaches and use the results. The performance data reported must be relevant to the *decisions* people must make. If that principle guides each new measurement approach introduced, officials will enhance their chances for improving decision making in the community and, thereby, make local government performance more responsive to community needs.

EXAMPLE 3.1 THREE DECISION MAKERS TELL OF THEIR MEASUREMENT USES

This dialogue excerpt, involving an elected commissioner from a large Michigan County, and the public works director and manager of a small Texas city, is from a HUD-sponsored conference on local financial management.*

Moderator

I'd like to address my first question to Charlotte Williams. From your vantage point as an elected commissioner in Genesee County, Michigan, how do you use performance measures?

Ms. Williams

We were able to use it to allocate manpower to the various departments and come up with what we knew we were going to have to do in a budget crisis, and that was reduction of manpower, which in some areas was between 20 and 50 percent of what was on board.

We were also able to determine if the desires and wishes of the citizens, the county so that they were not up in arms, angry, upset. They knew why we were doing it and they knew exactly what we were doing when it came to the time to adopt our final budget.

We were also able to determine if the desires and wishes of the citizens, and the resources available, were combined in a resourceful manner to

---

*Excerpted from "Workshop on Managing with Performance Measures," part of the Conference on Local Financial Management held in Detroit, June 7–8, 1979. The moderator was George P. Barbour, Jr., a consultant from Palo Alto, Calif. An edited transcript of this workshop was published as *Managing with Performance Measures in Local Government: A Dialogue* (Office of Policy Development and Research, U.S. Department of Housing and Urban Development, 1980), Washington, D.C.

complete our budget. We are still working in this area. We use a management analyst system to reduce our departments. In fact, in our County Clerk office, we are about to adopt a process whereby we will reduce the staff by 13 people before the end of this budget year going into next year's budget. The management analyst went into this department at the County Clerk's request because the Clerk knew it was going to have to happen. There was going to be a reduction in his department, money-wise, and he wanted to do it and organize the department the best possible way. We had arguments with department heads, and I mean real arguments, because they have asked for money to hire people that we had some questions about them doing. So we have sent members of [County Controller] McGraw's management analyst staff into those particular departments and even though department heads may disagree with their findings, we have been able to reduce budgets and we've even added in some areas that have used this system.

Moderator

David Bell is Public Works Director in Sherman, Texas and I'd like to direct the same question to him as a department head. How do you use performance measures in your city?

Mr. Bell

Sherman's performance measures system was being initiated as I came to work for the city and the first thing I used it for was as a way to help me evaluate the situation that I was getting into. People were looking at their performance and they were developing their indicators. I was able to work with the superintendents that I was to supervise, evaluate how well they were able to collect data, how well they were able to measure their performance. It just helped me get acquainted with the organization.

Since that time, I've also been able to use the measurement system on a routine basis to monitor various division activities and particularly the performance of the superintendents that work for me. Finally, as we developed better indicators, I was able to use the information that is generated through that system to justify things that I believe are right in managing the public works department of the city.

I can also use the information to speak with my manager or with my council and suggest things that I think need to be changed and how they can be changed and come back to the indicators and say why they need to be changed.

Moderator

It's amazing: you can see that performance measurement is used to reduce the budget as well as to justify a budget increase.

I'd now like to hear from the former city manager of Sherman, Texas, Ed Seegmiller, to give us a general management viewpoint of the use of performance measures.

Mr. Seegmiller

We need constantly to justify what we're doing. Without carefully collecting, analyzing, and monitoring the data as a useful tool, it's difficult to gain council support. Performance measurement has given Sherman's management the credibility needed in the community and in the council, and I think it gives the council credibility in the community.

EXAMPLE 3.2 THE DALLAS STREET INVENTORY SYSTEM

Duncan Rose, Formerly of the
Office of Management Services

One of the most frequently received service complaints in American cities involves street repair. What manager's office or street department has gone a day without receiving a call inquiring, "why isn't the chuckhole in front of my house repaired yet?" Most cities would like to have, as a service level objective, streets which are all safe and comfortable to ride upon and pleasing to look at. But few obviously can or will pay for such a high level of repair. As every street cannot be instantly and perfectly repaired when failures develop, management is confronted with a double-edged policy problem: *how much* street repair is sufficient and *which* streets get repaired?

In 1973 the director of the newly created Department of Streets and Sanitation Services in Dallas decided to initiate a systematic way to decide the "how much" and "which" issues and instructed the development of a street rating and inventory system. Over time, the system has become known as the street inventory system.

As developed, the street inventory system lists 52 pieces of information about each street segment in the city. Among the 52 descriptive elements are such items as block number, maintenance responsibility (city, county, state, etc.), class of street (freeway, thoroughfare, etc.), type of street surface, and most important, condition of street segment.

"Condition of street segment" is the heart of the system. Each segment of street can be rated into one of five categories ranging from A (good) to E (unacceptable). (A sixth category, U, is reserved for streets in fair or above condition but with a poor utility cut.*) Each category is carefully defined. Photographs of streets in each category are part of the definitions. The inventory is fielded annually by a small team of trained observers to insure consistency across the city. The observers cover all city streets by car and are spot checked by senior staff members. The street inventory data base, which was initially manual, was computerized during the second inventory to facilitate data analysis. The geographic information was gradually changed to be consistent with the street names and classifications used by the police department and other city data bases.

Using the descriptive information in the street inventory file, the Street Division can now accurately identify the number of lane-miles in each condition category. By establishing an average cost of repair per lane-mile by category, an approximate total cost of repair can be derived. In short, Dallas can reasonably estimate the cost of repairing and maintaining all streets in the city street system at a given repair service level (A, B, C, etc.). Also, by establishing criteria, priorities for the timing of repairs can be systematically established. An example of such repair priority might be: all thoroughfares in condition E, then D; followed by all secondary streets in condition E, then D; etc. The analysis of the first street inventory told Dallas policy makers that the streets were generally in a much poorer condition than they had thought. This was confirmed by Dallas's first household survey in which citizens gave the city very low ratings for street conditions and placed high budgetary priority on street maintenance relative to other services. Just as important, the street inventory analysis told the city manager and council what they would have to spend to bring street conditions up to specific levels of quality. Knowing what they would get for their money and, fortunately, having the resources available, the council approved a substantial increase in the street maintenance budget. Since then, the council and manager have used updated street inventory data each year to help decide "how much" to spend on street maintenance, and the Director of Street Maintenance has used the data to decide "which" streets to improve.

Over the years, the street inventory data base has been used by the city in additional ways not originally anticipated. It has provided a rationale for allocating Community Development Block Grant funds to street surfacing and resurfacing and repairs of curbs and gutters in community development target areas. The information has been used, in combination with other data, by the City Department of Housing Rehabilitation for the designation of intensive code enforcement areas. In 1978, the data were used by the Department of Public Works, again in concert with other information, for allocating capital improvement bond funds for street improvements. Several other city departments have also requested street inventory information.

---

*Refers to a poor repair made by a utility company after cutting into the street to fix a utility line.

EXAMPLE 3.3 PERFORMANCE MEASUREMENT IN IOWA CITY

Neal G. Berlin
City Manager

In Iowa City performance measurement is a simple way of learning essential facts about the city and services provided. Performance measurement provides an opportunity for determining community directions, facilitating political decisions by policy makers, determining program and project timing, and monitoring effectiveness and efficiency of city operations. The performance measurement approach used in Iowa City includes:

1. City council annual goal setting;
2. Quarterly operational and budgetary reports as part of a management by objectives program;
3. Other simple reporting mechanisms used by both the city council and management; and
4. Citizen input received in a variety of ways.

The city council annually identifies, in a goal setting session, 6 to 12 priorities for the city for the coming year. These goals provide both the foundation for emphasis in the annual budget preparation by department heads and the basis for reports to the city council in the coming fiscal year. In the following year the progress toward these goals becomes the basis for the next goal setting session.

Quarterly reports, usually on a single page per service division, are provided to the city council. These combine financial information and specific performance measurement progress toward objectives for the department or division. In reviewing these reports the city council generally will concentrate on identified problems or needs for goal modification.

Special performance measurement reports may develop out of the city council's discussion of the quarterly reports. For example, for the Community Development Block Grant Program, a special monthly report has been established for each neighborhood site improvement, with a specific progress report for each project.

To measure performance for each major capital improvement project and the overall status of the Community Development Block Grant Program, large charts which depict monthly progress are available in the city council's meeting room to inform it regularly of each project. It also establishes a future time line for each project. This assists the city council in responding to inquiring citizens.

Many other methods are used to provide performance measurement input to the city council and the staff. These include neighborhood planning and project progress meetings with citizens, informal meetings with employees, department head performance contracts, and citizen surveys.

Citizen surveys are an important part of the performance measurement process. Each month approximately 300 forms are sent to residents selected at random. The returns identify specific problems and also items of satisfaction. In addition, the questionnaire provides an opportunity for the city to indicate to the citizen sincere interest in citizen views. The form includes an invitation to call if there should be a problem at some future time together with the information necessary to insure that the concern receives prompt attention. The single page form asks a variety of questions, including attitudes about city services, level of response to previous citizen service requests, city services which the citizen would reduce or increase and how such changes would be financed.

The use of performance measurement in Iowa City has resulted in:

1. The city council and staff working together more effectively as a team;
2. The city council dealing more frequently with community direction and goals;
3. Both the city council and the staff tending to concentrate on the process of meeting specific goals or accomplishing specific tasks;
4. The city council having a more realistic understanding of the capabilities of the staff;
5. Increased pressure by the city council upon the staff for performance of *planned* work, and less pressure for ad hoc assignments;
6. Increased accountability throughout the system;
7. Improvement in the city council decision-making process;
8. The creation of a means by which the need for change in the system can be easily identified; and
9. Improvement in the information provided to citizens concerning community direction and government accountability.

EXAMPLE 3.4 DAYTON'S PROGRAM STRATEGIES

Paul R. Woodie
Assistant City Manager
Dayton, Ohio

In the 1960s and early 1970s, the City of Dayton adopted several "modern management" techniques such as program budgeting, management by objectives (MBO), and citizen surveys. In 1974, these were combined into a decision-making framework called "program strategies." As it evolved, Dayton's program strategies framework now includes: a strategic planning process, a five-year program budgeting structure, special client surveys as well as regular general citizen surveys, MBO and audits of the MBO program, special program evaluations, and a performance-based merit pay plan for executive level, senior, and middle managers.

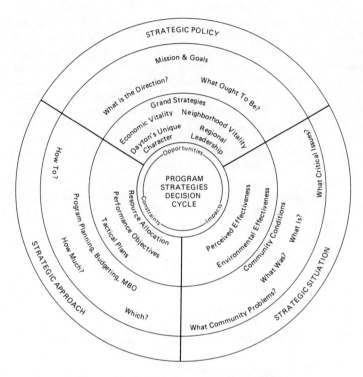

Figure 3-2. Dayton Program Strategies Guide.

The purpose of the program strategies framework is to provide the city commission with a practical means to articulate as well as to control public policy issues. Further, it is designed to insure the translation of policies and strategies into programs, and programs into desired outcomes. As shown in Figure 3-2, program strategies assumes a continuum of decisions, actions, and measurable results operating within three strategic dimensions. As summarized below, each dimension has its own set of key questions, and its own planning and measurement format:

DIMENSION	QUESTION	PLANNING AND MEASUREMENT FORMAT
Policy	What ought to be?	Policy goals and strategies
Situation	What was? What is?	Effectiveness measures, in terms of community conditions and perceptions
Approach	How to? How much? Which?	Tactical plans; resource allocation; program, management, and personal objectives

The program strategies process assumes that the purpose of all public policy is to control or alter certain community conditions through the delivery of municipal services. Though I will briefly describe each separately, the three dimensions are intended to work together as a continuum (hence the circle format of Figure 3-2), with the results in each dimension affecting the actions in all three. The three brief decision cases at the end of this example demonstrate this interaction.

THE POLICY DIMENSION

For a body of public policy to be more than an expression of lofty goals, it must be internally consistent, measurable over time, and reasonably achievable. In the Dayton decision-making process, the apex of the policy hierarchy consists of the following five grand strategies which are annually reviewed by the city commission at the commencement of the budget preparation cycle.

GRAND STRATEGIES: Policy goals for:
- Economic vitality
- Neighborhood vitality
- Dayton's unique character
- Intergovernmental affairs
- Urban conservation

Each of these five policy goals has a set of measurable objectives. For example, the goal of economic vitality is delineated by eight objectives such as "increase the number of jobs in the central business district." Progress toward each objective is annually appraised using verifiable indicators (how many jobs this year compared to last). All other strategies, departmental objectives, and major legislative actions are subordinate to these policy goals and tested against the set of objectives.

Just below these grand strategies are three- to five-year action plans called "strategy statements" which have been formally adopted for several issues, including transportation, land use, economic development, and social services. These statements are usually fashioned by a task force of citizens, policy analysts, and program operators. Each action plan includes documentation of current community trends, a set of strategy objectives, program priorities, and demographic targets. Most important, each statement must contain an impact assessment on each policy goal. For example, the transportation strategy describes a plan not only for the efficient movement of people and goods but must do so while enhancing economic vitality and neighborhood vitality. The consequence of this process resulted in the abandonment of public easement within neighborhoods in order to affect positively the perception of neighborhood integrity.

Without the hinge provided by the strategy statements, the policy goals would be merely rhetorical and the program objectives might be nothing more than bean counting.

THE SITUATION

In a political environment, the urgency of a given policy or strategy is dependent upon either the perception or reality of a community condition or trend. Both perception and reality are equally important to an elected official. For example, while downtown might statistically be the safest place to be in the city, there may well be a general feeling of insecurity on the part of both merchants and potential customers. To ignore one or the other fact might result in an irrational action by the elected officials. The city manager could well convince the city commission that no problem exists and, therefore, no action is necessary. *Or* the elected officials, under pressure from merchants, might order the deployment of additional police downtown resulting in a reduction of police protection elsewhere or a large increase in the police budget. Both solutions are incorrect. If indeed, the sense of security downtown is low, this will inevitably translate itself into loss of trade and loss of tax base. The mandate of our economic vitality goal would be adversely affected. However, putting extra police where there is no real crime problem is costly and inefficient. This problem did arise in Dayton. (Our response is described in the first brief case at the end of this example.)

That is but one example of the importance of combining verifiable "facts" about community conditions with public perceptions. This process results in "community condition statements," which exist for every major service, strategy, or new program. The statements are designed to provide decision makers with basic information about trends, perceptions, and demographics. As a part of this effort, the city has commissioned an annual public opinion survey since the early 1970s. This survey provides essential information on ongoing effectiveness of basic municipal services. In addition, special surveys are conducted periodically to appraise opinions and attitudes which affect human choice (e.g., location decisions of businesses), as well as special "client" surveys of the users of specific programs.

There is an important fact that should be remembered when using opinion surveys. Surveys are only useful in establishing a trend line. Analyzing a single survey and proclaiming that 65 percent of the general public believe streets are clean, *and this is good,* will only raise questions about the other 35 percent. Or, ranking satisfaction of one service over another may only mean that one is more popular than the other. (No one thinks the level of housing inspection is satisfactory.) What *is* important in determining program effectiveness is a comparison of one year to the next.

The importance of trends can be generally extended to all measures of community conditions. Rarely does periodic measurement identify a condition that is so hazardous to public health and safety that immediate, "all-out" action against the problem must take precedence over other city business. Generally, new programs, or changes to existing programs, to improve conditions can be considered in the context of overall community strategies during the normal planning and budgeting cycles. Policy and program effectiveness are determined by the *trends* of measured community conditions. Are they better this year than last? Are they worse? Are we winning or losing the game to reach our policy objectives?

THE APPROACH

Within the policy goals and strategies and in response to changing community conditions, programs are devised, modified, and abandoned; tactical plans are established, resources are allocated, and individual performance contracts are drawn. Objectives are seen as a means toward an end. Resources are generally the fuel.

As part of Dayton's long-standing management by objectives program, every program within the city or funded by the city has a set of annual objectives and corresponding performance measures. Overall, the MBO program involves a mix of both effectiveness measures and efficiency measures. The objectives are prepared by the departments in response to a budget message which includes the policy goals, strategies, and condition statements. After a determination by the policy analyst that the objectives are responsive, they are reviewed by the various neighborhood councils and appropriate task forces and submitted to the city commission as part of the "program strategies" document. Here is a sample of these program objectives and performance measures:

- *Objective:* To increase by 3 percent the level of perceived security among residents.
  Performance Measure: Percentage of public opinion survey respondents who classify neighborhoods as "safe."
- *Objective:* To limit the number of valid citizen complaints pertaining to waste collection.
  Performance Measures: (1) Valid complaints per 1000 housing units served; (2) Total number of valid complaints.
- *Objective:* To complete 95 percent of hazardous street and alley repairs within one work day.
  Performance Measures: (1) Number of hazardous street and alley repairs; (2) Number completed within one work day; (3) Percentage completed within one work day; (4) Percentage completed within three work days.

1980
PERFORMANCE REPORT

HOUSING AND NEIGHBORHOOD AFFAIRS

OBJECTIVE	CRITERIA	80 ESTIMATE	80 ACTUAL
Management/Housing and Neighborhood Affairs			
1. To design and implement, through Housing and Neighborhood Affairs, a voluntary paint-up/ fix-up project.	1a. Number of homes improved b. Number of neighborhood home improvement workshops	100 5	33 0
2. To determine the feasibility of the Housing Clinic concept as a judicial sentencing alternative for housing and environmental violators.	2. Date report submitted	3-10-80	12-79
	COMMENT: Study done in conjunction with the University of Dayton concluded such a concept would be feasible. Report submitted to Ohio Board of Regents but was not approved.		
3. To implement geographic housing and environmental services recommendations.	3. Date implementation completed	3-31-80	3-1-80
4. To prepare a procedure manual for holding Priority Board elections.	4. Date manual finished	2-29-80	2-29-80
5. *To assist in the planning and coordination of the Summer Environmental Clean-up and Neighborhood Youth Corps programs.	5. Percent of neighborhoods notified at least 30 days prior to implementation of programs	100%	100%
	COMMENT: Objective achieved.		

HOUSING CONSERVATION

Geographic Housing Inspection

OBJECTIVE	CRITERIA	80 ESTIMATE	80 ACTUAL
6. *To close 2,500 structural housing cases; and close 30% of those properties listed in the 1980 Worst First Property Inventory, and to have at least 65% of all occupied structures on the Worst First Property Inventory either closed or in legal order stage by December, 1980.	6a. Number of closed structural cases b. Number of structures in 1980 Worst First Property Inventory c. Number of Worst First closed d. Percent of Worst First closing e. Number of occupied open Worst First cases in legal order stage (12/31/80) f. Percent in legal order stage or closed	2,500 30% 65%	2,640 2,207 672 30% 610 58%
	COMMENT: Objective partially achieved.		
7. To complete on-site investigations of 90% of all citizen structural complaints within 2 work days and 100% within 5 work days.	7a. Number of citizen complaints b. Number of responded to within 2 work days c. Percent responded to within 2 work days d. Percent responded to within 5 work days	90% 100%	2,629 2,207 34% 92%
8. *To stimulate $2,000,000 in inspector initiated residential property improvements.	8. Dollars invested for residential property improvements	$2,000,000	$3,506,909
	COMMENT: Objective nearly doubled.		
9. *Through coordination with RECORP and CWDC, establish a process through which a portion of home improvement loans are directed to structures with open notice of violations and legal orders.	9a. Date process established b. Percent of CWDC home improvement loans to structures with open BHI's and legals c. Percent of BHI and legal order recipients receiving loan information	1-31-80 10% 100%	4-15-80 7% 100%
	COMMENT: Objective achieved.		
10. To secure owner consent to demolish 80% of those garages identified for removal under the Garage Demolition Program.	10a. Number of garages demolished b. Number demolished through Housing Inspection referral c. Percent demolished through referrals	150 120 80%	150 150 100%
11. *To develop and implement a structured case follow-up system which ensures cases proceed expeditiously through the enforcement process.	11. Date system implemented	3-30-80	3-30-80
	COMMENT: Objective achieved. Department indicates system has proven to be very successful.		

-42-

*High Priority Objectives

Figure 3-3. Excerpt from Dayton's 1980 Annual Performance Report.

Departments report performance against most objectives quarterly. Figure 3-3 shows an excerpt from an Annual Performance Report done by Dayton.

In addition to organizational objectives, for the past several years the city has had an incentive pay plan for management employees that centers on a set of personal and professional achievement objectives. The incentive pay plan was started with department directors and has recently been extended down to middle managers at the program level. The plan allows the city manager to apply the limited funds available for managerial raises differentially to reflect individual performance. It gives managers an extra incentive to achieve the city's objectives.

The Dayton Office of Management and Budget coordinates the MBO program and annually conducts a number of "MBO audits" and special evaluation studies of service agencies to verify reported performance to identify potential operating improvements.

THREE DAYTON DECISION CASES

Perception versus reality. As mentioned previously, in Dayton the statistical reality of low crime rates downtown was in direct conflict with citizens' perceptions of insecurity, as measured by citizen surveys. The *situation* of people feeling unsafe downtown threatened the *policy* goal of achieving economic vitality. Moving more police downtown, where there was little crime, would either significantly increase costs or leave other areas underprotected.

The proper *approach* was to define the problem as one of perception. Our response was to devise an action program whose singular purpose was to alter feeling of safety. It had two thrusts:

- Since the image of downtown was fostered by the media, we countered with a media campaign and a presentation to editorial boards.
- Since the perception of safety could be raised by a "police presence," we established a civilian force of uniformed parking control officers with walkie-talkies. The cost was half that of using police officers and was self-supporting through increased collections of parking fines.

In order to measure our program's success, we conducted an opinion survey of downtown merchants, downtown customers, and the general public *prior* to implementation to gauge the intensity of feelings of safety. After a year of experimentation, another survey was commissioned. There was a rather dramatic increase in the feelings of safety.

Efficiency versus effectiveness. In 1974, in response to low citizen satisfaction with the cleanliness of alleys, the city commission included in the five-year service plan a monthly alley cleaning program. Since this was a new program, we were able to employ the latest technology and the most efficient application of labor. Nevertheless, the general perception of cleanliness continued to decline. An evaluation suggested some minor adjustments and recommended a differential service in each neighborhood depending on the perception of cleanliness. Unfortunately, even this did not alter general feelings. As a result, at the end of the fourth year the decision was made to exclude the program from the next five-year plan. While the program was admittedly *efficient,* it was not *effective.* Because the ongoing evaluation was public and inclusive of both effectiveness as well as efficiency measures, the final decision was neither a surprise nor controversial. The department had a year to prepare for the close out and the commission was satisfied that we had tried.

The objective should follow the policy. Since the late 1960s the city had established a program objective to demolish 200 nuisance structures per year. After fine-tuning the program in the mid-1970s, we were able to meet the production requirement efficiently. Nevertheless, the commission and the neighborhoods were concerned. After drawing a *condition* statement, two facts emerged. First, the inventory of nuisance structures was growing at the rate of 300 per year. The city commission had unknowingly adopted an objective which permitted it to get farther behind the problem. Second, while demolition increased the sense of security in certain neighborhoods, it reduced the feelings of neighborhood prosperity in others. So the contribution to the neighborhood vitality *policy* goal was at best mixed. What was called for was a differential *approach* using demolition as one means, and sufficient resources to "deal" in a variety of ways with 300 nuisance structures.

CONCLUSION

Program objectives, even when measured, ought not to become the *end* product. Programs are *means,* not ends. The salient questions in any performance measurement system are — why are we measuring this, where have we been, and where are we going? Unless we can answer the latter, we may as well be counting beans.

4
Using Measurement to Improve Performance

People *use* measurement to make decisions to take *actions* to *improve service performance.* The intended result is more effective and efficient services — services that are more responsive to the needs and desires of the community, and that return more to the community for each tax dollar. Chapter 3 focused on the people who can use measurement and the decisions measurement helps them make. This chapter focuses on improving service performance.

The largest part of this chapter consists of examples written by local officials describing how they have improved performance in their communities with the help of measurement. The examples, grouped together at the end of the chapter, cover a variety of approaches to provide an idea of the many different ways communities can organize their performance measurement and improvement efforts.

In this part of the chapter, each of the general approaches covered in the examples is briefly described, providing an introduction to available performance improvement approaches. The general approaches covered are:

- Performance targeting and monitoring, such as management by objectives (MBO);
- Detailed measurement for making operational and organizational improvements, including:
  - Industrial engineering approaches (including operations research);
  - Organization development;
  - Performance incentives coupled with quality controls;
- Program evaluation and performance auditing.

These service improvement approaches are *not* mutually exclusive but can be combined in different ways for different uses. No one approach, or combination of approaches, is correct. The service and management problems in a community, the interests of its elected officials and managers, the abilities of its staff, and the resources committed, all have a bearing on the way performance measurement and improvement approaches will evolve to "fit" a community's own specific situation.

Inherent in any systematic approach to improving services are attempts to indicate and achieve *change*. The change can be a reallocation of resources: among services, among neighborhoods, among clients, among streets, among facilities, etc. Or the change can involve different policies and techniques for organizing and operating specific service programs. Often a change agent from outside the service program is used to help bring about change. The outside agent may be a consultant hired by the jurisdiction, or may be the city or county administrator's office, an office of management and budget, or an audit or evaluation office. In other cases, once the measurement system indicates a need for improvement and the desired change is agreed to by service program managers, it is left to the program managers to achieve the change (or service improvement) any way they can. The examples in this chapter provide an opportunity to compare different ways in which measurement can be used to help change service programs.

Some other important ideas examined in this chapter are these:

- *Different approaches to measuring and improving services tend to be complementary.* When a community uses two or more approaches, one approach often leads into another, or verifies the results of other approaches.
- *Selection of service programs* to improve — or at least to examine in detail — is an important issue in performance measurement. Several of the examples show how communities make these important selections.
- *A measurement program should be dynamic.* To remain useful and credible, the measurement program must change with changing conditions in the local government and with the changing needs of the community. Several of the examples, particularly the last two in this chapter, show how the evolution of service improvement approaches in communities has increased their usefulness.

PERFORMANCE TARGETING AND MONITORING
APPROACHES TO IMPROVING SERVICE PERFORMANCE

Performance monitoring involves periodic reporting of data for a consistent set of performance measures. Quarterly performance reports are fairly common, but actual reporting periods vary across communities: Charlotte, North Carolina, for example, uses three reports a year; Tacoma, Washington has used two a year. Some local governments use different reporting periods for different kinds of data. For example, a citizen survey may be done annually, while operational data are reported quarterly. This is the case in Dallas and San Francisco. In New York City, some operational data are reported monthly and some quarterly from operating departments to the Mayor's Office, which in turn makes two *Mayor's Management Reports* to the public each year covering selected performance measures.

Performance targeting means that the local government has set targets it will attempt to achieve for the performance measures reported. Targets that have been negotiated between different levels of management in an organization form the basis of management by objectives (MBO) approaches used in many communities, as indicated in the Iowa City and Dayton examples in chapter 3 and the Englewood, Ohio; San Francisco; and Charlotte examples in this chapter. In these five communities, the MBO objectives have been linked to the annual budget, making them targets for achievement within allocated resources. Note in Example 4.1 how Englewood's police objectives specify the cost increase allowable, if any, to achieve each objective. As shown in Example 4.2, San Francisco, aided by its automated budgeting and accounting system, includes unit cost efficiency targets within some of its objectives.

Performance targets are determined in a variety of ways. For example, they can be based on:

- *Historical data* (e.g., equal last year's performance, or improve on last year by X percent), such as Englewood's police objectives;
- *Engineered work standards:* Note in Examples 4.3 and 4.4 how the City of San Diego and Genesee County, Michigan use their industrial engineering techniques to set work standards for a department, then use those standards to target and monitor the department's performance;
- *Planned progress toward a longer-range community goal;* for example, increasing employment, increasing citizens' feelings of security, achieving equity of community conditions, completing planned steps in a community development project.

The most reliable targets of what an organization ought to be able to achieve are based on detailed studies of the service (see Examples 4.3, 4.4, and 4.7 on industrial engineering and program evaluation), such as engineered work standards used to target efficiency. Most performance targets used in local governments are *not* based on detailed studies. They are often based on historical data or the "expert judgment" of staff. These targets can be perfectly reasonable, so long as the local government does not equate the targets with *standards* for what is ideally achievable, and realizes that an agency that repeatedly achieves its targets may still have potential for substantial improvement.

Performance targeting and monitoring are most valuable when they are used to help achieve improved performance

Periodic performance reporting does not guarantee performance improvement. People must be prepared to make decisions based on the reports, and to set and achieve targets of improved performance. Selectivity in attempting improvement is an important part of achieving good results. A public official should take care in selecting programs and objectives for which large improvements will be sought, and those for which small improvements or the status quo will be considered acceptable. The periodic performance reports themselves can provide a valuable guide to those critical selections, as well as to basic policy decisions. All in all, there are three ways in which performance targeting and monitoring approaches can lead to improved performance:

- *Providing information to improve resource allocation and other policy decisions.* The Savannah example in chapter 2 is an excellent case of monitoring community conditions to help determine how public resources and service improvements should be allocated among neighborhoods.
- *Providing targets that "challenge" managers to improve services.* Alert managers of local service programs generally have a pretty good idea of the operational problems that exist in their services, and they usually know of a few things they can try on their own to help mitigate these problems. They may know where to shift an employee to relieve a bottleneck, improve response time, or reduce a backlog. They may know where supervision needs to be tightened, or where an extra quality control step added to existing procedures will improve effectiveness. MBO versions of performance targeting give service managers a chance to show they believe they can make some service improvements on their own, without "outside" help from the city or county administrator. Some performance objectives they negotiate become targets that challenge them for improvement. These performance improvements tend to be small, perhaps only a few percent, such as several of Englewood's police objectives shown in Example 4.1. These are the most prevalent improvements achieved through performance targeting. The cumulative effect of these small improvements for all services can be significant, as the pressure to increase the budget may be reduced just a bit in each service, and many small problems may never become big ones. Without the incentive of the "challenge" provided by the performance targets, however, many service managers may not make the extra effort to achieve these small improvements. In Example 4.2, San Francisco's MBO Don'ts List implies the need for this challenge by including conservatism and risk avoidance in objective setting as don'ts. As indicated in the Dayton example in chapter 3 and Example 4.11 on Phoenix, some communities have sweetened this incentive by basing managers' pay, in part, on the service performance they produce.
- *Identifying programs for detailed study.* The biggest service improvements involving measurement generally are achieved only after a careful examination of a service for operating problems and solutions, usually involving some "outside" intervention from a city or county administrator's staff, a budget or auditor's office, or a consultant. But any community has only limited analytic staff time or funds for consultants available for such detailed studies. The choice of which services to target for study and potential major

improvements is critical to getting the best results from a performance improvement program. Since some services may require capital investments or additional staff for significant improvement, thus affecting other scarce resources, that choice becomes even more important. The Englewood example shows how monitoring of citizen satisfaction helped identify four services as candidates for major improvement, and shows the reasoning process used to choose the one service in which this small community could afford to invest analytic time and new capital for equipment. The San Francisco example notes several cases in which MBO objectives and performance data focused mayoral and departmental efforts on important problems, leading to major performance improvements in a large city and county government. Example 4.9 on Charlotte shows how their MBO program and their monitoring of contractors' performance help trigger a number of the studies that city conducts of its service departments and contractors annually.

Top-level participation and careful preparation help translate performance monitoring into performance improvement

A pitfall to be avoided by any community embarking on a performance targeting and monitoring system is for paper processing to dominate the ultimate goal of such a system — to improve performance. Timely data collection and reporting are necesssary. But it is easy to let the pressure for filling out forms and preparing reports overwhelm any emphasis placed on developing useful objectives and performance measures, on meeting objectives, or on analyzing reports to help determine how to improve performance. One way to help insure that the "substance" (i.e., performance and objectives) of performance monitoring is taken at least as seriously as the "form" (i.e., collecting and reporting data) is to have top level, influential officials visibly participate in the measurement program. As described in Example 4.1, in Englewood the city manager met at first weekly, and eventually monthly, with managers from all departments to monitor actual performance against objectives. As described in Example 4.2, in San Francisco the mayor personally reviews departmental performance against objectives at the time of budget hearings and after the fiscal year is complete. The mayor's participation is highly visible through personal involvement in negotiation of departmental objectives and letters to department heads and commissions* acknowledging performance levels achieved, remaining problems, and expectations for further improvement. (See the mayor's letter to a department in Example 4.2.)

---

*In San Francisco, many departments report to independent commissions, with the mayor's authority coming more in development of the executive budget than in operational management. Thus, visible mayoral involvement during the budget process has been crucial to MBO's success.

Careful staff preparation is also needed to translate performance monitoring into performance improvement. In Englewood, the city manager purposely kept the monitoring system fairly simple due to the staff limitations, faced by any small community, for data collection and analysis. However, Example 4.1 indicates the careful preparation that went into the decision to select snow removal as the highest priority service for a major investment in improvement. In the City and County of San Francisco, where the MBO system is of necessity much larger and more complex than in Englewood, staff preparation has been thorough and has taken many forms. In San Francisco, it is impossible for the mayor to be well informed of all the objectives of all the departments at all times. The mayor's staff carefully analyzes past performance and proposed targets, takes care of as much negotiation of objectives as possible before mayoral involvement, and briefs the mayor on key objectives and performance issues in each department. Thus, the mayor is well prepared to participate in negotiation of budgets and objectives, and in departmental performance reviews. Example 4.2 includes a sample briefing paper the staff prepares for the mayor for these purposes.

But good preparation of the mayor or the city or county manager — or even of the chief executive's direct staff — can only carry improvement so far in a large city or county government. Far reaching improvement depends on developing strong managers and staff in the operating departments who understand performance measurement and how to use it to improve their own operations. San Francisco Mayor's Office staff have worked directly with hundreds of departmental managers and staff to help them develop credible objectives and select useful performance measures. The Mayor's Office has also prepared a series of brief, straightforward handbooks on the MBO system, for daily reference by departmental staff, including how MBO is related to the budget and accounting systems, how to develop objectives and performance measures, and how to analyze performance reports to identify problems and find ways to improve performance. This emphasis on preparation and development of departmental managers and staff — as well as mayoral staff — has been an essential ingredient in San Francisco's success.

DETAILED MEASUREMENT APPROACHES
FOR ACHIEVING OPERATIONAL AND
ORGANIZATIONAL IMPROVEMENTS

A service program or organization may be selected for special study for any number of reasons. Regular performance monitoring may have uncovered some weak aspect of the agency's performance. The council or commission may have singled out the program as having a high priority for improvement. The agency may have appeared as the subject of a newspaper article attacking waste in government. The program manager may have requested special help to solve a particular performance problem. Or the local government may have a sunset law or other policy requiring evaluation of every program in detail every five years or so, and it's simply this agency's turn in the barrel. Once a program has been selected, there are a number of ways a community can choose to study it in detail. However, the objective of the community is not to do a study. It is to improve performance.

Three categories of detailed performance improvement approaches are discussed here:

- Industrial engineering approaches (including operations research);
- Organization development approaches;
- Performance incentives with quality controls.

Some of these performance improvement approaches start with detailed studies that are intended to be followed by projects to implement service improvements. Other approaches, particularly some organization development techniques, combine the study and implementation phases into a continual process of problem solving, improvement, and evaluation. Each of these approaches requires careful examination of the operation and organization of a service program. These techniques generally involve the use of a "change agent" from outside the agency examined, whether government staff (e.g., from the budget office) or a consultant. In larger communities, a large service department with responsibility for many activities may already have on staff a person who is able to use industrial engineering or other approaches to help improve performance, and who thus serves as an internal change agent. When done properly, all of these detailed performance improvement approaches have in common:

- More detailed measurement and analysis than is usually required for performance monitoring in order to determine what needs to be improved and how to accomplish improvement; detailed measurement can also provide a "baseline" of the level of performance *before* change is introduced;
- Training, orientation, or other participation of operating staff to insure they can continue to provide improved performance after the change agent leaves;
- Performance measurement some time *after* implementation of improvements to determine how much service performance has actually improved.

The detailed performance improvement approaches often involve substantial investments of staff time, funds for consultants, or both. They also can generate extremely large payoffs in increased effectiveness and efficiency of services.

Industrial engineering approaches

Industrial engineering in private industry was an important part of the 1954 Broadway musical *Pajama Game,* in which a "time study man," stopwatch in hand, claimed to know how many stitches, per second, go into a pair of pajamas. Though their public sector use has not yet been honored by a Broadway show, industrial engineering techniques have proven successful in many local governments.

Perhaps the epitome of the industrial approach to performance improvement in the public sector is the one-person mechanized garbage truck used in some communities, including Phoenix and Scottsdale, Arizona. The driver — the only person with the truck — never has to get out of the cab. Large mechanized arms lift 90-gallon cans and empty them into the hatch on the truck with no visible human assistance.

Most industrial engineering approaches used in local government do *not* involve replacing people with machines; many do not require a stopwatch either. Generally, they involve improving the *methods* used to deliver service. Methods improvement can include scheduling the work better, organizing the work force better, or improving and standardizing the procedures that people working in the field or in offices use to do their daily tasks. Engineered work standards are often established as a result. Capital Improvements can be used along with methods improvements to increase performance further. Particularly if existing equipment needs replacing, a jurisdiction may want to buy new equipment that is better suited to the new methods or design new methods around more efficient modern equipment. However, improved procedures, organization, and scheduling often lead to performance improvements with *no* capital improvements. Because employees are better organized and managed, they can often accomplish more with extra individual effort. The slogan "work smarter, not harder" has been put into practice in many communities.

The City of San Diego, California has had an extensive work measurement program underway since 1975. As described in Example 4.3, San Diego's performance improvement staff has worked with city departments to develop engineered time standards for most municipal employees. They have been able to increase the level of service provided or reduce staff (generally by attrition) in programs they have studied. Their time standards become the basis for *performance monitoring* of each department studied. The activities of the performance improvement staff complement the city's *organization development* projects, described in Example 4.5 (see Example 4.10 for a description of the merger of these programs). San Diego now finds it useful to evaluate programs to insure that the right activities are being performed in the first place before submitting these activities to intensive work measurement studies. They also have a policy to restudy programs after five years to update standards and to achieve further improvement. Careful attention to selection of the first program to study (see selection criteria in Example 4.3) and to developing a well-trained analytic staff have helped build credibility for San Diego's program from the start, resulting in management's reliance on the performance information and improvements generated.

Industrial engineering techniques not only apply to operating field services such as sanitation, park maintenance, and vehicle maintenance. They also can be used to measure and improve the performance of many office services. Example 4.4 describes how the County Controller's Office for Genesee County, Michigan, has applied detailed measurement techniques to achieve significant white collar savings. Genesee applies the work standards it develops to a computerized labor cost-accounting system to establish rates of the productive use of personnel, to help identify overstaffed offices, and to provide information for budget preparation.

Another performance improvement approach that is sometimes grouped with industrial engineering techniques, and sometimes considered separately, is *operations research.* Operations research involves the use of mathematical models to simulate reality to help determine optimal solutions to operational problems. Measurement data can be used to develop and verify the assumptions that support the models, and to feed into the models so solutions can be calculated. Computer models have been used extensively for improving emergency services, such as determining police patrol districts or optimum ambulance locations. Over 100 communities have used computer models to determine the optimal number and location of fire stations. Akron, Ohio, has applied these techniques for planning and scheduling park services. However, not all models require the use of computers. "Paper and pencil" models that do not require advanced mathematics have been developed to design work schedules for extended hour services. Such models were initially tested by six California cities for work scheduling in libraries, wastewater treatment services, paramedic ambulance services, vehicle maintenance, and public beach services. They are applicable to almost any services with more than one shift or unusual hours of operation.*

Organization development approaches

A few local governments have taken *organization development* approaches to improve performance. Organization development (OD) looks at the total organization in four interrelated dimensions:

- Purpose of the organization: goals, objectives, and work performance targets;

---

*These models can be applied directly by using the *Work Schedule Design Handbook: Methods for Assigning Employees' Work Shifts and Days Off,* Office of Policy Development and Research, U.S. Department of HUD, Washington, D.C.

- Technology used: equipment and facilities;
- Work structure: work methods and procedures, supervisory structure;
- Staff: people working in the organization.

The approaches to measuring and improving performance discussed earlier in this chapter concentrate to varying degrees on the first three dimensions listed above. OD specialists consider the *people* dimension to be of equal importance to the others; they believe lasting improvements to an organization can only be maintained by building the internal capacity of the people within it. Good managers tend to adhere to this belief. Even if they do not use OD approaches to improve a program, they will not ignore the needs of its employees. OD specialists go further by explicitly insuring that employees (including managers and supervisors) are an integral part of the measurement and improvement process. They do not ignore the other three organizational dimensions. Instead, they work with all four together, often examining the interrelationships, to improve performance.

Many OD projects in local government have used the action research model to help identify and solve management or organizational problems. Briefly, action research* progresses through stages of gathering data, planning and implementing change, and evaluating the results of the process. Active participation of employees in all stages is stressed. As shown in Figure 4-1, in the action research model, there is continual feedback of information to the organization's personnel and repetition of the entire process to deal with new and unresolved issues. Action research does not terminate with an elegant solution. Rather, it provides practical answers to particular problems at specific times. The continual cycle of action research, in which new issues are constantly arising, makes organization renewal a continuing process and builds the capacity of individuals to respond positively to change.

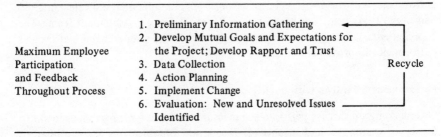

Figure 4-1. The Action Research Model.

*A detailed explanation of action research is available in: I. Chein, S. Cooke, and I. Harding, "The Field of Action Research," *American Psychologist,* Vol. 3, 1948, pp. 43–50.

The implementation process of a typical OD program operates using the following behavioral science principles and assumptions:

- An organization *and* the individual within it can achieve greater effectiveness.
- The most effective improvement efforts in an organization are those that are created and sought by all members of the organization.
- The best resource for improvement often lies with the knowledge and experience of the employees within the organization.
- A cooperative structure creates an opportunity for all members of the organization to participate actively in the planning and decisions that affect the social and technological improvement of their work.
- Many employees want to do their job better and will welcome the opportunity to contribute cooperatively to improvement.
- A significant improvement in the quality of life at work will increase employees' effectiveness, as well as the effectiveness and efficiency of the entire organization.

Organization development is a promising approach to improving public services. However, once an attempt is made to reach out to employees to learn their problems and ideas, some responsive action is extremely important. The initial intervention can raise employee expectations for action. Lack of action can cause employee motivation and performance to *decline*.

The City of San Diego has organization development specialists who use such techniques as action research, employee surveys and feedback, team building workshops, role clarification, management counseling, and supervisory training. As described in Example 4.5, they not only test that employee morale improves, but in some cases they have also made use of effectiveness and efficiency measurement to demonstrate that their OD techniques measurably improved service performance or provided direct cost savings. As Example 4.10 indicates, in 1980 San Diego's OD team was merged with the city's work measurement team. The complementary use of their different approaches has strengthened San Diego's performance improvement efforts.

Performance incentives with quality controls

Several communities use performance measurement as a basis for management or employee evaluation and incentives. Evaluation of objectives accomplished or levels of performance achieved can be the basis for determining promotions, performance bonuses, and other pay increases. There are also nonmonetary forms of performance incentives, such as allowing work crews to go home early when they have finished their assigned work for the day. In such programs, the "assigned" work will generally be a negotiated amount that is greater than the average amount performed before the incentive programs (e.g., longer garbage collection or street sweeping routes).

Performance incentives provide a viable way to reward managers and employees for good performance. They can see they have something tangible to gain by improving their performance. However, it is generally impossible to construct a practical, understandable incentive formula that includes every important aspect of a service. When there is something tangible to be gained, it is only human nature for people to try to maximize those performance elements built into the incentive formula, even at the expense of service quality or some other service aspect that may not be covered. Any explicit performance incentive program needs some form of safeguard or "quality control" to avoid being abused.

Incentive program safeguards can take several forms. Performance reports can be audited on a sample basis to verify achievements reported. Quality control can also be built directly into an incentive program to be sure work quality is not sacrificed for quantity. As described in Example 4.6, in a street sweepers' incentive program in Washington, D.C., a supervisor follows behind the sweeping crews to be sure an adequate level of cleanliness is achieved before allowing the crews to go home, if they have finished their work early. The District used, in part, an organization development approach to design and implement the incentive program. Employees suggested the program in the first place, and supervisors participated in designing new sweeping routes. The quality control, based on visual "trained observer" quality standards, insured that the incentives resulted in increased effectiveness as well as increased efficiency. The streets were cleaner with no added operating or capital costs. Neighborhood residents noticed the improvement, as measured by before-and-after surveys of citizen satisfaction.

Performance incentive safeguards need not always be as direct as verification audits and immediate quality controls. In communities that use incentives as only one of a variety of performance measurement approaches, data from other sources can be used to verify indirectly performance incentive results. For example, if citizen satisfaction with a service, as determined from surveys, falls while the service manager's performance objectives are achieved, some investigation may be warranted to see if the objectives are adequate to meet public needs, if they were actually achieved, or if they were achieved at the expense of quality or some service element not included in the incentive program. Both Dayton, Ohio (Example 3.4 in chapter 3), and Phoenix, Arizona (Example 4.11), use managerial incentives as one of several improvement approaches. Both communities have ample performance data from other sources to complement and safeguard the incentive program. Should problems arise, both cities have the ability to audit performance reports to verify achievements reported.

PROGRAM EVALUATION AND PERFORMANCE
AUDITING APPROACHES

Several names are used for a set of measurement approaches that often involve the most in-depth measurement studies of service organizations. Some of the names given to these techniques are program evaluation, performance evaluation, performance auditing, management auditing, and operational auditing. Since there is no standardization in this field, a name alone will not reveal what a jurisdiction is doing.* What these approaches have in common is the idea of *evaluation* of programs and services. The most comprehensive evaluations examine all aspects of a program, starting with whether the purposes and objectives of the program are properly defined, whether the objectives are adequate to meet important public needs, whether those needs actually exist, and whether that program is meeting those purposes and needs. More limited evaluations may examine narrower efficiency or effectiveness issues or may simply verify an agency's own performance reports. Program evaluations or audits always imply intervention by someone from outside the program studied.

Program evaluation and performance audit staffs use analysis techniques from industrial engineering, operations research, and organization development (e.g., employee surveys), and other disciplines such as economics and social research. A single evaluation may employ techniques from several disciplines, as in the comprehensive evaluation described in Example 4.7 on San Diego County. To meet this challenge, the San Diego County Office of Program Evaluation built a multidisciplinary staff from a wide range of professional backgrounds. Acting on requests from the Board of Supervisors, from the Chief Administrative Officer, and from operating departments, the Office of Program Evaluation served as a high-level problem solver that delved deeply into efficiency, effectiveness, organizational, and operational issues for even complex social programs such as Aid to Families with Dependent Children. Their recommendations often resulted in significant program changes, savings, and performance improvements.

Some performance auditing staffs actually live up to the word *audit* in that they do not report to management, but are selected by and report to some other body, such as the elected council. An *independent* city or county auditor must either be an elected official or, as is the case in Dallas, Texas and King County, Washington, must report directly to the elected council or commission. He or she also must be independent of all officials responsible for the management of operating programs (e.g., city manager, county administrator, or "strong"

---

*The auditing profession has strict standards for techniques referred to as "auditing," such as the "independence" of the auditor. But many management or budget offices that do not meet those standards refer to parts of their programs as audits. It is therefore important to look beyond names.

mayor) and accounting systems (e.g., finance director). Local auditors generally conduct financial audits, for which independence is a recognized professional standard. Some also conduct audits of legal compliance, particularly for federal grant programs. The Dallas and King County auditors conduct financial and compliance audits, but they are also mandated by their city and county charters to conduct audits of economy, efficiency, and effectiveness. The auditors' extra measure of independence can result in an extra measure of objectivity in their performance audits.

Because of the heavy staff commitment required to do evaluations, especially comprehensive evaluations, careful selection of programs to study is necessary to insure effective use of evaluation or audit staff. Program selection might be triggered by a performance monitoring system that shows consistently missed targets or inconsistent results (e.g., operating objectives achieved while citizen satisfaction drops). Programs might also be selected for study based on the interests of elected officials, total program costs, their visibility to the public, and general management observations. Selection might also be in response to a sunset law or other legal requirement, or to an "audit cycle" determined by policy rather than law.

As described in Example 4.8, the Dallas City Auditor uses a systematic process, involving the city council and city management, to determine which agencies will receive performance audits. The result is an annual audit plan scheduling agencies to receive comprehensive or limited scope performance audits during the fiscal year. The city council has final authority for approval of the annual audit plan. The timing of the audit planning process is coordinated with the city's budget preparation process so the council can consider audit priorities in the perspective of its spending priorities and can approve an audit workload that fits the constraints of the budget for the City Auditor's Office.

COMPLEMENTARY USE OF PERFORMANCE MEASUREMENT AND IMPROVEMENT TECHNIQUES

Many of the examples in this book include the complementary use of two or more performance improvement techniques by the same community. Charlotte, North Carolina is an excellent example of a community that combines a variety of measurement and evaluation techniques for more effective performance improvement.

As described in Example 4.9, performance targeting and monitoring is at the heart of Charlotte's performance measurement and improvement efforts. All city programs are targeted and monitored through a management by objectives (MBO) program. All human resource program contracts are targeted through objectives written into the contracts and are monitored by required performance reports to Charlotte's Office of Budget and Evaluation. The budget and evaluation staff evaluates all of these contracts for the city council. The performance reports guide the staff in doing each evaluation, helping them determine whether only a verification of acceptable performance is needed, or whether an in-depth evaluation should be done. Contract evaluations have often led to improved contractor performance or contract termination, as described in Example 4.9.

The Office of Budget and Evaluation also conducts program evaluations referred to as "performance audits" of operating departments. These audits are designed to verify performance reported in the MBO program, to determine the adequacy of objectives, and to identify potential operating improvements. Charlotte is attempting to audit the performance of all major city programs over a five-year period, though some audits may be triggered by MBO reports.*

The MBO program allows the Office of Budget and Evaluation to identify problems and achievements, and to work with departments to solve these problems and build on these achievements. The operating departments have been developing their own analysis capabilities so they can recommend and implement their own improvements. Charlotte is, therefore, in a good position to achieve many performance improvements because the MBO program establishes negotiated targets that "challenge" operating managers to improve services. The balance in analytic capability between the budget office and the operating departments creates a healthy atmosphere which fosters improvement, as budget and operating staff can better understand each other and work together.

When the same office that manages an MBO program also conducts program evaluations, a great deal of power is necessarily concentrated in one place. The strength of this arrangement is the ease with which monitoring of programs can be coordinated with evaluation for more effective performance improvement. Its weakness is the potential abuse of power, such as the budget director using the threat of an evaluation or "audit" to get departments to agree to particular objectives. Charlotte has avoided such a heavy handed approach, by placing a strong emphasis on improving performance at the initiative of operating departments. The development of analytic capabilities within the operating departments also serves to balance the "power" of the Office of Budget and Evaluation. Communities concerned with the abuse of power may want to separate performance monitoring and program evaluation functions into two different agencies. Coordination of these efforts so they will have a complementary effect is possible when they are separated, if a special emphasis is placed on communication among the officials involved.

---

*None of these "performance audits" would satisfy the auditing profession's standard of independence. Charlotte uses the term *audit* to distinguish these relatively narrow studies from more comprehensive (and more staff intensive) "program evaluations," such as that described in Example 4.7 on San Diego County.

PERFORMANCE MEASUREMENT AND IMPROVEMENT
PROGRAMS MUST CHANGE AS THE NEEDS OF THE
COMMUNITY AND THE LOCAL GOVERNMENT CHANGE

A few of the examples in this chapter describe or imply changes a community has made in its performance measurement programs in order to become more effective in achieving improvements. San Francisco, for example, has shown a continuing emphasis on developing and improving its MBO program, and has done extensive evaluations of the program. Charlotte's versatile programs are described as having evolved as management needs changed. As the needs of the community change, so too do the needs of the managers and policy makers who use a measurement program. To remain credible with its users and to translate measurement into better decisions and performance, a performance measurement and improvement program must change along with the community and the local government.

One of the most significant changes made by a community in recent years has been the integration of two City of San Diego programs referred to previously in this chapter. In 1980, San Diego merged its work measurement program (Example 4.3) and organization development program (Example 4.5) into a new, integrated unit, the Organization Effectiveness Program. The new unit is under the city's Financial Management Department.

While the city was pleased with the successes achieved by both of the original programs, over the years weaknesses became apparent in each. While leading to large savings and increases in efficiency, work measurement efforts have often seemed to result in decreased employee morale. Meanwhile, although important organizational benefits (e.g., improved communication and morale) were achieved through the organization development team's efforts, with a few exceptions (such as those described in Example 4.5), the team had difficulty quantifying the performance benefits of their projects. The merger was aimed at eliminating these weaknesses, and at making San Diego's already strong performance improvement efforts even stronger. As a result, the complementary use of two different performance improvement approaches has increased, strengthening the impact of both. Work measurement analysts and organization development specialists now often work together on the same project. Example 4.10 discusses the merger of the two programs and describes San Diego's resulting Organization Effectiveness Program.

The City of Phoenix, Arizona has had one of the longest standing and most acclaimed programs of performance improvement of any jurisdiction in the United States. In the late 1970s, however, a review of the program found it had stagnated to some extent, doing the same kinds of things it had done in its early years, but not achieving the same dramatic results. Phoenix had reached the point of diminishing returns for its detailed measurement and improvement efforts, directed and controlled almost exclusively by the budget office. Managers and employees in operating departments saw performance measurement as the budget office's issue, not their own. Example 4.11 describes how Phoenix has improved the situation by decentralizing improvement efforts, revising budgeting and measurement approaches, and instituting programs of organization development and performance incentives. Phoenix also made special efforts to increase organizational communication and provide recognition and rewards to employees who made significant contributions to performance improvement.

Phoenix learned it had to convince people that *effectiveness and efficiency are everyone's business.* In attempting to do so, the city government rejuvenated its performance measurement and improvement programs with increased participation and motivation. Phoenix also learned not to rest on past accomplishments, but to be prepared to modify its performance improvement efforts, as needed, to correct problems and to respond to a changing environment.

As described in Example 4.11, once Phoenix got its performance improvement programs moving again through its initial changes, it did not stop there. Phoenix continued with a series of dynamic, progressive changes over five years (and is probably still changing for the better). The most recent change described in Example 4.11, the creation of a Value Management Office which combines industrial engineering and organization development approaches to improvement, is particularly interesting in its similarity to San Diego's merger of the same two approaches (see Example 4.10). That two local governments with such impressive performance improvement records are both attempting to combine the same improvement approaches is worthy of note by all government officials.

IMPROVED DECISIONS AND IMPROVED PERFORMANCE: TWO SIDES OF THE SAME COIN

The use of measurement to improve decisions, as examined in chapter 3, and its use to improve performance, as examined in this chapter, are really two variations on the same theme. The object of the "improved decisions" is to *improve service performance* — to make services more responsive to community needs. Likewise, many performance improvement approaches involve *decisions based on measurement* — such as resource allocation decisions and decisions concerned with which services to study in detail.

Decision making and performance improvement are presented separately to show clearly two major perspectives communities take toward performance measurement. Dayton (see chapter 3) and Charlotte, for example, use many of the same measurement techniques. Dayton has consciously organized its measurement approaches into a "decision framework," while Charlotte views its measurement techniques as performance improvement tools. Yet, Dayton achieves significant operational improvements from its MBO and performance

incentive programs, and Charlotte's measurement uses include resource allocation decisions. Often a community's perspective on performance measurement
depends upon who provided the initial impetus for the measurement program or
who is the primary audience (e.g., the council or the budget director). Whether
a community consciously takes one or the other perspective, or both, the result
can be both improved decision making *and* improved performance.

Yet another important perspective on performance measurement involves its
use for public accountability and communication with citizens. Chapter 5 discusses how communication with citizens relates to the use of measurement in
improving decision making and performance. Additionally, the role played by
communication as the link between the performance of local government and
accountability to the public is examined in chapter 5.

EXAMPLE 4.1 PERFORMANCE MONITORING AND TARGETING IN ENGLEWOOD, OHIO

David A. Rubinstein
City Manager
Walker, Michigan
Former City Manager
Englewood, Ohio

The City of Englewood grew rapidly from the late 1950s to the late
1970s (from about 1,500 people to 13,500). But as the growth was
almost entirely residential, and the land use inefficient, the growth in
local public service needs exceeded the growth in tax base until a
financial crisis resulted in 1977.

It was from this springboard that the City of Englewood's performance
budget system and performance monitoring program were launched.

Performance monitoring can be a difficult task even for a large city
that can afford to provide significant staff and computer support. In a
small city where staff and computer support are often in short supply,
performance monitoring is even more difficult. It is, however, still
achievable and desirable.

Englewood's performance monitoring and targeting techniques have
included a management by objectives (MBO) system named "programmed objectives" and citizen surveys, both of which were linked to
each other (surveys were the source for some measures supporting
objectives) and to our new performance budgeting process.

Englewood's approach to performance monitoring was based upon
some important pre-implementation decisions. First, we decided to
place our emphasis on effectiveness measurement over efficiency
measurement. We felt heavy emphasis on the latter would require

excessive record keeping for accurate cost accounting, for which we did not have sufficient resources available. We had just completed (1977) a survey of a representative sample of our citizens as part of a project to write a new comprehensive community development plan. Citizen and user surveys were to become the key to our effectiveness measurement. In Englewood we used telephone, mail, and interview surveys. The mail survey was done in conjunction with our *Englewood Communique,* a newsletter mailed to every household with a return envelope (postpaid) and survey enclosed. This approach linked the performance monitoring system to our public relations program, a link which proved to be very useful when we had to demonstrate our need for a tax increase. The increase passed in 1978, during the height of nationwide public pressure for state and local tax reductions and limitations.

Our second decision was to establish benchmarks for all of our services and programs. These benchmarks, when missed, would put us into a "management by exception" mode and would cause us to delve more deeply for further information on a particular program or service. We used an MBO approach to negotiate these benchmarks with the department directors, and document them as written objectives. In the first year, each director was allowed to participate to the extent he or she desired. That year the city manager's office prepared objectives for many departments which were unable or unwilling to provide their own written objectives. The second year, negotiations centered on modifying the objectives.

Many of the benchmarks negotiated served as targets to "challenge" department directors to improve services and restrain costs. As the objectives are linked to the budget, they include the cost increases, if any, departments are allowed to help achieve them. As shown by some of the police department's objectives in Figure 4-2, the performance improvements negotiated are often small, but departmental efforts to achieve them within budgetary constraints save Englewood from the fate of either uncontrollable increases in service costs or deteriorating services in the face of inflation.

The third decision we made before monitoring performance was *not* to link the programmed objectives directly to the measurement of the success or failure of individuals, but to use them for measuring the success or failure of services and programs. A separate performance evaluation system for personnel was installed. We felt we could better tie these two systems together at some future date, if at all. Our chief concern was to avoid creating programmed objectives reports which would be manipulated to bestow glory upon all the participants, instead of fairly evaluating the relative success or failure of our services and programs.

Our fourth decision was that, with the exception of our surveys, we were not going to get into the data collection business. As a result of this decision, we used whatever information was available. There is a

Department of Police

Productivity Area	Indicator	Specific Measure	Data Source	1977 Actual	1978 Actual	1979 Objective
Crime Prevention and Control	Physical Casualties	Number and rate of persons (a) physically injured, (b) killed in course of crimes or nontraffic crime-related police work	Incident Reports	Number: (a) 60 (b) 0 Rate: (a) 5.0 (b) 0	Number: (a) 25 (b) 0 Rate: (a) 2.08 (b) 0	To reduce by 5% the total number and to maintain the existing zero rate, at a cost increase of 6%.
	Peacekeeping in domestic quarrels and other local disturbances	Percentage of domestic quarrels and other disturbance calls with no second call within 72 hours	Dispatch Records and Incident Reports	95%	94%	To maintain current percent of success rate, at a cost increase of 6%.
	Stolen Property	Percentage of stolen property that is subsequently recovered: (a) vehicles (b) other property value	Incident reports, arrest or special property records	(a) 80% (b) 49.3%	(a) 74% (b) 15%	To maintain vehicle recovery rate and increase other property recovery rate by 3%, at a cost increase of 6%.
Responsiveness of Police	Response Time	Percentage of emergency or high-priority calls responded to within 3 minutes and percentage of non-emergency calls responded to in 7 minutes	Dispatch Records	*Emergency* 75% 55% *Nonemergency* 83% 78%		To increase the rate of compliance with emergency response time to 80%. Retain nonemergency response time at approximate current levels at no increase in cost.

Figure 4-2. Englewood, Ohio "Programmed Objectives" Document (excerpt).

lot of it in all local governments. The police department routinely collects data which can be used for both efficiency and effectiveness measurement. The wastewater plant must report voluminous data to comply with its NPDES permit.* The water department must report water quality data to the state to show our water supply meets health standards. It can easily be determined how many tons of asphalt were used by the street department's spring "fill up the pothole" program and how many streets were resurfaced. Similarly, it is easy to determine how many tons of salt were used on the streets last year and the year before. The finance department is a great source of information on all departments and can be used extensively.

Our fifth decision was that we would not be overly critical of the departments' objectives in the beginning of the program. We would work to improve upon them as the subsequent years passed and as the department directors became more familiar with writing good objectives statements and the rest of the MBO process.

So much for philosophy; how did it work? The performance monitoring system was made part of our year-round budget calendar. Because we wanted our resource allocation decisions to be made on the basis of what we wanted to accomplish most (goals priorities), we prepared a Programmed Objectives Document early in our budget process. These objectives were negotiated in early June, reviewed by the city manager in early July, and approved by the city council at the end of July. These objectives, once established, were then monitored at regular "management review meetings" between the city manager and the staff. These meetings were weekly at first and eventually became a monthly event. The city council was briefed at least once a quarter. The briefing consisted of slides showing objectives, current performance trends, and comparisons of key activities to previous years and other "benchmarks." Unless the benchmarks were missed, discussion rarely got beyond understanding what each slide said. Citizen survey results were reported as they became available to provide citizen perception data that complemented information on department activities and accomplishments. New information was reported as needs changed, in order to maintain a dynamic reporting system.

One of the most important uses of performance monitoring information is the identification of service problems and success to management, the city council, and the public. Both long-range problems (e.g., growing service demands expected to exceed resources) and short-range problems (e.g., poor snow removal) are important to identify. Short-range problems identified by surveys allow us to demonstrate responsiveness to taxpayer needs and wants, and to fend off special interest demands and "squeaky wheel" complainants whose service requests

---

*National Pollution Discharge Elimination System permit issued by the state under the authority of the State and Federal Environmental Protection Adminstrations.

may not be representative of community needs. Careful selection of problems to address in depth is especially important for a small community like Englewood, whose resources for analytic studies, capital improvements, or new service employees are extremely limited. The following case illustrates how that selection process has worked in Englewood.

In the 1977 survey, a representative sample of our citizens was asked to rate all of our city services. They were asked to give each service one of three ratings: more than satisfactory, satisfactory, or unsatisfactory. The survey results clearly indicated four services as being "more of a problem" than the others. These services were street cleaning and repair — 19.5 percent unsatisfactory; water service — 24.2 percent unsatisfactory; sewer service — 20.1 percent unsatisfactory; and snow removal — 27.3 percent unsatisfactory. For comparison purposes, all other non-recreational services received between 0.5 and 7.0 percent unsatisfactory ratings. We wanted to be able to have a short-range, visible impact on at least one of these four problems. So we tried to identify which problem had the "most achievable" solution. Our reasoning process involved a closer examination of information already available on these services, and discussions with managers and staff familiar with the problems.

We decided the water service survey rating was due to the taste and color of the water and to the high water rates. As taste and color problems were produced by the "hardness" of our source of supply (wells) which could not be corrected without building a water treatment plant at a local cost of over $1 million, this was determined to be a long-term proposition at best. The sewer problem was related to sewage backups into basements caused by inadequate drainage, illegal cross-connections, aging sewer lines, and high rates. These problems were being addressed through a federal grant program, but their solution was also determined to be a long-term proposition. Also, the sewer fund was already operating in an actual deficit, and the water fund was very close to being in a deficit.

In examining the two remaining problems, our analysis showed the majority of street repair complaints were from new subdivisions which still had undedicated streets and were the responsibility of the developers. So the impact of improving street services in areas under the city's responsibility would be limited. This left snow removal.

On examining our snow removal problem, we first asked whether the poor survey rating was just due to heavy snows that winter, or whether our equipment, facilities, and procedures needed improvement. It did not take much examination to determine:

- Our equipment was old, too limited, and maintained in an unsafe, outmoded 65-year-old garage;
- We were caught short of snow removal personnel whenever there was a large snowfall;

- Routes had never been studied for efficient and effective removal;
- All of the problems except the garage were solvable in the short-run within available resources, and a new garage was an affordable and necessary longer-term capital investment.

On this basis, snow removal was given our highest priority and was identified as such to the city council and the public. The city invested in new equipment and made more personnel available for snow removal. The city also established a long-range goal of replacing our old city garage with a new and safe facility. The staff reviewed and changed snow removal routes and other operational methods. The next two winters turned out to have just as heavy snows as 1977, but we were ready for them. In 1979 the city again surveyed the citizens on snow removal and the improvement was dramatic. In an article entitled "You Asked For It — You Got It" in our city newsletter we reported the results. The percentage of people rating the service as unsatisfactory decreased from 27.3 percent to 11 percent — a big improvement.

Performance monitoring alone did not lead to the selection of snow removal as the service to improve. As the reasoning process described above implies, some "informed management judgment" was also used. No amount of data can *replace* a manager's judgment — but measurement can *sharpen* that judgment. "Informed judgment" could have identified other services in which short-range improvements were possible. But without the survey, we may not have picked a service of such concern to the public. This is particularly important when improvement requires new investments, as in our snow removal case, which should go to high-priority needs.

Although we picked snow removal as having the "most achievable" improvements in the short run, we did not ignore the other service problems identified in the survey. The survey warned us to keep an eye on those problems, and to work for long-range solutions—as we already were for the sewer problem.

In sum, performance monitoring and targeting helped Englewood keep service managers challenged to provide good services at reasonable costs, helped direct service improvement efforts and investments where they were most needed, and helped identify needed longer-range improvements. Performance monitoring is hard work, but it pays!

EXAMPLE 4.2 THE MANAGEMENT BY OBJECTIVES PROGRAM OF THE CITY AND COUNTY OF SAN FRANCISCO

R. Peter Henschel
Director
Resources Management Program
Office of the Mayor

In late 1978, the City and County of San Francisco began to develop a management by objectives (MBO) performance measurement, management, and budgeting system. City leaders hoped to provide public administrators with the tools necessary to perform more effectively. They also hoped to use MBO to better inform citizens on the operation of San Francisco's government. Today, MBO is used by nearly all city departments. The mayor and city officials use it to make budget decisions, to monitor and improve performance, strengthen management, and present service information to the public. In short, MBO has become a valuable system with many useful applications. A brief discussion of the MBO techniques and how they are applied in San Francisco is presented below.

WHAT IS MBO?

MBO is based on techniques firmly established in the private sector. With MBO, executives can carry out a comprehensive strategy for their organization. The organization establishes its long-range goals, the objectives it will fulfill in order to reach these goals, and specific measures it will use to assess its performance in meeting these objectives. Through this process, a system is established for the evaluation of performance by each organizational unit. Each manager plans, budgets, and manages his or her unit in order to achieve the organization's overall goals and objectives.

SAN FRANCISCO'S ADAPTATION OF MBO

In 1978, then-Mayor George Moscone decided to try to apply MBO to the administration of San Francisco government. The passage of Proposition 13 (which severely limits local property taxes in California), other budget cuts, and increased public scrutiny of local government, underscored the need to improve effectiveness and efficiency, and to assess government performance. Mayor Dianne Feinstein recognized the potential benefits of MBO, and encouraged its further development and implementation as part of her overall management improvement efforts.

By 1982, 55 city departments were on MBO. The mayor has continued to evaluate the usefulness of MBO, in order to insure that the system be as meaningful as possible. The MBO process, and some of the results to date, are summarized below.

The MBO process in San Francisco. Each year, city departments and the Mayor's Office work together to develop the goals, objectives, and specific measures they will concentrate on in the next fiscal year. The Mayor's Office encourages broad participation in developing departmental objectives and performance measures to help insure their usefulness to departmental managers. For example, over 150 managers and supervisors in Social Services were involved in initial development of performance measures for an agency with over 3000 employees. To assist departmental staff, the Mayor's Office has prepared and distributed a series of brief handbooks for staff to use as reference tools in their daily work. The handbooks describe the MBO system and how it relates to San Francisco's computerized budgeting and accounting system, and provide useful "how to" information to aid in developing objectives and performance measures, and in analyzing performance reports to identify problems and opportunities for improvement. Figure 4-3 shows an excerpt from one of these handbooks.

Departments collect data on their performance measures. The Mayor's Office helps departments monitor the data collection and enter the information into the computerized budget and accounting system. The system contains data on each department program, including the program's budget (detailed reporting of revenues and expenditures), performance objectives, and targeted and actual results for each performance measure. The computerized accounting system aids in cost accounting and calculation of many efficiency measures, which are often built into the program objectives, as in the objective:

To provide the citizens of San Francisco a clean, attractive, safe, external environment by cleaning 162,000 miles of public streets using less than $23.93 labor cost per mile in 1980–81.

Performance against an objective such as this one may be gauged by reporting data for multiple performance measures covering workload, efficiency, and effectiveness, as shown in Figure 4-4, a sample computer printout page from a quarterly detailed performance report.

In a few short years, departments' sophistication in their use of MBO has grown. For example, they have developed comprehensive long-range plans to reduce problems that became apparent through the MBO process and have used MBO to justify budget requests.

Twice a year Mayor Feinstein formally reviews each department's MBO performance. In the spring she uses MBO results for the first half of the fiscal year to evaluate department requests and develop the budget

2. OBJECTIVES MUST EXPRESS THE EXPECTED RESULT, NOT THE
    PROCESS FOR OBTAINING THE RESULT.

Examples:

RESULTS		PROCESS
To reduce congestion	not	To build a bridge
To decrease accidents	not	To provide stop signs
To improve cleanliness	not	To sweep streets
To reduce error rate	not	To decrease caseloads
To reduce the number of burglaries in the downtown area by 10%	not	To increase the number of patrol hours in the down-town area by 10%

But why did you build
the bridge there when
the congestion is
here??

I thought my objective
was to build a bridge
not to reduce congestion.

3. OBJECTIVES ARE EXPECTED TO BE SPECIFIC IN TERMS OF WHAT
    IS EXPECTED TO HAPPEN - NOT GENERAL.

Examples:

To reduce incidence of VD by X% by 6/30/80	not	To reduce disease
To reduce theft by X% by 6/30/80	not	To reduce crime
To reduce applicant waiting time by X% by 6/30/80	not	To reduce intake caseload

Figure 4-3. A page from San Francisco's *Program Performance Measurement Handbook*, Office of the Mayor, February, 1980.

```
MSC REPORT 93          RUN NBR: 80/12/04      CITY AND COUNTY OF SAN FRANCISCO          DEPT: 90 PUBLIC WORKS
* PROGRAM LEVEL *      DATE: 09/02/82         MANAGEMENT BY GOALS AND OBJECTIVES                                   DEPT PAGE:  32
                       TIME:    14:36         DETAILED PERFORMANCE REPORT

                                              FOR QUARTER ENDING:   JUNE 81

******* PROGRAM STRUCTURE *******      ********* ORGANIZATION STRUCTURE *********
MSA/COMM GOAL: 21 PUB WKS/FTRAN &COMRC/URBAN CONSERVATION
-PROGRAM  : 37 STREET CLEANING          -RESPONSIBLE ORGANIZATION: 900800 STREET CLEANING & LANDSCAPE MAINT
```

OBJ PM T O	OBJECTIVE MEASURE	SOU RCE	RPT 90	PERF/ TARGET		* ACTUAL PERFORMANCE AND TARGETS **					
						1ST QTR	2ND QTR	3RD QTR	4TH QTR	YEAR-TO-DATE	ANNUAL TARGET

LTA   TO PROVIDE THE CITIZENS OF SAN FRANCISCO A CLEAN, ATTRACTIVE, SAFE, EXTERNAL EN-VIRONMENT BY CLEANING 162,000 CURB MILES OF PUBLIC STREETS USING LESS THAN $23.93 LABOR COST PER MILE IN 1980-81

						1ST QTR	2ND QTR	3RD QTR	4TH QTR	YEAR-TO-DATE	ANNUAL TARGET
10 I	CURB MI CLEANED MECH (CONTROLLED)	U	N	PERF: TARG:		20,654 23,437	26,265 25,000	28,454 26,562	32,540 29,687	107,913 104,686	104,686
11 I	CURB MI CLEANED MECH (UNCONTROLLED)	U	N	PERF: TARG:		6,740 6,250	6,716 6,250	7,548 4,687	7,186 3,125	28,190 20,312	20,312
12 I	CURB MI CLEANED MANUALLY - CETA	U		PERF: TARG:		7,924 9,360*	7,830 9,360*	6,841 9,360*	7,339 9,360*	29,934 37,440*	37,440*
13 I	TOTAL CURB MILES CLEANED	U		PERF: TARG:		36,318 39,047	41,811 40,610	42,843 40,609	47,065 42,172	168,037 162,430	162,430
18 -	PROGRAM LABOR HOURS	U	N	PERF:		99,440	99,440	0	0	198,880	
20 D	LABOR COST/MI - MECH CONTROLLED	U	N	PERF: TARG:		$15.98 $15.33	$12.96 $15.33	$12.86 $15.33	$11.48 $15.33	- -	
21 D	LABOR COST/MI - MECH UNCONTROLLED	U	N	PERF: TARG:		$6.13 $12.51	$7.24 $12.51	$8.17 $12.51	$4.66 $12.51	- -	
22 D	LABOR COST/MI - MANUAL - CETA	U		PERF: TARG:		$28.12 $44.41	$34.87 $44.41	$31.33 $44.41	$20.17 $44.41	- -	
23 D	TOTAL LABOR COST/MILES	U		PERF: TARG:		$17.63 $23.93	$17.62 $23.93	$16.31 $23.93	$14.40 $23.93	- -	
30 D	NO. OF STREET CLEANING COMPLAINTS	U	N	PERF:		2,364	1,860	1,172	1,058	-	
31 D	PERCENT VALID COMPLAINTS	U	N	PERF:		58 %	38 %	37 %	32 %	-	

Figure 4-4. Computer printout page from a San Francisco Quarterly Performance Report.

for the coming fiscal year. In the fall, after the end of the fiscal year on June 30, the mayor assesses each department's use of MBO, suggests revisions where appropriate, and proposes how the department can apply the system to policy issues or operational problems. The visible, personal participation of the mayor has been a vital part of the success of MBO in San Francisco, and the mayor's staff works hard to keep her well prepared for such participation. Figure 4-5 shows a sample briefing paper prepared by staff for the mayor's budget review, pointing out the significance of selected performance objectives, half-year results against targets,and recommendations for the coming year. Figure 4-6 shows a mayoral letter to a department based on a year-end assessment of MBO performance.

A variety of public reports use specific MBO results. These include the mayor's budget message, departmental annual reports, and reports on specific issues of concern to the Board of Supervisors and the public. In addition, department heads evaluate the performance of individual managers according to MBO results.

MBO benefits. In 1981 Arthur Andersen and Company and the mayor each conducted evaluations of the use of MBO for fiscal year 1979–80, when the system was used by 13 of the largest city departments. The studies revealed that the benefits of MBO outweigh the costs. These include tangible financial benefits, such as increased revenues and decreased expenditures. MBO also produces less tangible benefits. These include:

- Improved quality or reliability of servies;
- Improved availability of serrices;
- A more meaningful budget process, where departments state what level of services they will provide for their budget dollars;
- Better understanding of what is expected of individual managers and departments, so efforts are better coordinated;
- Better planning, so managers learn to anticipate the needs of the department and the public;
- Better management of all resources, including personnel, equipment, supplies, and space, as well as dollars;
- An improved ability to identify problems encountered within the department, or within individual programs or services.

Specific performance improvements. Recent uses of MBO in significant efforts to improve performance include the following:

1. The Municipal Railway (Muni) cut the number of lost service hours by 50 percent in one year, largely by concentrating on this MBO objective. The mayor and Muni officials anticipated the serious problems with maintenance of diesel equipment by

MAYOR'S BUDGET REVIEW   1982/83

DEPARTMENT   Public Works – Gas Tax/Road Fund   DEPT. NO.   90

PROGRAM/DIVISIONAL DESCRIPTIONS

PROGRAM (Division)   Engineering – Traffic Operations

Discuss significant service level impacts at recommended level and significant organizational issues.

Functions: The Traffic Operations program provides the signs denoting the schedule for mechanical street sweeping; investigates traffic complaints for stop signs, traffic lights, and other traffic control devices; provides the Department of Electricity with funds to maintain street signals; and engages in traffic planning.

Five major items account for the $964,000 expenditure increase:

1. Funding of three temporary positions as permanent ($101,000) for traffic signal investigation work.

2. One hundred sixty-three miles of street cleaning signs requires $295,000 in temporary salaries.

3. Engineering services for purchase and installation of new signs ($119,000).

4. Completion of a pavement rating survey indicating the condition of every street in San Francisco and the priority which street repair work is needed. This will assist in the proper administration of a $7 million to $18 million capital program over the next three years ($359,000).

5. The provision of an additional $98,400 to the Department of Electricity for maintenance of traffic signals for salary standardization and one additional electrician.

Personnel: one position – in the Traffic Sign Maintenance area is made permanent.

****

Significant Performance Objectives

	81/82 Target	81/82 6 mos. Actual	82/83 Recommended
1. To complete 80% of traffic and parking investigations within 10 working days.	75%	75%	80%

Significance: This objective indicates that traffic and parking investigations are done in a timely manner. This sometimes results in reduced claims against the City.

	81/82 Target	81/82 6 mos. Actual	82/83 Recommended
2. To complete 90% of traffic sign repair items within 10 working days.	90%	84%	90%

Significance: This objective indicates that traffic signs are repaired in a timely manner.

	81/82 Target	81/82 6 mos. Actual	82/83 Recommended
3. To evaluate the pavement condition of all streets.	--	--	100%

Significance: By conducting a pavements rating survey, DPW can effectively identify and prioritize the streets that require street maintenance work.

	81/82 Target	81/82 6 mos. Actual	82/83 Recommended
4. To install new mechanical street sweeping signs (on 163 miles of street covering at least 3 new mechanical routes).	0	0	163

Significance: The completion of this objective will indicate that 100% of the areas targeted for mechanical street sweeping are concluded in the activity. In the current year 81/82 the target was only 90 miles of which 70 miles have been completed in the first six months.

5.

Significance:

Figure 4-5. Sample budget briefing paper for mayor.

OFFICE OF THE MAYOR
SAN FRANCISCO

DIANNE FEINSTEIN

September 10, 1981

Mr. John Sanger, President
  and Members
Public Utilities Commission
Room 287, City Hall
San Francisco, California 94102

Dear Commissioners:

I recently reviewed the Commission's Annual Management
By Objective Performance Report for the fiscal year 1980-81. I
want to take this opportunity to personally congratulate you,
Mr. Sklar, and all of those members of the staff who contributed
to the clearly documented results of creative cooperation. The
bottom line of your efforts is clearly going to be better service
for the people who use the Municipal Railway.

Under the umbrella of MBO and the need to improve productivity
through settting objectives and "working smarter", you have shown
that real improvements can be made.

I want to emphasize my satisfaction with the improvements in
these areas:

  . On street vehicle availability and reliability. The
     reduction in breakdowns is particularly encouraging.
     The average percent of time the fleet was available on
     the street was met or exceeded all targets, except for
     motor coaches. In most cases, an overall improvement of
     30% in reliability also occurred. Our preventative
     maintenance program has clearly helped keep reliability
     up.

  . The sharp reduction in lost service hours and in
     unscheduled overtime. For example, lost sevice hours
     for cable cars averaged only 1.8% - a real improvement
     over the 5% of the prior year. Overall, lost service
     hours were cut by 50%. The new inspection program also
     seems to be contributing to the improvements.
     Unscheduled overtime was cut by 36%.

  . The encouraging, though preliminary, findings of the
     Transit Line Coordinators pilot project are that we may
     have found at least part of the solution to our

Figure 4-6. MBO Performance Review Letter from mayor to a department.

"bunching" problem. For example, Presidio Division
increased its runs arriving on time by 10% from 38% to
48%. Overall, for the pilot program, "bunching" was
reduced by 27%. This means better service on the 1, 5,
21, 30 and 41 lines.

- The reduction in passenger complaints by about a third,
  from 164 in January to 104 in June - a clear indication
  of progress.

- The 50% improvement in the availability of data
  processing service.

- The 13% reduction in industrial accidents over prior
  year levels. This shows the value of solid,
  comprehensive training programs.

- The Finance Bureau's success in obtaining over $40
  million in grants for capital projects.

- The discipline shown by all by refraining from
  supplementals that require new funds.

However, as you well know, improvements are still necessary in
many areas. For example, we still appear to have problems in
availability and reliablity for diesel buses and, while there has
been improvement in METRO scheduling, progress is still needed.

I believe these results show that improvements can be made when
we set measurable objectives and work creatively to meet them. I
am particularly pleased that a focus on results, with a specific
set of targets to achieve, has been not only accepted but
encouraged by your staff. Regular quarterly reviews by staff to
you are a key part of this program and I am pleased that they are
occurring.

Improved management and productivity requires creative
cooperation in a partnership between not only Commission and
staff, but between management and labor. For this reason, I also
am pleased that the PUC has embarked upon way to harness the
potential of employees in forging solutions to often difficult
operational problems. The private sector has already shown us
that labor-management committees structured for this purpose can
not only work but also reduce grievances in the process.

I applaud you and your staff at all levels for making the
progress shown, and hope that we have now established a new set
of higher standards and objectives to reach.

Warmest regards.

Sincerely,

Dianne Feinstein
Mayor

DF/PH:qrh

Figure 4-6. Continued

using MBO statistics. They were able to plan for most effective handling of the problems, so that the crisis was relatively short and not as severe as it might have been.

2. In 1980–81, the treasurer/tax collector's MBO objective to reduce the time needed to examine safety boxes of deceased persons led to an increase in fees collected from $66,000 to $100,000 and an elimination of the inspection backlog.

3. The Department of Public Health increased environmental health inspections of licensed operations by 15 percent. Based upon MBO information the department discontinued a health hazard appraisal and risk reduction program that had very low public support. Because of problems in billing and collection performance, the department set MBO targets to improve procedures and train staff better.

4. The Police Department reduced police response time from 7.8 minutes for priority calls to 4.6 minutes. MBO results are used to determine which police functions should be emphasized in each precinct.

5. The Port Commission negotiated leases of $10.8 million — worth $900,000 more in revenue than targeted — while spending $80,000 less than targeted on maritime operations. The department has set MBO objectives to remodel specific Port facilities, and coordinate them with its Five Year Capital Improvement Plan. MBO objectives focused department efforts for the first time on the persistant problem of crime downtown, which is now significantly lower.

6. MBO statistics were used in the development of a comprehensive plan to make San Francisco's Public Library system as up-to-date and useful as possible. The Public Library will apply data on library usage, population composition in each branch area, and user costs to develop a system that most efficiently serves San Francisco.

7. MBO data for the Airport indicated the need to emphasize reduction of airfield and traffic accidents, while demonstrating the effectiveness of security and accident procedures. A survey of passengers led to revision of performance targets and objectives.

In sum, each department has adapted MBO to better set its priorities and assess its performance. MBO statistics apply to a diverse set of city services as the few examples presented above demonstrate. MBO is used in all aspects of city administration, from targeting specific service improvements to increasing revenues.

Problems encountered and improvements planned. While it has only used MBO for a few years, the city has found the MBO program to be an essential part of efforts to improve San Francisco's government. In addition to being enthusiastic about MBO, the mayor and city departments continue to try to improve its operation. In addition to identifying the benefits of MBO in San Francisco, the 1981 evaluations of the process identified problems encountered since MBO development began in 1978. This led to the following MBO Don'ts List which has helped guide further MBO development:

1. *"Don'ts" in Initial Implementation:*
   - Delegating executive direction of the program to lower levels within a department or unit;
   - Creating a "paper mill" with forms and procedures;
   - Emphasizing system techniques over the system's expected results;
   - Implementing too quickly;
   - Having objectives not supported by adequate plans or data;
   - Failing to blend individual objectives into the whole (i.e., losing "the big picture").
2. *"Don'ts" in Obtaining Staff Cooperation:*
   - Omitting participation by subordinates in setting objectives;
   - Leaving out staff managers in the implementation process;
   - Failing to reward performance;
   - Lacking ability or willingness to delegate.
3. *"Don'ts" in Setting Expectations and Obtaining Staff and Management Use of MBO:*
   - Considering MBO a panacea for all management or performance problems;
   - Failing to provide feedback to the individual manager;
   - Failing to revise the system based upon experience;
   - Being impatient for results;
   - Omitting periodic reviews of performance;
   - Omitting refresher training with respect to refinements and failing to give managers new to the system the necessary exposure.
4. *"Don'ts" in Finding the Right Initial Compromise:*
   - Endeavoring to be too conservative, or to "hedge" on objectives and targets of performance;
   - Trying to quantify performance where the managers were not ready with the data to back up expectations;
   - Emphasizing short-term objectives;
   - Negotiating objectives without the necessary "guts" or taking of necessary risks.

In further improving the MBO process, the Mayor's Office and departmental managers will try to tie MBO performance more closely to specific budgets and develop incentives to improve performance. They will identify areas where small systems improvements should enhance

MBO performance. And, of course, city administrators will continue to revise MBO objectives and performance measures to better administer San Francisco's government. At present, they are focusing on changes needed in the city's personnel management process in order to tie hiring, classification, and performance evaluation procedures more directly to MBO results.

EXAMPLE 4.3 WORK MEASUREMENT AND PERFORMANCE IMPROVEMENT IN THE CITY OF SAN DIEGO

Libby Anderson
Director
Financial Management
Department

Until 1973, in the City of San Diego, most financial planning (with the exception of the Capital Improvements Program) was done on an annual basis. That year, we completed our first long-range planning effort, a six-year plan for the operating budget. Much to our dismay, the six-year plan demonstrated that the city faced a deficit in the future. Revenues were not going to keep pace with expenditures. Alternatives were developed to meet this deficit, and they included (1) increase taxes; (2) reduce service levels; and (3) improve efficiency. We chose the last alternative.

In 1975 the Productivity Improvement Program (PIP) was established in the Financial Management Department, under the city manager. The staff consisted of administrative analysts led by a supervising administrative analyst. All were generalists who went into the program with no specific industrial engineering training. A consulting firm was hired to train the staff and guide us through our first study. This approach left us not only with improvements in one operating division, but also with a staff capable of improving the performance of other city operations. We now have an intensive one-week course developed for all new analysts. A consultant is brought in for two days and staff conduct the remainder of the training.

In implementing PIP, we expected to realize savings. It was felt that workers without time standards do not work as efficiently as those who have standards. We were looking for the same amount of work from a reduced staff, or an increased amount of work from the same staff. Also, we wanted to develop a rational link between workload and staffing.

The Equipment Division of the General Services Department was the subject of the first study. The department showed a strong interest in being involved in the initial study. The selection for our first study was based upon the following criteria:

- A division performing a representative cross-section of functions to which industrial engineering principles could be applied;
- A division with relatively uncomplicated work processes that could be studied in a short period of time to maximize benefits;
- A division with a relatively large number of employees working on a relatively few work processes to minimize the cost per employee covered by the study;
- A division whose management expressed an interest in a performance improvement study.

The Equipment Division is responsible for the maintenance, repair, and service of all city-owned automotive and industrial equipment, except that of the fire and police departments. Maintenance and service activities are performed on a two-shift basis at three stations. Light units maintained include cars, pickup trucks, and auxiliary equipment; medium units include small dump trucks and crew trucks; heavy units include refuse packers and large dump trucks; industrial units include bulldozers, motor graders, and motor sweepers. At the time of the study, the division maintained and serviced 630 light units, 314 medium units, 287 heavy units, and 303 industrial units. At that time, the division had 165 staff members and a total operating budget of $5,400,000.

The functions selected for study were general automotive, heavy industrial equipment repair, service stations, and mobile service units (day and night shifts), preventive maintenance, and welding and fabrication (day and night shifts) at all three stations.

Industrial engineering techniques employed included:

- Work distribution charting, to learn how evenly or unevenly the workload was distributed among workers, crews, and facilities;
- Work description, to be sure every job task was clearly understood;
- Process and work flow charting, to identify missing or duplicative procedures, bottlenecks in the work flow, and ways to simplify work processes;
- Developing and documenting methods improvement opportunities;
- Work measurement (work sampling and time studies) to identify the proportion of time staff spent on each task (including "productive" and "unproductive" time), and to develop engineered work standards;
- Developing and implementing a performance reporting system, to monitor progress toward achievement of work standards.

Significant benefits resulted from the study. Annual savings of $387,000 were identified in the Equipment Division. These savings were realized principally by staff reduction of 27 positions, all of which were accomplished through attrition.

As more studies were performed, we refined our techniques and expanded our process. In 1978 we added an evaluation component to precede the work measurement study. This insures standards will be set on doing the right amount of work on the right job in the right way. The work measurement study determines how long it should take to do the work and what staffing requirements are at various workload levels. Once the study is complete and recommendations adopted by management, a performance monitoring process we refer to as a "proj-

THE CITY OF SAN DIEGO, CALIFORNIA QUARTERLY PRODUCTIVITY REPORT	DISTRIBUTION: 1. Original & one copy to Deputy City Manager 2. One copy to Financial Management Director 3. File one copy

DEPARTMENT Park & Recreation	DIVISION Park Maintenance	QUARTER ENDING Sept. 30, 1979

PROGRAM ELEMENT/SECTION	MEASURED POSITIONS	PRODUCTIVITY PERFORMANCE* LAST QUARTER	THIS QUARTER	PERCENT DEVIATION FROM 100% THIS QUARTER*
1. Mowing	14	88.9%	85.1%	−14.9%
2. Sweeping	8	87.0%	93.2%	− 6.8%
3. Trees	8	86.7%	80.2%	−19.8%
4.				
5.				
6.				
7.				
8.				
9.				
10.				
11.				

WHEN THIS QUARTER'S PRODUCTIVITY PERFORMANCE DEVIATES ± 10% FROM 100%, INDICATE FACTOR(S) CAUSING DEVIATION BELOW:

1. Productivity performance below 100% because of equipment breakdowns and employees in on-the-job training status.

3. Productivity performance below 100% because of delay in obtaining scheduled replacement vehicles. (Currently only two vehicles available out of seven assigned.)

SIGNATURE (DEPARTMENT HEAD)   DATE 12/18/79

*These are efficiency measures that show the *percentage of standard achieved,* as discussed near the end of Chapter 2. They compare actual work completed to the amount that "should have" been completed based on engineered work standards.

Figure 4-7. The City of San Diego, California Quarterly Productivity Report.

ect maintenance system" is put into place. This system includes submission of a Quarterly Productivity Report (see Figure 4-7) to the city manager and feedback to the workers on their performance. An analyst is assigned as liaison to each maintenance system. This analyst insures the ongoing validity of the data being reported by conducting periodic audits (e.g., checking under the hood to see if truck XYZ did indeed have its radiator changed, or going out to Fifth and Broadway to see if the curb is painted), and by making adjustments as necessary when new equipment or methods are introduced. Finally, five-year restudies are scheduled for all projects.

Our studies sometimes also produce unexpected spin-off benefits. We have found that in bringing fresh eyes to look at departmental operations objectively and intensively, improvements are often revealed which are not seen by those involved daily in getting the job done. For example, in studying the Police Department, we wondered why Police Academy students were enrolled in the Safety Retirement Program set up for emergency services. Was the danger of falling off a chair or being poked in the eye with a pencil such that our recruits ought to be in this more expensive retirement unit? No, this retirement classification was required because police recruits were sworn in prior to commencing academy classes. This practice was changed as a result of our observations. Police recruits are now not sworn in until field training begins. For the first five months of their training, they are included in the General Retirement Program like the rest of us pencil pushers. The city saves $359,000 annually in reduced retirement contributions.

The Productivity Improvement Program in the City of San Diego has been a success. The accrued program costs from fiscal year 1975 through fiscal year 1979 were $1,105,301. Accrued savings for the same period were $9,164,325. These savings have been realized with no decrease in service level. Additionally, the program provides an improved level of management information. Employees know what is expected of them. Supervisors can evaluate the performance of their units. Division heads can track how well each section is doing, and the city manager gets an overview of the city's overall performance record. The reporting system brings problems to the surface which adversely affect performance, such as equipment downtime, high turnover, and service level declines. Because reports are made quarterly, steps can be taken to remedy problems before they become insurmountable. Budgetary and operating decisions have frequently been based on PIP study results.

Work measurement is a management tool; in and of itself, it means little. Its value lies in its use by management. Because of the high degree of credibility which staff has earned, management places heavy reliance on information generated by the program.

Work measurement and other industrial engineering techniques have become even more powerful tools in San Diego since they have been used in concert with organization development techniques as part of our new Organization Effectiveness Program (OEP). San Diego's organization development efforts are described in Example 4.5, and the interdisciplinary OEP is described in Example 4.10.

EXAMPLE 4.4 MEASURING AND IMPROVING OFFICE WORK IN GENESEE COUNTY

Richard G. McGraw
County Controller

Genesee County, Michigan, is a large urban county governed by an elected board of 14 commissioners, and several elected department heads. In 1974, at the onset of fiscal stress in the county, a management analysis staff was started under the controller, the county's chief appointed financial management officer. The staff has since studied many diverse agencies, ranging from the county animal shelter to the Treasurer's Office, circuit courts, and County Clerk's Office. Because of the functions performed by Genesee County, much of the staff's measurement and improvement work has focused on office activities. This has taken special creativity, since office people rarely produce a tangible physical product.

Industrial engineering techniques, when applied to offices rather than factories or field services, must account for the variety of tasks office workers perform with little or no pattern of repetition. Thus a variety of measurement techniques are needed for many office studies. An office methods analyst must be skilled in basic work measurement techniques, have the vision to see the essence of a situation before getting lost in the details, and the imagination to modify and mix standard techniques to meet the situation. As of mid-1979, the Genesee County management analysis staff consisted of three people: a director with six years experience in finance and work measurement; a senior analyst with 19 years experience in industrial engineering; and a recent college graduate with a mathematics degree.

Along with work measurement, detailed studies of county departments have included management and employee interviews, office layout analyses, telephone and equipment analyses, labor projections, procedure development and documentation, and work simplification. The general process followed by many of our studies has five steps:

1. *General reconnaissance:* A quick examination is done of the project, including personnel, their location, and their attitude toward the study;
2. *Preliminary study:* A preliminary plan is prepared based on the reconnaissance information. Tentative work measurement techniques are tried (usually for two to three days) in order to refine the plan and identify problems;

3. *Detailed study:* The analyst selects the measurement and analysis techniques to be used, prepares a final study plan, and conducts a detailed study (which usually takes four to five weeks);

4. *Procedures development:* Work procedures are refined to improve efficiency and work quality and are *written down* to establish consistent policies and insure that all phases of a job have been identified. All phases of work must be included in order to establish accurate work standards. Written procedures also facilitate training of employees;

5. *Work standards development:* Once improved procedures are established and performance estimates obtained from the study, work measurement devices (e.g., stopwatch analysis) will be selected to establish time standards. The standards will be tested through continued measurement as improved procedures are implemented. The procedures and standards will be modified, if necessary.

Genesee County has a computerized cost-accounting system, including a labor distribution process that summarizes hours and activities of employees for many departments. When work standards are applied to the labor distribution data, manpower utilization rates are determined showing the percentage of available employee time used "productively." Generally, if manpower utilization rates below the 85 to 95 percent range are reported consistently for a work unit, there is an opportunity to reduce personnel for that unit. Rates that go up and down with some regularity may indicate opportunities for reducing staff by revising employee work schedules to match the workload. Study results and information from subsequent performance monitoring are considered when the county's budget is prepared. Position allocations take into account targets for improved operating performance.

Our recent study of the County Clerk's Office used a wide variety of measurement techniques, of which five are described below:

- *Time ladders:* Time ladders are logs maintained by the employees being studied. On forms designed for ease of showing the start and end of each activity in sequence, each employee records his or her activities over the entire work day. See Figure 4-8 for a filled-in time ladder log. Time ladders tell a methods analyst the general task categories of each employee, and the time used to perform various activities.

- *Work sampling:* Work sampling is extremely useful for measuring nonrepetitive work. Simply put, work sampling involves an analyst making numerous observations (e.g., every 10 minutes throughout the work day, repeated for several weeks) of all employees of a work unit, and noting down the activity each employee is performing at each observation point. There are a number of variations

NAME _John Doe_   DATE _4-3-79_

POSITION _Court Clerk_ _____ UNIT or OFFICE _____

TIME CODE	VOL.	TIME CODE	VOL.	TIME CODE	VOL.	TIME CODE	VOL.	TIME CODE	VOL.	TIME CODE	VOL.
8:00		9:30		11:00		12:30		2:00		3:30 Counter	
2		32		2		32 Desk		2		32	
4		34		4		34		4 Filing		34 Desk	
6 Desk		36		6 Posting		36		6		36 Counter	
8		38		8		38 Counter-Atty.		8		38	
10 Work		40		10		40		10		40 Desk	
12		42 Posting		12		42 Phone-Public		12 Restroom		42 Counter	
14		44		14		44		14		44	
16 Pull		46		16		46 Desk		16		46 Desk	
18 Files		48		18 Filing		48 Phone-Public		18		48	
20		50		20		50		20 Court		50	
22 Filing		52		22 Restroom		52		22		52 Filing	
24		54		24		54		24		54	
26 Phone-Transf.		56		26 Counter		56		26		56 Phone-	
28 Attach File		58		28		58		28 Counter		58	
8:30 for Court		10:00		11:30 Filing		1:00		2:30		4:00 Counter	
32		2		32		2		32		2	
34		4		34		4 Posting		34 Counter		4	
36		6		36		6		36		6	
38		8 Break		38		8		38		8 Desk	
40		10		40		10		40		10 (Judicial	
42		12		42		12		42		12	
44		14		44 LUNCH		14		44		14 Report)	
46 Court		16		46		16		46 Counter-		16	
48		18		48		18		48		18	
50 (Pleas)		20		50		20		50 Judge E.		20	
52		22		52		22		52		22	
54		24		54		24		54		24	
56		26 Court		56		26		56 Counter		26	
58		28		58		28		58		28	
9:00		10:30 (Attachment)		12:00		1:30		3:00		4:30	
2		32		2		32 Computer		2		32	
4		34		4		34		4		34	
6		36		6		36		6 Break		36	
8		38		8		38 Posting		8		38	
10		40		10		40 Filing		10		40	
12 Phone-Dist.		42		12		42		12		42	
14 Court		44		14		44		14		44	
16 Desk		46		16		46		16 Desk		46	
18		48		18		48		18		48	
20 Work		50		20		50 Attach		20		50	
22 Phone-		52 Posting		22		52 Atty		22 Restroom		52	
24 Public		54		24		54 File		24		54	
26		56		26		56		26 Desk		56 Counter	
28 Posting		58		28		58		28		58	
9:30		11:00		12:30		2:00		3:30 Counter		5:00 Desk-Phone	

INSTRUCTIONS:

1. When you stop doing one task and start another, draw a line across the column.
2. Enter the proper job description of work completed in the columns indicated.

Figure 4-8 Sample time ladder.

involving the timing and techniques for making observations. Work samples can lead to estimates of the proportion of time employees spend on each activity, as well as the percentage they spend on "productive" activities. Figure 4-9 shows a summary of work sampling observations for a period of one week for a work unit studied in the County Clerk's Office.

County Clerk — Legal Division
Work Sample — Judge B.
April 10–April 17, 1979

Activity Description	Employee E	Employee L	Employee B	Module Total	Module %
Praecipes	9	6	2	17	1%
Counter Work	67	31	33	131	12
Conferring	14	14	11	39	3
Court	114	3	6	123	10
Phone	13	5	7	25	2
Posting Cases	19	74	40	133	12
Posting Journal Sheet	16			16	1
Attic	11	14	8	33	3
Journal Sheet	25			25	2
Judicial Report	6	15	20	41	3
Desk Work	17	19	16	52	4
Judicial Cards	7	21	2	30	3
Index Cards	1	18	15	34	3
Sentences & Probation	5			5	0
Sort Papers	2	24	21	47	4
File	3	5	5	13	1
New Case	1	4	8	13	1
File Papers	2	22	13	37	3
Judgments	1	21		22	2
Walk	17	13	9	39	3
Pull Files		1	4	5	
Court Preparation		2	4	6	
Administration Building			38	38	3
Cashier			21	21	2
Deposition			17	17	1
Mail	4	1	3	8	1
Paper Shredding			47	47	4
Other	11	8	16	35	3
Subtotal Productive	365 93%	321 81%	366 93%	1,052	89%
Non-Productive	8	17	3	28	2
Extended Lunch	1	4	9	14	1
Break	15	25	15	55	5
Rest Room	4	26		30	3
Personal	0	0	0	0	0
Total Paid Observations	393	393	393	1,179	100%

Figure 4-9. Work sampling summary.

- *Stopwatch analysis:* Once improved procedures are developed and broken down into discrete tasks, an analyst uses a stopwatch to measure how long it takes an employee to complete each task. This is particularly useful for establishing work standards.
- *Fractionated professional estimates (FPE Times):* Individuals who have a working knowledge of an operation (e.g., employees who perform the operation, or their supervisors) are asked to break down each work activity into discrete tasks which can be measured. The individuals then give their professional estimates for the length of time needed to complete each discrete task. These FPE times can be used to construct time standards for each activity, which can be verified to an extent by work sampling and by examining monthly totals of activities and employee hours.
- *Determination of constant and nonconstant operations:* Constant operations are those performed for a fixed time per month or per day. Nonconstant operations are those that generally vary in employee time applied and unit count per day or month. This distinction is important for the calculation of manpower utilization rates.

Figure 4-10 shows a manpower utilization report for the General Division of the County Clerk's Office. Note the manpower utilization rate was only 49.7 percent (lower right-hand corner of report). Based on the work measurement study, more efficient procedures were implemented and the number of authorized positions in the division were reduced from 17 to 9. As a result, the manpower utilization rate increased to 90.3 percent.

When surplus staff are identified, Genesee County tries to avoid employee layoffs. Whenever possible, employees are transferred to other departments (with no loss in pay) in which the need for additional staff has been identified. Whenever possible, surplus positions not transferred are not eliminated until vacancies occur.

Office cost control involves specialized application of industrial engineering techniques. It requires many technical skills plus imagination, aggressive leadership, and the ability to plan a complete program and "sell" the concepts at all organizational levels in government. Measurement and reporting must be done in a manner significantly different from the way they are done in a factory or field service that has a clear-cut product. The analyst must learn to think in larger terms to develop control for economic and effective management. These practices have paid off handsomely for Genesee County. In 1979 the annual budget for the management analysis team in the Controller's Office was $87,617. In the team's first five years, the results of their studies yielded the county a total of $2,252,345 in savings.

GENESEE COUNTY GOVERNMENT
MANAGEMENT ANALYSIS SECTION
MANPOWER UTILIZATION REPORT

Department COUNTY CLERK

Division GENERAL

Month APRIL

Std. No.	Operation Name (Non-Constant)	Item Measured	Std. (hours)	Items Processed	Std.Hrs. Earned
GC001	Issue Marriage License	Each License	.428	374	160.072
GC003	Certified Copies of Vitals	Dollars of Fee	.035	$8,587	300.545
GC011	Birth Registration	Each Certificate	.126	687	86.562
GC012	Death Registration	Each Certificate	.314	268	84.152
GC013	Passport Application	Each Application	.446	238	106.148
GC201	Assumed Name Filings	Each Certificate	.200	234	46.800
GC022	Assumed Name Expiration Notice	Each Card or Envelope	.033	400	13.200
GC023	Copartnership Filings	Each Certificate	.200	13	2.600
GC024	Copartnership Expiration Notice	Each Card or Envelope	.033	30	.990
GC025	Limited Partnership Filings	Each Filing	.500	2	1.000
GC026	Notary Commission	Each Commission	.080	135	10.800
GC027	Notary Commission 2nd Notice	Each Card or Envelope	.035	12	.420
GC028	Concealed Pistols License	Each License	.303	40	12.120
GC031	Cashier	Each Transaction	.014	2,439	34.146
	Total Non-Constant Standard Hours Earned				859.555

Std. No.	Operation Name (Constant)	Std. Hrs.	Mult. by Working Days	Monthly Std. Hr.	Std.Hrs. Earned
GC101	Cash Reconciliation	2.0	20		40.0
GC301	Clerk-Concealed Weapons Licensing Board			8	8.0
	Total Constant Standard Hours Earned				48.0
	Total of All Std. Hours Earned				907.0

POSITION/HOUR SUMMARY

I.   Number of Authorized Positions
II. Total Work Days Covered 17/20
III. Authorized Hours:
   A. Regular 27.20
   B. Overtime .... -0-
   C. Temporary .... -0-
   D. Borrowed .... -0-
   Total (A thru D) 27.20
IV. Non-Productive Hours
   A. Vacation 88.4
   B. Holiday 136.0
   C. Personal 167.3
   D. Loaned 480.0
   E. Other 24.0
   Total (A thru E) 895.7
V. Net Available Hours (III-IV) 1824.3
VI. Total Standard Hrs. Earned
   A. Total Non-constant standard hrs. earned ... 859.0
   B. Total constant daily hours earned 40.0
   C. Total constant weekly hours earned .... —
   D. Total constant monthly hours earned 8.0
   E. Total constant yearly hours earned .... —
   Total (A thru E) 907.0
VII. Manpower Utilization (VI ÷ V) 49.7

Figure 4-10.   Genesee County, Michigan Manpower Utilization Report.

**EXAMPLE 4.5 USING ORGANIZATION DEVELOPMENT
TO IMPROVE PERFORMANCE IN THE
CITY OF SAN DIEGO**

Richard L. Hays, Former
Organization Effectiveness Supervisor

In 1976 with partial financial support from a HUD grant, the City of
San Diego started its first full-scale organization development (OD)
effort in its Communications and Electrical (C&E) Division. The OD
project produced substantial improvements in both employee morale
and organizational performance. The organization development and
training team that led the C&E effort has since gone on to work with
similar success in other operating departments. In 1980 the team was
moved to the Financial Management Department to become part of a
new unit called the Organization Effectiveness Program (OEP), which
merged the city's work measurement and organization development
staffs. This action firmly institutionalized OD as a performance improvement technique in San Diego. The merger and the OEP are described in
Example 4.10.

The San Diego OD staff employs an "action research" approach
when working with a department, involving data collection, planning
and implementing change, and evaluating results. Feedback to, and
participation of, employees is stressed throughout the action research
process, so new issues will surface and be acted upon during implementation, and employee groups will develop the ability to communicate
better and solve their own problems after the OD specialists leave. Some
of the specific activities we use vary from project to project. Those
used on the C&E project provide a good picture of our general process.

The Communications and Electrical Division maintains all of the
city's street lights and traffic signals, repairs parking meters and collects
meter revenue, and operates microwave transmission stations and a
broadcast facility for nonpolice and nonfire field communications
("station 38"). The C&E project activities were:

- *Data collection:* Two kinds of information were collected:
  - *Organizational and employee data* to measure personnel
    satisfaction, organizational climate, leadership practices, use of
    training opportunities, and motivational conditions. The team
    used meetings with management, one-on-one interviews of
    employees by OD staff, and written employee surveys to
    collect this information. Several good employee surveys were
    available. The team drew from the *Minnesota Satisfaction
    Questionnaire* (University of Minnesota), the *Survey of Organ-
    izations* (Institute of Social Research), and the *Job Diagnostic*

Survey (Yale University). Their interviews with employees included questions concerning their perceptions of the performance of their organization. Much useful information, such as absenteeism, turnover, and grievance history, was available from division records.

- *Service performance data:* Some time before this OD project, San Diego's work measurement staff had developed work standards for many C&E activities, and implemented a performance monitoring system to track performance against standards. This made it easy to track efficiency measures. Also, because of the legal implications of much of C&E's work (particularly emergency repairs), division records contain considerable information from which effectiveness measures could be drawn (e.g., number of emergency repairs begun within one hour). Client satisfaction data were obtained through telephone surveys of citizens who reported problems or made service requests, and mail surveys of other city departments that use C&E services.

- *Team building workshops:* Eleven team building workshops were held for C&E employees, starting with a three-day workshop for C&E managers, followed by a three-day workshop for C&E supervisors and nine two-day workshops for individual work groups. With OD specialists as facilitators, workshop participants went through exercises and discussions to build skills in communication, problem solving, conflict resolution, and decision making. Employee interview and survey data were fed back to participants to help them identify key organizational issues. *Action planning* was begun toward the end of the workshop. Participants learned a "creative problem solving format," which they applied to develop an action plan for resolving each organizational issue they had earlier identified. Part of each action plan included developing a process to monitor progress in resolving the issue.

- *Ongoing consulting* by the OD staff helped C&E managers and supervisors continue their planning and *implementation* efforts to resolve issues after the workshops, and to facilitate ongoing communication, staff participation, and feedback of interim results. This consulting was also aimed at building C&E's internal capacity to identify and resolve organizational issues in the future, after the OD team left.

- *Miniworkshops for supervisory training:* This was one approach implemented to help resolve a range of issues identified in the workshops. The OD staff organized a series of one- to two-hour meetings of C&E supervisors to cover specific topics for which training needs were identified. Topics covered included stress reduction, effective discipline, employee motivation, and effective use of time.

- *Evaluation:* Project evaluation consisted primarily of before-and-after comparisons of organizational, employee, and performance data collected, as well as assessment of issue resolution. To provide some verification that changes measured were due to the OD project rather than external forces, staff obtained the cooperation of other organizations to serve as "quasi-control groups." Staff could not arrange a true control group within San Diego's C&E Division, but the City of Long Beach allowed San Diego to use their organization that provided equivalent services as a control group for the employee surveys. The San Diego Building Division also served as a control group for employee surveys. Street light and traffic signal crews of the California Department of Transportation served as a control group for some of the work standards-related efficiency measures. While the C&E Division showed substantial improvement for many measures, the control groups showed no significant change.

After initial data collection activities to establish baseline information for feedback and evaluation, the C&E project took about one year to complete. During that time, 194 organizational issues were resolved out of 245 identified. The remaining issues were resolved, for the most part, by the division in the next year following the project. Some highlights of improved practices implemented were:

- Improved intergroup problem solving among design engineers, electricians, and electronic technicians. Together they identified cost savings that would be immediately instituted on existing projects. The regular intergroup meetings they established should help keep costs of electrical design, materials, installation, and operations from growing too fast.
- A screening process for repair requests to reduce the number of times repair crews are sent out unnecessarily.
- A switch to purchasing certain electrical parts that had previously been made in-house at a higher cost than the purchase price.
- Redistribution of certain types of work to certain crews that were better equipped for the work, and that could do it in less time at lower total labor costs than would the previous crews.
- Improved collaboration with other departments, allowing C&E to get critical vehicles back from repair in an average of 1.5 days per breakdown rather than one week. This greatly reduced the loss of productive labor time due to vehicle repairs.
- Reduced hours of operation of station 38. Since 80 percent of station 38's broadcast activity took place during the day, Monday through Friday, its night and weekend emergency operations were shifted to the Fire Department's communications center, which could handle the increased workload.

Employee surveys indicated substantial gains in key organizational dimensions, such as leadership, employee satisfaction and motivation, and organizational climate. Division personnel data showed reduced turnover and absenteeism after the project. This is particularly significant since these changes occurred during the campaign to pass California's Proposition 13 which severely limited local property taxes in the state. The campaign, which was particularly strong in southern California, featured a considerable amount of negative public comment about public employees and governments. Several efficiency improvements occurred, highlighted by: a 29 percent increase in a combined efficiency index (weighted by work standards) for the street lamps and traffic signal section; cost per unit for one year for repair and maintenance of signalized intersections was reduced from $829.00 to $723.24. Effectiveness improved as measured by increases in the numbers of repairs made within preset time limits (e.g., street lights relamped within three days). The client satisfaction surveys (for both citizens and city departments) showed a high level of satisfaction before and after the project. Improvements to which dollar benefits could be attached were worth about $130,000 to the City of San Diego the first year: about $70,000 in direct savings, and about $60,000 worth of staff time made available for more productive use (e.g., completing more repairs).

A more recent OD project (completed in 1980) was a Total Program Management (TPM) project involving three California cities: San Diego, Long Beach, and Manhattan Beach. TPM is a process developed by the U.S. General Accounting Office and has previously been tested by agencies in federal, state, and local governments. TPM involves the use of efficiency and effectiveness measures, client satisfaction data, and employee morale and satisfaction data. As is clear from the C&E project, San Diego's OD approach already embodied these principles. Improvements implemented in San Diego's Building Inspection Department as a result of our TPM project are valued at about $145,800 in annual benefits: about $58,000 worth of direct savings due to reduced overtime, and about $87,800 worth of staff time put to more productive use (e.g., completing more inspections).

Many of the methods improvements made as a result of San Diego's OD projects could have been identified by other means, such as detailed studies by management or industrial engineering consultants. The big difference is that departmental employees, including managers and supervisors, came up with the answers − and the questions − by themselves. The OD staff served mainly as skilled facilitators of the process used. The extra benefits from helping employees identify their own problems and solutions are not calculable in dollars but are extremely valuable for two reasons:

- Employees are better motivated to implement improvements they have identified for themselves.

- The organization and the people within it are left with an increased ability to communicate and to identify and solve problems.

**EXAMPLE 4.6 PERFORMANCE INCENTIVE PROGRAM
TO IMPROVE STREET CLEANING IN WASHINGTON, D.C.**

Doug Lee, Formerly of the
Office of the City Administrator

Although the City of Washington, D.C. has been increasingly mechanizing its street cleaning operation, most of the streets and alleys are still cleaned manually due to traffic congestion, parked cars, and citizen opposition to restricted parking regulations. The Bureau of Street and Alley Cleaning in D.C.'s Department of Environmental Services is responsible for the cleaning of streets and alleys. It has a work force of about 400 employees and a budget of around $8 million. A manual cleaning truck crew consists of four sweepers, two loaders, and one truck driver. The sweepers spread along both sides of the street and use brooms to sweep the litter and dirt into piles. The loaders use shovels and brooms to pick up the dirt piles and load them into the truck which follows the sweepers.

The street cleaning operation has been plagued with many problems — truck breakdowns are very frequent, schedules are inadequate, there are no work standards, managers are complaint oriented, and workers are difficult to control. An analysis of street cleaning performance data indicated that cleaning routes were completed only 51 percent of the time, the truck breakdown rate was around 25 percent, workers often loitered for several hours at the end of work periods, quality of sweeping was sometimes very poor, and absence without leave was averaging 50 hours per worker per year.

A performance improvement project was initiated to increase the frequency of and to improve the quality of cleaning without adding resources. It was part of a larger effort, the Neighborhood Services Improvement Project (NSIP), partially funded by a grant from the U.S. Department of Housing and Urban Development. NSIP was designed to demonstrate how comprehensive, integrated use of industrial engineering techniques, organization development applications, and citizen participation can improve performance in services which preserve and improve the physical condition of residential neighborhoods. NSIP was coordinated by the performance improvement staff in the Mayor's Office with active involvement from line managers of the service delivery agencies (NSIP is further discussed in chapter 5).

The project team first met with the crew members assigned to the test site to solicit suggestions to improve performance. The crew members, including truck drivers, broomers, and loaders, expressed enormous frustration over their work. They indicated that morale was low, absenteeism was high, trucks were old, and supervision had been confusing, mainly because there were too many people giving them orders. *The workers also said that they could and would do more work if they were given some incentives.* The street cleaners suggested that they be given a "fair day's work" and allowed to go home when they had finished that assignment. The city's household refuse collectors had for many years been performing under such a system, known as the "task system," whereby they can leave when the route is finished, or when they have collected four truckloads of trash, as specified in the union contract.

When the incentive proposal was made to street cleaning managers, it was rejected due to unhappy experiences with the refuse collectors.

It was pointed out that the waste collectors left significant spillage under the "task system" by being in a rush to go home early. Further, it was felt such an incentive program would escalate antagonism and arguments between supervisors and workers. The managers were convinced that the quality of street cleaning would drop significantly even if the supervisor checked behind the workers. Street cleaning managers made a counterproposal, recommending that cash bonuses be used as an incentive to get workers to do more work.

When the project team talked to the workers about the alternative of using cash bonuses instead of the task system as an incentive, the crews rejected the proposal and expressed strong feelings about their desire for a "task system." The project team then took a "task" incentive proposal, including quality controls, to the department director. Approval to test this task incentive was obtained largely due to top management desires to evaluate the quality controls.

The project team then worked with the test neighborhood's street cleaners, especially the field foreman and crew leadmen, to prepare for a system that would increase cleaning without sacrificing work quality. First, the field foreman was trained on a quality standard considered acceptable after a street is cleaned by a crew. Taking advantage of the visual rating system based on photographic standards, developed by the Urban Institute of Washington, D.C., the project team arranged for the field foreman to be trained by the trained observer who systematically rated the cleanliness of streets in D.C. The visual rating system was modified to create a quality control standard for street cleaning. The Urban Institute system employs a seven-step scale in half points from 1.0 (very clean) to 4.0 (very dirty) to rate the cleanliness of streets. The quality control standard, on the other hand, requires a clear differentiation of "acceptable" cleanliness and "unacceptable" cleanliness. Therefore, any street that was rated on the scale as 1.0 was deemed acceptable. If a street or part of a street received a rating of 1.5 or higher on the photographic rating scale, the crew would be required to reclean the street before being allowed to go home.

The project team then briefed the crew members on the conditions and constraints of the incentive program. Team members described in detail the quality control system. The presentation was highlighted by photographs illustrating streets in the test area which met the quality standards and those which did not. The photographs served as a reference for the crew in understanding the quality control system. Next, the routes were redesigned by the field foreman, the leadmen, and a project team member. Since the foreman and the leadmen were extremely familiar with the routes and the cleanliness of the test site, they were able to create balanced routes.

The task incentive was finally implemented a few days later with the field foreman driving behind the truck crew checking the quality of cleaning. Upon sighting a block which did not meet the quality standard, the foreman would write down the route number, the street segment, the side of the street, and the location of the leftover litter on a specially designed form. The field foreman would send the crew members back to reclean before they were allowed to go home.

The following improvements were made under the task incentive program:

- Frequency of cleaning each street was doubled from once in two weeks to once per week, without adding any new staff or equipment.
- Efficiency of street cleaning, measured in square yards swept per labor hour, increased 42 percent.
- An average of 1190 square yards was recleaned per crew-day under the quality control system.
- In before-and-after surveys conducted as part of NSIP, the percentage of residents who considered dirty streets a "major problem" dropped from 42 percent before the project to 30 percent after the project.

As a result of these performance improvements, the task incentive program was expanded from one neighborhood to an entire ward (out of eight wards in the city) and from once in every week to every day.

EXAMPLE 4.7 SAN DIEGO COUNTY OFFICE OF PROGRAM EVALUATION

Marilyn K. James
Former Project Manager
Office of Program Evaluation

The San Diego County Office of Program Evaluation was created by the county's elected Board of Supervisors in 1974. The staff was built up of persons from multidisciplinary backgrounds, including systems analysis, statistics, accounting, finance, economics, and public administration. At the office's inception, it reported directly to the Board of Supervisors. It was later shifted into the county's Office of Management and Budget. Assignments were received directly from the county's chief administrative officer as well as the Board of Supervisors. In addition, many requests for technical assistance came from operating departments.

The Office of Program Evaluation received assignments to conduct program evaluations (which included both effectiveness and efficiency analyses) in several diverse functions of county government. Many of these evaluations were in public welfare, including the Food Stamp Program, General Relief Program, and Aid to Families with Dependent Children (AFDC) Program. Other evaluations covered, for example, the county's personnel policies, in-house leasing program, permit processing system, juvenile justice system, voting system, custodial and building maintenance services, and conservatorship program.

One of the most comprehensive evaluations the office undertook was of Aid to Families with Dependent Children, which serves over 27,000 families in the county. In fiscal year 1976-77, over $101 million was being provided in AFDC assistance grants, with a net county cost of about $21 million. Administrative costs for the program ran about $9 million, with a net county cost of over $2 million.

While the form and structure of the AFDC program are largely dictated by the federal and state governments, the day-to-day management of the program in California is the responsibility of each county. However, the state monitors local government operations closely and penalizes counties which exceed state-established guidelines for cost containment. For example, when staffing exceeds state norms, as was the case before the evaluation in San Diego, state cost reimbursements are reduced and county taxpayers are required to carry a larger percentage of the program's administrative cost. This was the context in which the San Diego County Board of Supervisors assigned the AFDC program to the Office of Program Evaluation for study.

The project examined diverse concerns that had been raised by members of the Board of Supervisors, the public, and the media, including:

- The adequacy of the total amount of benefits available to AFDC clients in San Diego County;
- The effectiveness of local work and training programs:
- The AFDC participation rate of elegible households in San Diego County;
- The usage levels and capacities of local welfare facilities, especially as related to the projected local case load growth;

- The possibility of alternative client processing systems which would retain or improve the quality of service and reduce administrative costs.

The evaluation used measurement tools from diverse disciplines such as industrial engineering, quality control, and organizational development. These tools included work measurement and systems analysis of all operations to identify inefficiencies, random samples of client case files for service quality, client and employee surveys to determine their perceptions of service quality and organizational problems, and the use of census data to determine participation rates of eligible people.

The final report, presented to the Board of Supervisors in May 1977, contained 92 recommendations. Fifty-two of the recommendations were efficiency related, and the remaining 40 concerned effectiveness.

Following the completion of the evaluation, an implementation team was formed to test and to refine the recommendations which came out of the evaluation. Based on the results of a 10-month pilot implementation project, total program administration savings attributable to the evaluation exceeded $2.1 million annually. Much of the savings were due to significant gains in worker efficiency in processing clients. The efficiency gains were the result of systemwide improvements which allow the workers to "work smarter, not harder." For example, a new client screening system "screens" out ineligible clients earlier in the processing system, thus saving worker time. This improvement, along with many others, resulted in workers being able to process about 20 percent more clients per day. In addition, the quality of service to clients improved. For example, the amount of time required for an AFDC applicant to receive initial aid was reduced by one third.

Many of the project's methodologies and findings have been shared with other government organizations, at the local, state, and federal level. The evaluation received a 1979 National Association of Counties Achievement Award.

EXAMPLE 4.8 PERFORMANCE AUDITING AND ANNUAL AUDIT PLANNING IN DALLAS

James R. Fountain, Jr.
Assistant City Manager
Former City Auditor

In April 1976 the citizens of Dallas voted to amend the city charter provisions governing the duties of the city auditor. Two fundamental changes were made:

- Responsibility for the city's accounting system was transferred from the city auditor to a newly established Office of the City Controller, under the direction of the city manager.
- The duties of the city auditor with regard to internal auditing were expanded to include reviews of the economy, efficiency, and effectiveness of operations, as well as the more traditional financial auditing functions.

The amendment to the charter was the first step in creating an independent, broad-scope internal audit function for the city, unencumbered by operational responsibilities. To help carry out its new responsibilities, the Dallas City Auditor's Office developed and implemented an annual audit planning process. The city council accepted the idea and included the following requirement in the council resolution defining the responsibilities and administrative procedures of the Office of the City Auditor:

Before the beginning of each fiscal year the City Auditor shall submit an annual audit plan to the City Council for approval. The plan shall include identification of the scope of each audit to be conducted in terms of the organizations, programs, functions, and activities to be audited and in terms of the audit elements to be addressed.

The Annual Audit Plan serves the following purposes:

- Provides clear and current authorization for each audit conducted by the office;
- Facilitates efficient planning for individual audits;
- Assists the city auditor in coordinating internal audit activities with state and federal auditors and with the city's independent auditors;
- Provides a basis for determining the funding level required to carry out internal audit responsibilities;
- Provides prior notification to city department managers of the general scope and timing of audit work to be done in their departments;
- Provides a basis for determining the type and extent of additional staff training or outside consulting services required to conduct audits;
- Provides criteria for evaluating the performance of the city auditor in carrying out the responsibilities of the auditor's office.

The process used to develop each year's audit plan allows both the city council and city management to be involved in the selection of audits so that the information needs of both can be met. The city council has final authority for approval of the plan.

PERFORMANCE AUDIT PROGRAM

Generally accepted standards for the internal auditing profession call for regular audits to appraise the economy and efficiency with which resources are employed, the effectiveness of the organization in achieving its objectives, and its compliance with applicable legal provisions. The Dallas City Auditor's Office includes in this program:

- *Comprehensive performance audits:* This type of audit encompasses a review of all aspects of the auditee's operations with respect to compliance, economy, efficiency, and effectiveness. The resulting information should provide a basis for long-term policy decisions, as well as generate suggestions for improving operations.
- *Limited scope performance audits:* This type of audit focuses on a specific aspect of auditee operations, such as the efficiency of personnel use or the cost-effectiveness of procurement policies. These audits are normally conducted in response to specific information requests from the council or management, and focus on identifying opportunities for improving operations.

SELECTING AUDITS FOR THE ANNUAL AUDIT PLAN

The financial audits and some other projects of the Office of the City Auditor are defined based on a long-range plan for the office. The long-range plan is updated each year during January and February, with primary responsibility of selection of audits and projects resting with the city auditor.

The conduct of *performance audits* is directly related to the current information needs of the city council and city management. For this reason, *a separate process has been developed for selecting specific performance audits to be included in the Annual Audit Plan.* The steps in the process are described below.

1. *Identify candidates for audit.* Requests for audits are solicited from the mayor, members of the city council, the city manager, and departments reporting directly to the council (e.g., Dallas transit system, parks and recreation). To facilitate the request process, Audit Request Questionnaires are provided (see Figure 4-11). The city auditor and assistant city auditors, upon request, assist respondents in completing the questionnaires.
2. *Confirm audit requests.* After all questionnaires are received, they are analyzed by the audit staff and a tentative audit prospectus is prepared for each. Each prospectus is discussed with the requestor to insure the request has been properly interpreted.

INSTRUCTIONS: Complete a separate form for each audit requested. Attach any information or documents to this form which may be pertinent to determining the need for the audit. Return the completed form to City Auditor, 3FS City Hall, before 5:15 p.m., July 2, 1979. Please do not hesitate to call Jay Fountain at 670-3222 should you require any assistance.

Description of Entity to be Audited

Scope of Audit (Check all that apply)

☐ Program Results
☐ Productivity
☐ Management Review
☐ Compliance

Circumstances Leading to the Request

☐ Budget   ☐ Increase
               ☐ Decrease
               ☐ Overrun
☐ Lack of Program Information
☐ Adverse Publicity
☐ New Program
☐ New Management
☐ Follow-up to Previous Audits/Studies
☐ Need to Increase or Improve Services
☐ New Legal Requirements
☐ New Policies
☐ Other (Please explain)

Please list the questions this audit should answer. (Use reverse or additional sheets if necessary.)

Please give any other information you feel is necessary for the understanding of this request. (Use reverse or additional sheets if necessary.)

SUBMITTED BY:

_____   _____
          Signature   Date

_____
          Title

Figure 4-11. Audit Request Questionnaire

3.   *Establish audit priorities.* Relative priorities for each audit candidate are set by the mayor and the city council. A priority ranking ballot (see Figure 4-12) is distributed which indicates, for each audit candidate, the proposed scope and the source of the request.

PROPOSED ANNUAL AUDIT PLAN

Based on the long-range plan and the performance audit selection process, the city auditor prepares a proposed Annual Audit Plan for the next fiscal year. The proposed plan includes:

1.   A cover memorandum summarizing the contents of the plan;
2.   A list of audits and projects to be conducted;
3.   A prospectus for each audit on the list (Figure 4-13).

ADOPTION OF FINAL AUDIT PLAN

After establishment by the council of the city's service and funding levels for the coming fiscal year, including the city auditor's budget, appropriate revisions will be made in the proposed Annual Audit Plan. The revised plan is submitted to the council for adoption by resolution.

ANNUAL PLANNING SCHEDULE

The planning schedule shown in Figure 4-14 illustrates the timing of each step in the annual planning process during the fiscal year. The process is initiated in January with the revision of the long-range plan, which is approved by the city council in early March. During March and April, the city's budget is prepared and submitted to the city manager. Concurrent with budget preparation and extending through the month of May, the Annual Audit Plan, including a project-based budget, is prepared. The council receives the proposed Annual Audit Plan in early June, and workshop sessions are held as necessary to allow the council to review the plan, obtain explanations from the city auditor, and make any desired revisions. After appropriate revisions are made, the final Annual Audit Plan is approved by the council in mid-July. If any revisions to the city auditor's budget are required by the council, these will be made in late July and submitted to the city manager. The council then considers the city auditor's budget along with the rest of the city budget, and final approval is given through adoption of the appropriations ordinance in late September.

During October, the Annual Audit Plan is distributed, and the managers of programs to be audited during the year are notified. If refinements in audit planning procedures are considered desirable, they

LIST OF AUDIT CANDIDATES
FOR PRIORITY RANKING BY CITY COUNCIL

INSTRUCTIONS:

1. You have 100 points to distribute amoung the audits listed below. The more important an audit is to you, the more points it should receive. Any single audit may receive as little as zero or as many as 50 points, so long as the total number of points for all audits does not exceed 100.

2. Enter your point ratings in the blank beside the appropriate audit in the column headed "Score". It is important that you use all of your points.

3. After completion, please sign and date each page and return to the Office of the City Auditor.

Score	Audit	City Council	City Manager	Department Head	City Auditor	Other
_____	13. Street abandonment to adjacent owner.	X				
	Scope: Program results, compliance.					
	Objectives: Review and evaluate current policy with regard to equity; review and evaluate sufficiency of internal controls.					
_____	14. General code enforcement.	X				
	Scope: Comprehensive.					
	Objectives: Determine whether the current code enforcement structure is achieving city goals as efficiently and economically as possible.					
_____	15. Street Lighting	X				
	Scope: Management review, program results.					
	Objectives: Determine whether street lighting on major freeways is adequately monitored, and evaluate the speed and efficiency of corrective action.					
_____	16. Equipment Services	X				
	Scope: Management review, productivity.					
	Objective: Determine whether Equipment Services provides vehicles to City departments at reasonable cost.					

Source of Request

_____   _____
Signature   Title

Figure 4-12. Audit Priority Ranking Ballot.

CITY OF DALLAS
OFFICE OF THE CITY AUDITOR
ANNUAL AUDIT PLAN

AUDIT PROSPECTUS FOR _____ GENERAL CODE ENFORCEMENT

SCOPE OF AUDIT	☐ Financial ☒ Control System Review ☒ Program Results	☒ Compliance ☒ Productivity

PRIMARY AUDIT OBJECTIVES

One of the most important and pervasive of the City's functions as a municipal corporation is the establishment and enforcement of ordinances intended to promote the social and economic welfare of its citizens. Enforcement activities cover a multiplicity of areas and are assigned to a wide range of City departments. The auditors will seek to develop a comprehensive profile of these activities and their complex interrelationships. Analytical work will then be performed to accomplish the following primary objectives:

- Review and appraise the various administrative control systems employed to ensure that code enforcement activities comply with relevant laws and regulations, to monitor and control the effectiveness of code enforcement in achieving legal and policy objectives, and to promote operational efficiency.

- Determine whether code enforcement activities are generally achieving legal and policy objectives.

- Identify opportunities for achieving established objectives more economically and efficiently.

Audit work from a previously authorized review of the code enforcement activities of the Department of Housing & Urban Rehabilitation will be updated and incorporated with the planned work.

PERFORMANCE TARGETS

☒ New Audit   ☐ Previously Authorized
Start Date: March 1, 1980
Report to Council: December 1, 1980
Audit Hours: 3,542
☐ Consultant Fees:

ANTICIPATED BENEFITS

☒ Financial	☒ Stronger Internal Control
☐ Directly Recoverable Costs:	
☒ Policy Alternatives	☐ Other:

Figure 4-13. Sample Audit Prospectus.

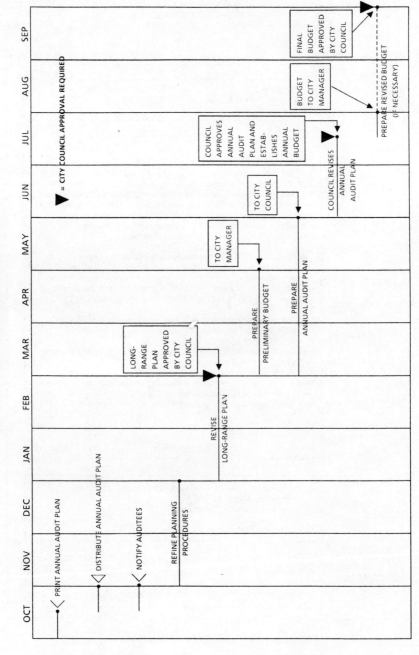

Figure 4-14. Audit Planning Schedule.

are made during November and December, prior to the initiation of the new planning cycle on January 1.

As with any organization, the need for unscheduled projects sometimes comes to the attention of the Dallas City Auditor's Office. For these contingencies, we budget some unscheduled staff time for "consultations with the city manager." This "consulation time" consists of brief investigations into problems needing immediate attention that may not be covered by the projects scheduled in the Annual Audit Plan. If the need for a large-scale unscheduled project becomes apparent, we refer it to the city council for approval. If the council wants us to do the new project, we ask the council to identify planned projects we can postpone to free staff for the unscheduled work.

To date, the response to the Annual Audit Plan process has been very favorable. Both the city council and city management understand they are an important part of the process. The process confirms the city auditor's accountability to the council. Further, there have been no questions raised by auditees with regard to the need or authority for specific audits. In several cases they had already begun to identify problems and enhance control systems, leading to a more constructive environment for the audit.

EXAMPLE 4.9 PERFORMANCE MEASUREMENT AND IMPROVEMENT IN CHARLOTTE, NORTH CAROLINA

Tom Finnie
Deputy City Manager, and
Pam Syfert,
Director, Budget and Evaluation

Performance measurement and improvement are often linked together. It is extremely important, however, that the emphasis be put on improvement. Charlotte's measurement efforts revolve around extensive performance targeting and monitoring, in the form of a management by objectives (MBO) program and performance contracts for human services. Our MBO system encourages the operating departments to make improvements at their own initiative, and it provides useful budget information. Performance contracts help human service contractors understand the level of performance expected of them. But we don't stop at targeting and monitoring performance. We make active use of program evaluation techniques, most notably internal performance audits and contract evaluation, to make sure our measurement efforts lead to performance improvements.

Using performance targeting and monitoring at the heart of performance measurement and improvement efforts has several advantages, such as:

- Early detection of problems before they require comprehensive program analyses or complete program overhauls, which are generally time consuming and expensive;
- Goals, objectives, and performance data against which to conduct performance audits;
- The basis for monitoring the results of the recommendations from most one-time program evaluations or improvement studies;
- A sense of fairness in which all departments are subject to monitoring or analysis;
- A professional image. Major business leaders in Charlotte have responded positively to the city manager's aggressive use of the well-recognized business concept of MBO.

Charlotte's MBO, performance auditing, and contract evaluation programs are described further below.

MANAGEMENT BY OBJECTIVES

Charlotte primarily uses its MBO program to monitor service effectiveness and service quality. The program contains approximately 400 objectives, which are monitored through three performance reports a year:

- A five-month status report (see excerpt in Figure 4-15);
- An eight-month progress report tied to the "objectives budget," listing the coming year's objectives;
- A year-end report.

Reports of performance against objectives focus on exceptions: problems and achievements. In many cases the problems relate specifically to the budget. Sometimes achievements spur further improvements. Some examples are outlined below:

- A performance report precipitated discussions with Charlotte Neighborhood Centers' personnel when that department failed to reach its goal of increasing clients by 40 percent. The result was a freeze on certain positions because of decreasing workload and consideration of a change in program direction.
- The Water Meter Reading Division was failing to meet the objective of reducing its backlog. When this failure was highlighted in a performance report, an analysis of the problem was initiated, leading to the addition of temporary positions. By the next performance report, the backlog had been reduced.
- The Street Cleaning Division has consistently met its goal of maintaining a high level of cleanliness, based on a five-point visual rating scale. This achievement has led to an effort to improve

Department:	Public Works	Program:	Environmental Health and Protection
Division:	Sanitation	Activity:	Refuse Collection—Residential

Objective 1: Maintain clean, uncluttered properties and reduce possible health hazards by adhering to a regular schedule of twice-weekly pickups for residential units and businesses. Maintain level and quality of service so that no more than 25 percent of the crews under any foreman receive more than 5 valid resident and business complaints per month and that no more than 25 percent of the foremen have crews that exceed the monthy five-complaint limit.

Status of Achievement: In order to measure the level and quality of refuse collection services, data will be gathered and reported as shown below:

Objective Achievement

Objective Measures	July	August	September	October	November
Number of Service Requests	1798	2283	1692	1715	1978
Number of Crews With More Than 5 Complaints/Month	31	34	25	21	13
Number of Foremen With Crews Having More Than 5 Complaints Per Month	14	14	13	12	8
Percentage of Crews With More Than 5 Complaints/Month	35%	39%	28%	24%	15%
Percentage of Foremen With Crews Having More Than 5 Complaints Per Month	93%	93%	87%	80%	53%

Objective Resolution Statement: Provide a narrative indicating whether the objective has been met or not. If the objective has not been achieved, explain what factors have contributed to the lower level and quality of refuse collection service.

Concentrated efforts are being made to meet this objective. There is a progressive decrease in the percentage of foremen and crews receiving complaints. These efforts will continue to further decrease the complaint percentage so that this objective can be met.

Figure 4-15. Excerpt from Five-month Performance Monitoring Report
of Charlotte, North Carolina.

effectiveness and efficiency further by evaluating the frequency of cleaning streets and basing the cleaning schedule on need.

PERFORMANCE AUDITING

To provide depth to the MBO program, Charlotte also does performance audits focusing on a department's objectives, as well as on efficiency and effectiveness questions. The audit reports are used primarily by department heads to make improvements in objectives, performance reporting, work scheduling, and work assignments, and to help set priorities. In programs with work crews, work sampling is used to determine if crew sizes are too large or small.

The performance audits provide useful program information for the budget office and a basis for performance improvements. Here are some examples:

- *In Landscaping:*
  - As a result of work sampling, recommendations were made to trade off better equipment for a reduction in tree trimming personnel.
  - As a result of field observations, recommendations were made for discontinuing some types of services which were not required.
  - Certain recommendations were made to improve Landscaping's reporting against objectives. The data backing up performance reports were verified as accurate in most cases; data collection improvements were made where accuracy problems existed.
- *In Traffic Engineering:*
  - Poor planning and scheduling procedures were identified and recommendations made for improvements.
  - Certain positions approved in the budget were recommended to be held vacant pending the outcome of work sampling.
  - Because of poorly defined objectives and confused reporting, training classes in management by objectives were held for section heads in the Operation Division.
- *In Sanitation:*
  - Operational changes were recommended to increase quality of service as measured by complaints of missed pickups and spilled trash.
  - Inaccurate data were identified in performance reports, and recommendations made to improve data collection and reporting.

All major city operations are scheduled to have a performance audit completed over the next five years.

CONTRACT EVALUATION

Charlotte's Budget and Evaluation Office is responsible for evaluating all human resource programs contracted for by the city's Community Development Department. The Budget and Evaluation Office and the Community Development Department cooperate in writing performance contracts that include the following elements:

- *Objectives:* The contract objectives include targets for the number of clients to be served; the desired impact on clients; and client satisfaction levels, which are measured through user surveys in selected programs.
- *Performance reporting requirements:* These specify the frequency of reports to be submitted by the contractor, the type of reports, and the format in which the data will be presented.
- *Type and quantity of services to be provided.*

The contract objectives and performance reports give the Budget and Evaluation Office the basis for evaluating contractor performance. Evaluations will vary from routine verification of reports that indicate good performance to investigations into the reasons objectives were not met.

As a result of these evaluations, changes have been made in the human resources programs:

- *Some contract programs have been terminated:*
  - The cost per client of an accounting assistance program was considered too high compared to similar tax assistance services. This program was terminated after the evaluation.
  - A methadone treatment program was not renewed after the evaluation revealed that it did not serve the number of clients targeted and that the same treatment was available to clients from other sources.
- *Many contract programs have been modified:*
  - After an extensive evaluation of the city's nonprofit housing corporation, the scope of services was revised to coordinate better with the city's housing priorities; rehabilitation goals were set in the contract and certain functions, such as property management, were eliminated because the evaluation concluded that these functions were not having an impact on providing additional housing.
  - The Meals for the Elderly Program was modified so more meals were prepared and served on site, instead of being catered. This change was made after clients, in an evaluation survey, rated catered meals significantly lower than on-site meals.

- A contract providing household services for the elderly and handicapped was changed to increase weekly service hours per client. The evaluation pointed out the time provided for assistance was not adequate to make clients more self-sufficient.
- A successful tutoring program was expanded into new target areas after test results showed the program was successful in meeting its goals.
- Additional counselors were added to an education contract after the evaluation showed the objectives for the percentage of clients completing courses were not being met. No cost was added to the contract for this change.

It is Charlotte's experience that contract objectives, performance reporting, and evaluation result in better services for clients. Programs are better administered when agencies and contractors know what is expected and know their performance will be measured and reported to the city council.

FACTORS CONTRIBUTING TO CHARLOTTE'S SUCCESS

Charlotte started its MBO program in 1971 and gradually added the other performance measurement and improvement approaches. The following factors appear to have been instrumental to the good results Charlotte has achieved:

- *Top management continuity and support:* Charlotte has been fortunate that City Manager David Burkhalter provided consistent leadership and support from 1971 through 1980. Every effort has been made to make measurement and improvement systems practical, to avoid putting the city manager in the position of having to support whimsical and obscure recommendations.
- *Right person, right place, and right idea:* The person responsible for the operation of the measurement and improvement systems has to want to use them, and has to be in a position to implement decisions. The budget office is the agency that can best reconcile MBO and evaluation recommendations with decisions to increase or decrease spending.
- *Programs were never oversold:* The idea of the MBO system in Charlotte was not to save the world or to recreate it in the image of a systems analyst. It was simply to improve the budgeting process, which in Charlotte is very much a management process. Better council and public understanding of the budget, contract evaluations, and performance audits were valuable spin-offs from the MBO system, but were not solemn promises made in the beginning to sell the system.

- *Evolutionary, flexible programs:* The Charlotte programs are not rigid. The appropriate analysis tool is used for the appropriate problem. Programs have changed and will continue to change to meet new management needs.
- *Reasonableness:* Charlotte's MBO forms are simple, and departments are encouraged to revise objectives whenever necessary. Paperwork and data collection are kept to an absolute minimum.
- *Balance:* Every effort is made to encourage a healthy balance between analysis capability in the operating departments and in the Budget and Evaluation Office. Recommendations for improvements are expected to come as much if not more from departments; implementation is almost always the responsibility of the operating department.

Charlotte's performance measurement and improvement programs did not reach their current levels overnight, but developed gradually. Our implementation experience would suggest: start by covering the entire jurisdiction with performance objectives; respond to and reward those departments that show interest; use basic, commonsense measures and techniques in the beginning and let sophistication develop over time; pray for top management continuity; and try to ignore unjust criticism. Some improvement is better than none and the millennium of local government management is not going to come in some great quantum leap.

EXAMPLE 4.10 SAN DIEGO POSTSCRIPT: ANATOMY OF THE MERGER BETWEEN THE CITY'S PRODUCTIVITY IMPROVEMENT PROGRAM AND ORGANIZATION DEVELOPMENT AND TRAINING PROGRAM

Trudy J. Sopp
Supervisor
Organization Effectiveness Program

In July 1980, a merger took place between two successful City of San Diego programs — the Productivity Improvement Program (PIP) and Organization Development and Training (OD&T). These programs are separately described in this chapter in Example 4.3 (PIP) and Example 4.5 (OD&T). City Manager Ray T. Blair elected to combine these two sections to form the innovative Organization Effectiveness Program (OEP). Under the direction of the city's Financial Management Department, OEP has become a powerful integration of administrative (work measurement) analysts and organization development specialists. This merger serves as a study in the evolution and refinement of the resources needed to conduct results oriented performance improvement in the public sector.

BACKGROUND

Over the years as the PIP and OD&T programs became more visible and active, it was easier to evaluate their strengths and weaknesses. The PIP emphasis on cost cutting through staff reductions and the view of PIP staff as "outsiders" by departments eventually had an adverse effect on employee morale. Specifically, employees' sense of control over their work environment, job security, and feelings of participation in work-related decisions suffered. Weaknesses in the OD&T approach involved the difficulty of quantifying qualitative organizational changes such as better management practices, more frequent and effective communications, role clarification, and improved problem-solving abilities. As well, organization development techniques take time and patience and organizations in crisis and pain have little tolerance for either.

The city manager sought a merger in order to strengthen PIP and OD&T, and address the ever increasing demands on city departments for performance improvements in a post-Proposition 13 era. The intention was that PIP would benefit from the "human factor" and participatory emphasis on methodology of the OD&T approach and, concomitantly, OD&T would improve its documentation and analytic abilities through a realistic employment of PIP's work measurement and methods improvement technology. Essentially, PIP techniques would be placed within the context of organization development processes and climate-setting approaches.

OEP AS A FUNCTIONING UNIT

The purpose of the consolidation was to integrate administrative analysts and organization development specialists in the same performance improvement efforts in selected departments. There was no interest in having the two separate programs merely coexist under one roof. To accomplish this structural and programmatic goal, the supervision was decentralized with one organization development supervisor managing the section and four project leaders (composed of two OD specialists and two administrative analysts) heading teams of analysts and OD specialists. Although professional staffing varies, there are approximately three OD specialists and six administrative analysts in the OEP section. To augment staff and contribute to the development of the public administration field, OEP offers an administrative internship program for graduate students.

The merger required a unification of staff, philosophies, and ideologies. The OEP has four goals that when used together form the foundation of its working philosophy. These goals entail working jointly with city departments, employees, and citizens to:

- Improve efficiency and effectiveness;
- Increase citizen or user satisfaction with services;

- Save money through direct cost reductions or increase service levels without corresponding cost increases;
- Improve employee job satisfaction.

The OEP is not interested in meeting one goal at the expense of the others. Rather, through implementing engineered work standards with human resource management techniques, OEP strives to accomplish all four goals using them as cornerstones for its intervention. Since department managers and their staffs are integral to determining the focus of any OEP project that affects them, they are involved in identifying how OEP goals will be met and what new standards, if any, will be set for their departments.

Two points about the new OEP are important to note. First, the OEP resides in a department that reports directly to the city manager. This gives it the authority it needs to facilitate change, as well as access to decision making and information resources. Second, a merger of this sort has a training requirement. Analysts and OD specialists came together with different backgrounds and skills. Although it is sufficient to create a climate and structure where these skills complement one another, the staff asked for more. The analysts and OD specialists wanted to expand their skills to include the strengths and talents of each approach. This was an unanticipated consequence of the merger but one that has led to a stronger, more well-rounded staff.

As a combined unit, OEP services include: consulting with department managers, staffing requirement studies, work flow charting, team building workshops, supervisory training, survey construction and administration, facilitation of meetings, goal and objective setting, creative problem-solving workshops, and others. Services often range from large comprehensive projects (one to two years in length) developed to realize major changes in organizations and operations, to smaller, more flexible projects developed for specific performance improvement needs, to specialized projects for one-time interventions.

By mid-1982 several projects have been conducted with interdisciplinary teams. These projects have worked well with an equal emphasis on all four OEP goals. For example, in 1980, a "restudy" of the Equipment Division was conducted by an interdisciplinary team. (See Example 4.3 for a description of the original 1975 Equipment Division PIP study.) In the Equipment Division Restudy Project data collected by the administrative analysts were used as the basis for a team building session of managers and employees conducted by an OD specialist. Using OD techniques such as conflict resolution, creative problem solving, and communication exercises, the OD specialist worked with the analysts and Equipment Division managers and employees to facilitate the effective use of important efficiency and user satisfaction data. What might have been an adversarial relationship took on a participatory structure and insured "buy in" from the top and bottom of the client organization. The analysts offered their expertise on how to gather and interpret such data and the OD specialist guided the process in such a way as to encourage participation and accurate problem identification and problem solving. This combination of skills complements one another and produces the performance improvement results within a structure both managers and employees can accept.

Clear project goals have been identified as a key ingredient to successful interdisciplinary intervention. In a multiskilled team everyone must know the purpose of the intervention so skills can be directed best.

We are pleased with the OEP in the City of San Diego. A waiting list of department managers anxious for OEP services is a distinctive mark of our success. As we refine our integration we feel the future offers the further development and strengthening of a model performance improvement program.

EXAMPLE 4.11 THE PHOENIX EXPERIENCE: EVOLUTION AND CHANGE

Patrick Manion
Assistant to
the Mayor

Since 1970 the City of Phoenix, Arizona has used extensive performance measurement and improvement programs to increase the efficiency and effectiveness of city services. In the 1980s, performance improvement is still a strong theme in Phoenix, but the orchestration of improvement efforts throughout the city government is quite different. Some changes have evolved as natural refinements of measurement and improvement processes, while other adjustments were made by direct intervention to correct deficiencies that had developed. The result is a shift from highly centralized measurement and improvement programs, primarily dependent on the budget office for direction and control, to programs that directly involve executives and middle managers throughout the government, and reach out to encourage all city employees to participate in improvement efforts.

Phoenix initially developed, with the assistance of an outside consultant, an industrial engineering based work planning and control program with heavy emphasis on time standards, major systems studies, technological improvements, and performance monitoring. At one time, the performance of over 2500 employees (then 40 percent of the work force) was monitored in regular reports that measured employee efficiency against designated time standards. In the early 1970s major efficiency gains were reported and significant cost savings realized.

Among Phoenix's most successful industrial engineering applications were the introduction of new technology and crew reductions in garbage collection, improved planning and scheduling of building inspectors, and improved methods for treasury collections. In garbage collection alone, the cumulative results of improvements since 1971 have meant cost avoidance of over $25 million of expenditures.

Also in the early 1970s, the city began evaluating effectiveness through Program Analysis and Review (PAR) Studies. The PARs developed comprehensive goals and objectives for service programs (the first time this had ever been done in Phoenix), assessed the effectiveness of existing service levels, evaluated alternative service levels, and examined selected policy issues in detail. The primary results of the early PARs, completed during the period of a strong economy and new federal revenue sharing money, was to document existing service levels and their effectiveness for city council review. As a result of these studies, some services were added or increased, such as implementation of a Fire Emergency Medical Service and expansion of the street seal coat program. The PARs also led to some service reductions such as reduced residential street sweeping frequency and a reduction in the frequency of uncontained trash collection.

As the initial PARs were completed, the use of comprehensive goals and objectives was expanded to all departments and became incorporated into the budget review process. In the mid-1970s, PAR studies focused on specific policy issues such as "the appropriate level of equipment replacement," "the level of city funds for social programs," and "alternatives for reducing police response time for critical calls for service."

As the performance improvement activities in the mid-1970s evolved, some difficulties developed in keeping the program as dynamic as before. Specifically, the following problems were identified:

- Time standards were outdated for many activities because analysts had insufficient time to maintain the multitude of standards that constantly required change as city operations expanded and procedures were altered.
- Department heads had lost interest in the monthly performance reports that were monitoring efficiency because most measures showed little or no change. (Our analysis found that once initial improvements had been made, efficiency rates often would remain static for long periods. We became convinced that, for many activities, periodic work sampling is a better, less expensive management tool than a continuous work standards reporting system.)
- Some department heads considered the comprehensive goals and objectives that had been developed to be strictly part of a budget exercise and had not made use of the objectives for managing

their departments, as had been intended. The consensus, even in those departments that used objectives, was that the performance measures backing up the objectives were too detailed and not sufficiently results oriented. Consequently, much information was collected and reported without being used.

Some of Phoenix's problems were symptoms of an overly centralized process in which department managers and staff has no "ownership." They saw the measurement and improvement efforts as budget office issues and not their own.

In 1977, City Manager Marvin Andrews set objectives for revitalizing the performance improvement efforts, improving organizational communications, and placing more responsibility for city activities with executives and middle managers. Actions undertaken to achieve these objectives included implementation of an organizational development program, establishment of a performance achievement system for executives and middle managers, and appointment of a Citizens Productivity Advisory Committee to work with staff to review and evaluate the directions of the improvement efforts.

Phoenix initiated an organizational development (OD) program in the spring of 1977. Citywide and departmental five-year organizational development plans were completed in the fall of 1977. The departmental OD activities provided the link between department activities and achievement of the city's organizational objectives, as well as a framework for employee participation in setting objectives and planning how to achieve them. In 1978, the city started using periodic employee attitude surveys as one way to determine the degree of success in improving communications flow and morale.

Also in 1977, Phoenix started a performance achievement program for executives and middle managers. The performance achievement program combined management by objectives with incentive pay. Management employees set job accomplishment objectives, in consultation with their superiors, to be measured over a specific period of time. The objectives help managers plan staff workloads and serve as yardsticks to measure managerial performance. Performance achievement plans are reevaluated annually or whenever significant changes in work situation occur. Managerial salary levels are open, within a given range, to allow flexibility in compensating individuals for varying degrees of performance against their objectives. While organizational development helps increase participation in setting objectives, performance achievement plans give managers an extra incentive to achieve them.

The Citizens Productivity Advisory Committee, whose eleven members represented banks, educational institutions, manufacturing firms, utilities, and private service organizations, completed its six-- month study in April 1978. The committee's recommendations focused on five opportunities for improvement: communication, training, accountability, organization, and program results. The performance achievement program and OD efforts were already starting to address the accountability and organization issues. The committee report gave reason for optimism, as it concluded: "The potential for productivity gains within the City of Phoenix is very high. There is great support for an effective citywide program from all levels of management. There is an honest individual desire for measurement of effort and effective utilization of City resources."

In response to the committee's recommendations, City Manager Marvin Andrews instituted changes in reporting relationships with renewed emphasis on training, communication, recognition, and results. In the fall of 1978 the city manager appointed a department head critique committee to evaluate the budget process. As a result of the committee's findings, several improvements were made. These included a new service level trends report highlighting major performance measures, and giving a simpler, clearer picture of *program results* than was previously available. The trends report replaced the comprehensive goals and objectives that many departments found too detailed. Figure 4-16 shows a typical, highly detailed comprehensive goals and objectives report that was discontinued. Figure 4-17 shows a much simpler service level trends report. Also, Phoenix's zero base budgeting process was simplified, decreasing the paperwork involved and increasing the use of summary information. The zero base budgeting process relies on departments developing service level impact statements for various levels of funding.

In 1979-80, as part of the plan to make departments feel more responsible for their own performance, seven operations analysts from the Management and Budget Department were assigned to work for line departments. Under this decentralized concept, the operations analysts report directly to department heads during their assignments. The operations analysts, however, continue to receive technical guidance through a central coordinating office. The operations analysts are also periodically rotated among departments as assignments are completed and other performance improvements are identified in different activities.

The central coordinating office initially continued to operate out of the Management and Budget Department. As the focus of the program continued to shift from less emphasis on the hard industrial engineering measures to a more behaviorist approach, management recognized a need to further modify the administration of the program. In March 1982 a new Value Management Office, reporting directly to the City Manager's Office, was created. The Value Management Office was formed by merging the coordinating unit for the decentralized operations analysts in Management and Budget with the organizational development and training activity in the Personnel Department.

TRAFFIC ENGINEERING

PROGRAM:

SUBPROGRAM: OPERATIONS

ACTIVITIES:

Objective:
Service Level:
Percent of
Objective:

Signals	Street Lighting and Meters	Signs	Marking and Delineation	Construction Traffic Control
• Replace 8" diameter signals with 12" diameter signals on 120 intersections over the next six years • Currently maintaining the desired rate of 20 replacements a year (100%) • Replace 1,000 pedestrian signals with new design to meet national standards within four years • Replacement program not yet under way due to technological problems • Convert 60 span-wire signals to mast-arm at 10/year	• Install continuous one-side lighting on all major streets • Of 421 miles of major streets 172 miles have continuous one-side lighting (40%) • Install two-side lighting on all fully developed major streets • Currently two-side lighting on 64 miles of 145 miles of Class A-1 major streets (44%) • Reconsider current City policy requiring petitions for midblock lighting in new subdivisions	• Replace 25,000 regulatory and warning signs on a 6-year cycle (approximately 4,200/year) • Current replacement rate 1,500/year (35%) • Replace 15,000 street name signs on a 10-year cycle (1,500/year) • Current replacement rate 500/year (33%) • Install all signs within ten days of work order • Currently requires 15 days on average (67%)	• Restripe all streets with average daily traffic flow exceeding 30,000 on a 3-month cycle • All streets on current 8-month cycle (37%) • Restripe all streets with average daily traffic flow from 10,000 to 30,000 vehicles on a 4-month cycle • All streets on current 8-month cycle (50%) • Restripe all streets with average daily traffic flow of less than 10,000 vehicles on a 6-month cycle	• Inspect traffic controls on major projects weekly • Currently being done (100%) • Review plans for City initiated and major private construction in the right-of-way • Currently being done (100%) • Make presentations to interested groups on proper control practices as needed • Currently being done (100%)

- Current rate 6/ year (60%)
- Monitor all signals at intersecting major streets quarterly
  - Currently being done (100%)
- Monitor all other intersections every six months
  - Currently being done (100%)
- Replace all obsolete vehicle detection equipment by June, 1974
  - Final phase of schedule will remove all obsolete equipment within fiscal year (100%)

- Current policy can be more efficient
- Maintain prescribed maintenance levels of Electrical Maintenance Division, Salt River Project, and Arizona Public Service
  - Currently being done on a complaint basis only (70%)
- Remove unnecessary lighting where required
  - Currently being done (100%)
- Replace 1,000 overage meters within 5 years
  - Program not underway at present time (0%)
- Perform preventive maintenance on all meters
  - Now being done

- All streets on current 8-month cycle (75%)
- Restripe all crosswalks every nine months
  - Currently being done (100%)
- Remove unnecessary markings and delineations
  - Currently being done (100%)

Figure 4-16. A highly detailed report from Phoenix.

ANNUAL BUDGET — PAGE ___

SERVICE LEVEL TRENDS

DEPARTMENT/DIVISION Phoenix Civic Plaza	ACTUAL SERVICE LEVEL PRIOR YEAR	BUDGETED SERVICE LEVEL CURRENT YEAR	ACTUAL SERVICE LEVEL CURRENT YEAR	NEXT YEAR SERVICE LEVEL WITH	
				BASE REQUEST	BASE AND SUPPLEMENTAL REQ.
Number of events booked and serviced annually	988	925	925	925	975
Number of conventions serviced	25	23	35	28	33
Annual Attendance	813,138	750,000	825,000	750,000	850,000
Average staff hours per event	112.5	124.3	124.3	124.3	126.1
Revenue generated from rentals and events	$811,640	$815,000	$850,000	$815,000	$900,000*
Average occupancy percentage					
Symphony Hall	65.6	65	65	65	70
Exhibit Hall	38.1	40	40	40	45
Assembly Hall	39.7	40	40	40	45
Meeting Rooms	59.4	60	55	60	60
Estimated convention delegate spending	$14.6 Million	$20.0 Million	$28.0 Million	$20.0 Million	$38.9 Million
Ratio of estimated economic impact of conventions to Civic Plaza operating budget and Convention Bureau support	$4.90/$1.00	$6.00/$1.00	$8.22/$1.00	$6.00/$1.00	$10.50/$1.00
Results of annual opinion survey of services provided					
Conventions	7.9	8.0	7.5	7.0	8.0
Theatrical and consumer shows	8.7	8.5	8.2	8.0	8.5
Local users	8.4	8.5	8.2	8.0	8.5
Public	6.9	7.5	7.5	7.0	7.5

(0-3 Not Satisfied/ 4-6 Satisfied/ 7-8 Pleased/ 9-10 Very Pleased)

*Assumes Rental Rate Increase

44-142D
Rev. 11-78

CITY OF PHOENIX, ARIZONA

Figure 4-17. A simplified report from Phoenix.

The new Value Management Office combines the industrial engineering and behaviorial approaches to performance improvement with the resources to direct citywide training activities. Analysts are available both from the central Value Management Office and at decentralized locations to provide assistance in the form of consulting services to departments. Analysts can provide organizational development program training to foster better communication and problem-solving skills as well as perform detailed system studies and staffing allocation and scheduling reviews. The Value Management Office works closely with the Management and Budget staff in their policy analysis and general management studies, and with the City Auditor's staff in their program audits.

City departments also have made significant performance improvements using their own staff resources. On occasion, the city still uses outside consultants to assist with particular problems. For example, a consultant study issued in July 1982 identified over $1 million in potential savings through improvements in the city's airport maintenance operations. Other major performance gains initiated by departments include contracting some landfill operations, consolidating uncontained and contained garbage collection crews, converting to a work week of four 10-hour days in police patrol, using more efficient equipment in street maintenance to reduce crew size, and improvements in grant accounting procedures.

Another outgrowth of the renewed performance improvement efforts has been the resurgence of the employee suggestion program. By increasing cash awards to 10 percent of the annual savings (up to a maximum award of $2000), and by publicizing the program heavily to employees, participation and savings have increased dramatically. Annual cost savings have been documented at $1 million from employee suggestions. For 1980 and 1981, the City of Phoenix was recognized as the outstanding governmental unit for employee suggestions by the National Association of Suggestion Systems.

The overriding message of the changes made in the Phoenix performance improvement programs since the mid-1970s is that *efficiency and effectiveness are everyone's business.* We found evidence that the message was getting through when a 1980 Employee Attitude Survey showed improvement over the initial survey done in 1978. Performance improvement efforts will be successful in the long run if people throughout the organization can understand them, recognize their importance, and feel they will receive recognition and rewards if they contribute to performance improvement. Phoenix has been building not only performance improvement skills and understanding, but also motivation for improvement throughout the organization. As a result, our performance measurement and improvement programs have been revitalized. With continued top management and council support, the potential for ongoing improvement appears to be very strong. However, as Phoenix's former Mayor, Margaret Hance has said, "We must not be content to rely on our past accomplishments." We must continue to modify and adapt our program, as necessary, to correct deficiencies and react to a changing environment.

5
Communicating with the Public for Improved Accountability

Using measurement to help make decisions and improve performance, as discussed in chapters 3 and 4, implies *accountability* for decisions and performance. Performance measurement gives public officials a tool to achieve performance accountability. Workers, supervisors, and middle managers are accountable to upper level managers for their performance, or their crews' or organization's performance, and the upper level managers are in turn accountable to elected officials. This is particularly clear in local governments using approaches such as management by objectives (MBO), in which performance reports are used to hold service managers accountable for achieving their targets. It is even clearer in places like Dayton and Phoenix, where achievement of objectives is linked to managerial pay. Those are forms of *internal* accountability of lower level public officials to higher level officials. This chapter examines *external* accountability: the *accountability of a local government and its officials to the public* it serves.

This chapter is concerned less with the actual measurement of performance than it is with *communication with the public*. Without good communication, how can local officials be sure they understand the public's best interests, and how can they get the message across that they are trying to make government performance responsive to those best interests? *Communication is the link between performance and accountability.*

This chapter describes various levels of communication between a local government and its citizens:

- Government reports and presentations *to the public* to let them know about problems and performance, as well as publicity about government performance;
- Government conducted surveys in which the government asks its citizens questions and uses their answers to help direct public policy;
- Service improvement efforts that include citizen participation to help identify problems and contribute to solutions;
- Citizen involvement approaches in which citizens get to ask questions of their own and make policy recommendations early in the government decision-making process, giving their views a good chance of being accepted.

Examples based on local government experiences for each of these levels of communication are provided, including four at the end of the chapter contributed by local officials.

REPORTING PERFORMANCE INFORMATION
TO THE PUBLIC

Improving accountability to the public is a scary notion to many public officials. Performance measurement uncovers both good and bad performance. Using measurement for policy and management purposes may be a fine idea, but why make that information public? Why risk calling attention to problems people might not otherwise notice?

Public officials in many communities have found it to their advantage to make performance information public. They have found when they take the initiative in reporting performance information to the public, they have control over the manner in which the information is disclosed. They can highlight improvements in their public performance reports and describe what the government is trying to do about problems made apparent by the data. This is far preferable to letting someone else, such as the local press, decide what information about public performance should be made public.

Many local governments make performance information public as part of their annual budget process. This allows program performance to be seen in the context of program cost. Other jurisdictions issue separate reports on performance. In either case, good public reports are those that can be easily understood by the reader. They are never purely statistical. Good public reports contain enough supporting narrative to be understood by the public. They also sometimes use graphics to help make key points. The idea is not just to provide performance data, but to communicate clearly how well the community is doing. There is no standard way of presenting performance data to the public; several communities have used creative approaches.

Dayton, Ohio's *Program Strategies* document is released to the city commission, the public press, and Dayton's neighborhood "priority boards" (citizen groups involved in the budget process). It includes the proposed budget and service objectives for the coming fiscal year, as well as prior performance versus objectives. Figure 5-1 shows excerpts from some of the special colored pages included in this document to report on community condition and satisfaction trends. Statistics, graphics, and explanatory narratives are used to make the conditions reported understandable. Dayton publicly reports conditions over which the government has little immediate control (e.g., property value, traffic noise, employment) but which are important to citizens, as well as conditions and perceptions over which the government has some control (e.g., feelings of security, street and alley conditions). In addition, Dayton reports national and

COMMUNITY SECURITY

CRIME PREVENTION
CRIME CONTROL
CRIMINAL ADJUDICATION
DETENTION AND REHABILITATION

NEIGHBORHOOD SAFETY INCREASES

The map on the right indicates a rise of 4% in the citywide perception of neighborhood safety during 1981. The 1981 level of 90% represents a 22% increase over the 1974 level of 68%. The highest level of perceived safety was in the FROC neighborhood (96%).

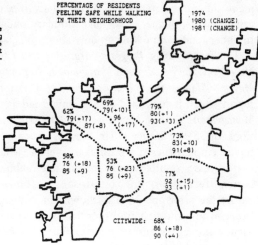

PERCENTAGE OF RESIDENTS
FEELING SAFE WHILE WALKING
IN THEIR NEIGHBORHOOD

1974
1980 (CHANGE)
1981 (CHANGE)

CITYWIDE: 68%
86 (+18)
90 (+4)

GOOD NEIGHBORS MAKE RESIDENTS FEEL SAFE

Reasons for Feeling Safe in Neighborhood

Reason	% Citing
Good Neighbors	43%
Unafraid	32%
Low Crime	13%
Good Police	3%
Other	9%

Females cited good neighbors as the reason for safety (49%) more frequently than males (35%). Males were more likely to cite being unafraid (38%) than were females (26%).

75% THINK POLICE RESPONSE IS QUICK

Police Contact/Response

	1974	1979	1980	1981
Called Police	35%	44%	44%	37%
Quick Response	49%	72%	66%	75%
Helpful	59%	61%	61%	72%

The percentage of respondents feeling that police response was quick to their call increased 9% in 1981. The percentage of those who found the police to be helpful increased 11% from 61% to 72%.

ACTUAL RESPONSE TIME DECLINES

Response Time

1979	1980	1981
12 min.	15 min.	14 min.

Figure 5-1. Excerpts from Dayton, Ohio's "Program Strategies" Document.

regional trend data in some cases to help readers put Dayton's performance in perspective.

Charlotte, North Carolina's *Objectives* document (excerpted in Figure 5-2), submitted for debate to the city council and made public, is the city's primary proposed budget document. Yet it is mostly narrative with few dollar figures. For each program it emphasizes goals, selected objectives, and achievement highlights from the previous year. Only summary budgeted positions and dollar figures are shown for each program. Narrative "budget notes" describe reasons for changes from the previous year. While city council members also receive a much larger budget document with detailed schedules, they give the *Objectives* document the most attention. In the *Objectives* document the goals, objectives, achievements, budget notes, and summary budget figures are all shown in easy-to-understand form taking up only about one page or less per program.

Unlike Dayton's *Program Strategies* and Charlotte's *Objectives* documents, New York City's *Mayor's Management Report* is not a budget document. The *Mayor's Management Report* is a City Charter mandated public performance report which is published in September and January of each year. The *Mayor's Management Report* contains selected performance data and narrative descriptions for 35 city agencies. The September report is the city's annual performance report emphasizing the prior fiscal year's (which ended the previous June 30) performance results versus targets and annual performance targets for the current fiscal year. For comparison, performance results from the fiscal year before the prior one are also shown. In January, an interim fiscal year report is issued listing the first four months actual versus targeted performance for each agency as well as annual targets. For most performance measures it also lists preliminary targets for the forthcoming fiscal year (staring 6 months later) based on current performance experience, new improvements planned, and the city's projected financial plan for that year. Both reports also contain a section describing citywide performance improvement initiatives and an executive summary with both citywide and agency-specific highlights. While the *Mayor's Management Report* is not a budget document, the performance targets take into account current budget allocations and future financial plans. Also, the citywide section describes many improvement efforts throughout the city government which are aimed specifically at helping to balance the budget without raising taxes or reducing services. While the *Mayor's Management Report* is large enough to seem imposing to some people (as much as 600 pages) it is actually a summary of the performance data collected in the city's Executive Planning and Reporting System, in which some larger agencies' individual management plans or reports are as big as the entire *Mayor's Management Report*. The report's clearly written agency narrative sections include agency missions, accomplishments, problems, and plans for improvement. The narratives make the performance data understandable, and, along with the citywide section,

Building Inspection

Goal
Promote public safety and a quality environment by reviewing plans and inspecting buildings to ensure compliance with regulations regarding minimum building, zoning, electrical, plumbing, mechanical and housing standards.

SERVICE LEVEL NOTES
FY 83 Objectives
• Inspect and cause the repair of approximately 215 housing units per month in order to insure that the overall condition of the housing stock does not deteriorate.
• Answer 96% of an estimated 1000 complaints concerning zoning or housing code violations within eight work hours.
• Review all building plans for single-family homes in one work day.
• Conduct special occupancy inspections of all nursing homes, day care centers, restaurants and lounges once every three years, for a total of 560 inspections over a three year period.
• Maintain a productivity rate of nine inspections per inspector day.

Current Achievements
• The number of housing units repaired averaged 200 per month, approximately 6% below the objective.
• 493 of 511 (96%) housing complaints and 82 of 114 (72%) zoning complaints were answered in one day.
• Plan reviews of each of the 455 single-family structures were completed in one day. However, the number of plans submitted has dropped by half over last year's level.

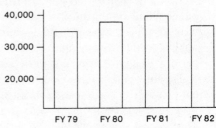

BUILDING INSPECTIONS
(eight months data)

PRODUCTIVITY NOTES
• Five car radios were eliminated from inspectors' vehicles and replaced by beeper service for a savings of $6,000.
• One zoning inspector was reassigned to cover all office functions for an auto allowance savings of $2,000.

BUDGET NOTES
Operating Budget
The recommended budget reflects a $143,050 increase from the FY 82 level. This increase reflects a full year's cost of the reclassification of the Building, Electrical, Plumbing and Mechanical Inspectors' positions and increases in auto allowance rates, legal advertising costs and data processing charges.

RECOMMENDED BUDGET

	FY 82	FY 83
Positions	70	70
Operating Budget	$1,612,489	$1,755,539

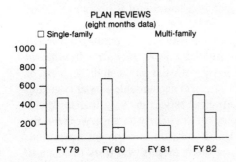

PLAN REVIEWS
(eight months data)
□ Single-family   Multi-family

• The inspector productivity ratio averaged 9.3 inspections per inspector day.

Figure 5-2. Excerpt from Charlotte, North Carolina's "Objectives" Document.

make the *Mayor's Management Reports* useful reference documents on city and agency performance, rather than just collections of statistics. Figure 5-3 contains an excerpt from an agency narrative.

In the mid- to late-1970's, Washington, D.C., issued annual reports to the public titled *Improving Program Performance* (excerpted in Figure 5-4). These were exemplary reports for describing performance improvement efforts to the public, particularly in their use of narrative and graphics for making program performance understandable to the public.

Phoenix, Arizona has made an extensive number of reports public on individual program evaluation and performance improvement projects. In July 1979, it issued a report describing its wide array of performance improvement approaches. Most of the report is dedicated to "briefs" on individual improvement efforts. As shown in Figure 5-5, each brief not only describes the problem addressed, solutions, and results, but also provides the name, address, and phone number of the city department to contact for more information.

ADVANTAGES AND PROBLEMS OF PUBLICIZING
GOVERNMENT PERFORMANCE

Of course a written report is not the only way to let the public know about government performance. All generally accepted public relations techniques, such as press conferences and releases, public service films and messages for media use, and presentations at citizen meetings, are useful for communicating performance information to the public.

Public officials who communicate well with the public concerning government performance have found they can make publicity work to their advantage in several ways. They can build their credibility with the public and the press, as performance reporting suggests a desire to be held accountable as well as greater sensitivity to problems of effective and efficient service delivery than most citizens ascribe to governments. This display of sensitivity in turn weakens the credibility of those who make demagogic attacks on government operations. Officials can also use publicity to motivate the managers who work for them to improve performance and meet targets. Since there are severe constraints on the financial incentives governments can offer their staff, all other motivational tools are extremely important. The possibility of getting a good or bad write-up in a public report or in the local press can spur many people to pay attention to performance improvement. Finally, good communication on government performance can have a useful educational effect on citizens and the press. It can help citizens understand public problems better as well as how the government is trying to solve them. This can be particularly helpful when citizen cooperation can significantly reduce a problem or contribute to its solution. When a government's plans for improvement are made clear to citizens, they may relent in their

DEPARTMENT OF HEALTH

The Department of Health (DOH) provides services to promote, maintain, and enhance the health of the City's residents. These include monitoring and surveillance of infectious disease; control and elimination of health hazards from environmental sources (such as radiation or rodent infestation); providing diagnostic, treatment, and preventive health services in child health, tuberculosis, venereal disease, school health, and other areas; setting and monitoring City standards of care for handicapped children, the newborn, and for day care services; maintaining the registry of all births and deaths occurring within the City; and certifying staff and monitoring operations of all clinical laboratories. In addition, forensic medical services are provided through the Office of Chief Medical Examiner.

GENERAL PUBLIC HEALTH

Immunization

A Citywide student immunization compliance rate of approximately 99 percent brings to successful culmination the two years of intensive efforts by the Department of Health, the Board of Education, and the Mayor's Task Force on Immunizations (chaired by the City Council President). Nearly 104,000 students were innoculated between July and December 1981 in a combination of special in-school immunization clinics (41,469) and Department walk-in clinics (62,476), whose hours were expanded during the first four weeks of the school year to accomodate increased demand.

The success of the two-year immunization drive is best measured by the dramatic decrease in the City's measles, mumps and rubella incidence. For Calendar 1981, mumps decreased 14.4 percent, rubella 47.6 percent and measles 91.2 percent compared to Calendar 1980. The Federal Centers for Disease Control define a disease eradicated in a specific area when that area has been free of that disease for a minimum of four weeks. Throughout Calendar 1981, 67 percent of the City's 183 zip code areas remained completely measles free, and for the last four weeks of 1981, 97.7 percent of the areas were measles free. Incidence has fallen from 1,210 cases in Calendar 1980 to just 106 in 1981. New York City has become the urban leader of the nation's measles eradication effort.

Tuberculosis Control

The tuberculosis control indicators present a mixed picture. The most important indicator, the number of new cases of tuberculosis (503), shows no change for the first four months of Fiscal 1982, as compared to the same period in Fiscal 1981 (501). This suggests that incidence is leveling off after having increased 7 percent in Fiscal 1981. The other critical indicator, the percentage of Citywide cases completing 12 consecutive months of treatment, rose to 69 percent during the first four months of Fiscal 1982 from 58 percent for the same period of Fiscal 1981.

On the negative side, due to turnover and Federal actions (described in the last Mayor's Management Report) the tuberculosis control program will not return to its full staffing levels until February 1982. Consequently, the percent of DOH-treated cases that demonstrate remission within 6 months of treatment fell to 59 percent for the first four months of Fiscal 1982, significantly lower than the 74 percent Fiscal 1981 annual figure. The Department expects improved performance once up to full staffing.

Figure 5-3. Excerpt from an Agency Narrative in New York City's
"Mayor's Management Report," January 30, 1982.

PARKING OPERATIONS

Parking meter revenues have more than doubled in the last two fiscal years, so that in FY 77 collections totaled $2.8 million (see Figure 01). In addition, the percentage of meters out-of-order on any day has decreased from 10% to 1%, while maintenance crew productivity has risen 19% in the past year. These dramatic gains occurred primarily as a result of improvements installed by an interagency project team charged with redesigning parking meter operations. The City's parking meter system not only generates needed revenues for the District, but also facilitates improved traffic flow and increased business activity.

The project to improve parking meter operations began in January, 1976, after a management review identified opportunities for further maximizing revenue yields and for improving management practices in the areas of rate structure, coin collection, coin counting, and meter maintenance. Because responsibility for the system's operation was divided between DOT and the Department of Finance and Revenue (DFR), staff from those agencies were assigned to the project along with technical assistance staff from OBMS.

After a detailed study of the District's parking meter system, parking meter management practices of six major cities, and coin handling and collection procedures of several private companies, the project team made a series of recommendations, all of which were implemented by September, 1977. These improvements included:

- *Parking meter management responsibilities consolidated.*
- *Collection system redesigned and collection responsibilities contracted out.*
- *Standard meter maintenance procedures established.*
- *Parking meter equipment and facilities upgraded.*
- *Parking meter management information system implemented.*

Figure 01

INCREASE IN PARKING METER REVENUE

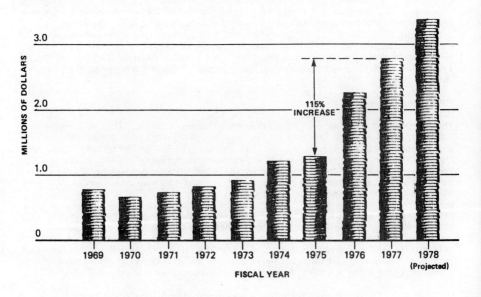

Figure 5-4. Excerpt from Washington, D.C.'s "Improving Program Performance."

ENGINEERING

ENGINEERING INSPECTIONS
CONSTRUCTION PROGRESS REPORT

PROBLEM

The Inspection Section of the Engineering Department prepared a weekly construction progress report. These reports were prepared to give detailed explanations on each construction project in the City. After an evaluation by the management staff in the Engineering Department, it was determined that their report was not needed. There were already two sources for the same information. These reports were as lengthy as 27 pages each, with an average of 15 pages each.

SOLUTION

This multipage weekly report, at the suggestion of an inspection supervisor, was reduced to a single page, monthly report. With an average of 50 reports per month this relieved a significant amount of staff and inspectors time.

RESULTS

The implementation of this suggestion reduced a voluminous amount of paper work to a bare minimum for the processing of this particular report. The total dollar savings for both staff time saved in typing, filing and printing cost and paper cost amount to over $28,000 the first year.

CONTACT
Engineering Department (602) 262-6561
251 West Washington
Phoenix, Arizona 85003

ENGINEERING CONCRETE SPECIFICATIONS

PROBLEM

In 1978, cement was in short supply. This slowed housing, street and commercial construction projects.

SOLUTION

The City of Phoenix reviewed its concrete specifications and reduced the cement content by one-half bag per cubic yard. This allowed the City to continue street projects where sidewalks, median islands, and curb and gutter construction were part of the design. Also, the Engineering Laboratory is now in the process of preparing a new specification of Portland cement concrete for use nationally. This new specification will incorporate the use of a waste product — fly ash — as an additive to concrete. This will result in monetary savings and provide a concrete with improved workability and good quality.

RESULTS

Reduced cement content expanded the supply of concrete. It also resulted in a cost savings on City projects of $118,000.

CONTACT
Engineering Department (602) 262-6561
251 West Washington
Phoenix, Arizona 85003

NUCLEAR ASPHALT CONTENT GAUGE

PROBLEM

In the past, one of the biggest problems facing a paving operation has been a fast and accurate determination of the asphalt content of a bituminous mix. As in most cases, the given mix had been laid and compacted long before the results were known.

SOLUTION

A sophisticated new method for testing asphalt quantity that uses space age techniques and reduces test time by a dramatic 63% is utilized by the Phoenix Engineering Department. The test method operates by passing fast neutrons from a radioactive source through a helium detector tube. Hydrogen atoms, which are prevalent in asphalt, slow the travel of the neutrons and the slower-moving neutrons can be counted by the helium detector tube. The number of counted neutrons is directly proportional to the amount of asphalt, the moisture content and the amount and quality of the aggregate in the sample.

RESULTS

The results are particularly dramatic when the method is applied to the 300,000 tons of asphalt that the City of Phoenix must test each year. Traditional methods require some 2,000 hours to take the samples and test them, as compared to the new method which cuts the test time to 750 hours. The new method also provides results in 15 minutes after the sample is taken as compared with a day, or more, for the more familiar methods. Annual savings to taxpayers and developers amount to an estimated $15,000.

CONTACT
Engineering Department (602) 262-6561
251 West Washington
Phoenix, Arizona 85003

Figure 5-5. Excerpts from Phoenix, Arizona's Productivity Program Report.

pressure for ad hoc requests (e.g., rebuild my street now!) if they see that the plans will address their problems in due course. Citizens with a better understanding of local government, and the belief that their public officials are genuinely trying to improve performance, are less likely to want to constrain their officials through severe tax or expenditure limitation measures.

Premature publicity can create problems for performance measurement and improvement efforts. Good communication with the public is important, but a local government should make sure it is well prepared before giving a lot of publicity to its performance measurement and improvement efforts. Public officials should have confidence in the accuracy and usefulness of the data reported. Wide publication of inaccurate or meaningless performance reports could discredit government efforts at improvement. Local government agencies often need a year or so to get used to a new system of performance measurement before they can consistently define understandable measures and report reliable data. Agency managers need to develop confidence in a measurement process and in their ability to meet performance targets. A major publicity effort could threaten managers who have not developed that confidence. Managers who feel threatened may not cooperate with the process or may purposely provide inaccurate data to make their programs look better. Local governments often wait until they have one or two success stories of well-documented improved performance before they publicize a measurement program. That is not a matter of spreading only the good news and hiding the bad; it is a sensible approach which allows credibility to be built with the public that future objectives will be achieved. It also fosters confidence within the government that the objectives are achievable.

CITIZEN SURVEYS PROVIDE COMMUNICATION
AS WELL AS MEASUREMENT

As mentioned in chapter 2, and as noted by public officials in several examples in chapters 3 and 4, citizen surveys are a useful way for local governments to communicate with citizens both to identify priorities and problems and to measure service effectiveness. Surveys reach those citizens who do not have the time, or enough interest in a single issue, to attend public hearings or community meetings. Surveys can provide information from a broad sampling of the entire community, rather than just those who complain or make special requests. Surveys can also be limited to particular neighborhoods or target populations of interest (e.g., owners of small businesses) or to the users of a particular service. Surveys allow a local government to obtain useful information from its citizens in a *controlled* way, *often allowing the compilation of trends and comparisons of responses by neighborhood or other target populations.*

Citizen survey information can be grouped into four categories

1. *Citizen ratings of "satisfaction" or "quality" of services,* such as satisfaction with recreational opportunities and facilities; the odor, taste, appearance, and pressure of local water; the timeliness of services received; and the courtesy and dignity of treatment by government employees;

2. *Citizen "perceptions" of community conditions,* such as feelings of security from crime;

3. *"Factual" data otherwise difficult to obtain accurately,* such as estimates of the number of rat sightings in a neighborhood; criminal victimization of citizens; participation rates (i.e., the number of *different* persons or households using a service) for parks, libraries, transit, or other services; postservice condition of clients who receive health, employment, or other social services; particular service problems (e.g., repeated sewer backups);

4. *Citizen priorities for service improvements, increases, or decreases,* such as which community or neighborhood problem needs the most attention, which services should be increased, and which cut back. Local officials often find survey questions on citizen priorities useful, particularly when faced with the need for overall cutbacks or tax increases. These types of data are particularly subject to bias, often representing a "popularity poll" of services rather than objective information. For example, no one has ever heard of a majority of citizens in a community suggesting that fire services should be cut back, even though local governments often find they have more forces deployed than they really need for good protection. Some officials fear that citizens' "uneducated" responses to priority questions will tie their hands in planning future actions. Other officials feel this information will give them an early warning when a particular action they feel must be taken will be unpopular, causing them to prepare a better case for their proposal in advance so they can hold firm against negative reaction.

Figure 5-6 shows some citizen satisfaction rating questions from a Randolph Township, New Jersey, survey. Figure 5-7 shows questions seeking factual data and citizen perceptions of community conditions asked on a Dallas, Texas, survey.

**Surveys limited to "public outreach" can be
extremely simple and inexpensive**

Iowa City's *monthly* survey, referred to in chapter 3, costs next to nothing to administer. A one-page questionnaire (see Figure 5-8) is simply mailed to 300

TOWNSHIP OF RANDOLPH

CITIZEN SURVEY

EFFECTIVENESS OF BASIC MUNICIPAL SERVICES

The Time Survey began _____.

Hello, my name is _____, and I am a member of the League of Women Voters. Randolph Township has asked us to take a survey of services the Township provides, so, with your permission, I would like to ask the (   ), over 18 years old, living in your home a few questions.

1. To begin with, how long have you lived in Randolph Township?

    1. ( ) 1-3 months (terminate interview)
    2. ( ) 3-6 months   3. ( ) 7-12 months
    4. ( ) 1-3 years   5. ( ) 3-5 years
    6. ( ) over 5 years   7. ( ) refused/don't know

The first series of questions I would like to ask are about recreation.

2a. How would you rate Randolph's recreational opportunities, within reasonable traveling distance of your home, for males, ages four to twenty? Would you say they are excellent, good, fair, or poor?

    1. ( ) excellent   2. ( ) good   3. ( ) fair
    4. ( ) poor   5. ( ) don't know 6. ( ) refused

2b. For females of the same ages, within reasonable traveling distances of your home?

    1. ( ) excellent   2. ( ) good   3. ( ) fair
    4. ( ) poor   5. ( ) don't know 6. ( ) refused

2c. How would you rate recreational opportunities for adult males ages twenty to sixty?

    1. ( ) excellent   2. ( ) good   3. ( ) fair
    4. ( ) poor   5. ( ) don't know 6. ( ) refused

2d. For females ages twenty to sixty?

    1. ( ) excellent   2. ( ) good   3. ( ) fair
    4. ( ) poor   5. ( ) don't know 6. ( ) refused

2e. How would you rate Randolph's recreational opportunities for senior citizens?

    1. ( ) excellent   2. ( ) good   3. ( ) fair
    4. ( ) poor   5. ( ) don't know 6. ( ) refused

Figure 5-6. Excerpt from Randolph Township, New Jersey's Citizen Survey.

4. On the average, about how often have you, personally, ridden on the Dallas city buses in the past 12 months --almost daily, weekly, monthly, less than once a month, or not at all?

ALMOST DAILY	1
WEEKLY	
MONTHLY	3
LESS THAN ONCE A MONTH	4
DON'T KNOW OR NO ANSWER	8

5. During the past 12 months, how often have you or anyone else in this household--including children--visited the Dallas Public Library [IF NEEDED: either the main downtown library or any one of the branch libraries]--was it almost daily, weekly, monthly, less than once a month, or not at all?

ALMOST DAILY	1
WEEKLY	2
MONTHLY	3
LESS THAN ONCE A MONTH	4
DON'T KNOW OR NO ANSWER	8

6. During the past 12 months, have you or any other household member visited or telephoned the Dallas Public Library for some service other than for borrowing books?

   [IF YES, ASK:] What other service did you contact the library for most often?

NO, NOT AT ALL FOR OTHER SERVICES	0
YES, CONTACTED LIBRARY TO:	
GET OTHER INFORMATION OR ANSWER TO A QUESTION:	
IN PERSON	1
OVER THE TELEPHONE	2
BORROW MATERIALS OTHER THAN BOOKS	3
ATTEND LIBRARY PROGRAMS	4
ATTEND ADULT BASIC EDUCATION CLASSES	5
BROWSE AND RELAX	6
OTHER SERVICES NOT LISTED ABOVE	7
DON'T KNOW OR NO ANSWER	8

7. For what reasons don't you or other members of this household use the library more often--I mean, what kinds of things would make the library more convenient, enjoyable, or useful, so that you would want to use it more often? [PROBE:] What other reasons? [INTERVIEWER: RECORD NO MORE THAN TWO REASONS, BELOW]

For Office Use

Figure 5-7. Excerpt from Dallas, Texas's "Citizen Profile" Survey. (continued next page)

13. Now, we would like to find out what people think about the quality of this neighborhood--and the kinds of things that may be problems. As I ask about different kinds of problems, please tell me whether you feel it is a very serious problem, a somewhat serious problem, only a small problem, or not a problem at all in this neighborhood . . .

a. First, what about the level of noise in this neighborhood-- is it a very serious problem, a somewhat serious problem, only a small problem, or not a problem at all?

VERY SERIOUS PROBLEM	1
SOMEWHAT SERIOUS PROBLEM	2
ONLY A SMALL PROBLEM	3
NOT A PROBLEM AT ALL	4 **
DON'T KNOW OR NO ANSWER	8 **

b. [IF NOISE IS A PROBLEM, ASK:] What type of noise is a problem in this neighborhood?

TRAFFIC NOISE	1
INDUSTRIAL OR FACTORY NOISE . . .	2
AIRCRAFT NOISE	3
PEOPLE OR CHILDREN	4
ANIMALS	5
GENERAL NOISE (UNSPECIFIED) . . .	6
OTHER NOISE NOT LISTED ABOVE . . .	7
DON'T KNOW OR NO ANSWER	8

* 14. What about junked or abandoned cars--is this a very serious problem, a somewhat serious problem, only a small problem, or not a problem at all?

VERY SERIOUS PROBLEM	1
SOMEWHAT SERIOUS PROBLEM	2
ONLY A SMALL PROBLEM	3
NOT A PROBLEM AT ALL	4
DON'T KNOW OR NO ANSWER	8

15. What about vacant lots that are not taken care of--what kind of problem is this in your neighborhood? [PROBE IF NECESSARY:] Is this a very serious problem, a somewhat serious problem, only a small problem, or not a problem at all?

VERY SERIOUS PROBLEM	1
SOMEWHAT SERIOUS PROBLEM	2
ONLY A SMALL PROBLEM	3
NOT A PROBLEM AT ALL	4
DON'T KNOW OR NO ANSWER	8

20. Do you have any problems with rats, mice, or other small rodents? [PROBE IF NECESSARY]

VERY SERIOUS PROBLEM	1
SOMEWHAT SERIOUS PROBLEM	2
ONLY A SMALL PROBLEM	3
NOT A PROBLEM AT ALL	4
DON'T KNOW OR NO ANSWER	8

Figure 5-7. Excerpt from Dallas, Texas's "Citizen Profile" Survey. (continued)

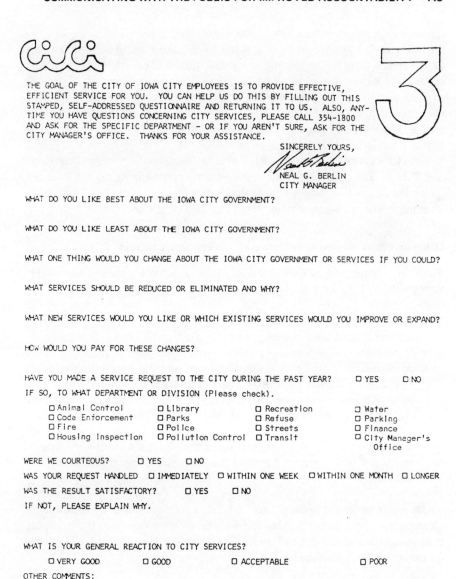

THE GOAL OF THE CITY OF IOWA CITY EMPLOYEES IS TO PROVIDE EFFECTIVE, EFFICIENT SERVICE FOR YOU. YOU CAN HELP US DO THIS BY FILLING OUT THIS STAMPED, SELF-ADDRESSED QUESTIONNAIRE AND RETURNING IT TO US. ALSO, ANY-TIME YOU HAVE QUESTIONS CONCERNING CITY SERVICES, PLEASE CALL 354-1800 AND ASK FOR THE SPECIFIC DEPARTMENT - OR IF YOU AREN'T SURE, ASK FOR THE CITY MANAGER'S OFFICE. THANKS FOR YOUR ASSISTANCE.

SINCERELY YOURS,

NEAL G. BERLIN
CITY MANAGER

WHAT DO YOU LIKE BEST ABOUT THE IOWA CITY GOVERNMENT?

WHAT DO YOU LIKE LEAST ABOUT THE IOWA CITY GOVERNMENT?

WHAT ONE THING WOULD YOU CHANGE ABOUT THE IOWA CITY GOVERNMENT OR SERVICES IF YOU COULD?

WHAT SERVICES SHOULD BE REDUCED OR ELIMINATED AND WHY?

WHAT NEW SERVICES WOULD YOU LIKE OR WHICH EXISTING SERVICES WOULD YOU IMPROVE OR EXPAND?

HOW WOULD YOU PAY FOR THESE CHANGES?

HAVE YOU MADE A SERVICE REQUEST TO THE CITY DURING THE PAST YEAR?   □ YES   □ NO

IF SO, TO WHAT DEPARTMENT OR DIVISION (Please check).

□ Animal Control	□ Library	□ Recreation	□ Water
□ Code Enforcement	□ Parks	□ Refuse	□ Parking
□ Fire	□ Police	□ Streets	□ Finance
□ Housing Inspection	□ Pollution Control	□ Transit	□ City Manager's Office

WERE WE COURTEOUS?   □ YES   □ NO

WAS YOUR REQUEST HANDLED   □ IMMEDIATELY   □ WITHIN ONE WEEK   □ WITHIN ONE MONTH   □ LONGER

WAS THE RESULT SATISFACTORY?   □ YES   □ NO

IF NOT, PLEASE EXPLAIN WHY.

WHAT IS YOUR GENERAL REACTION TO CITY SERVICES?

□ VERY GOOD   □ GOOD   □ ACCEPTABLE   □ POOR

OTHER COMMENTS:

_____
SIGNATURE (Not required)

Figure 5-8. Iowa City, Iowa's Monthly Survey.

residents each month at bulk rate postage. No pretense is made that the 30 or so responses each month provide a statistically accurate sample. But then this survey is *not* used for budgeting, program evaluation, or long-range planning. Instead, the survey is used as an outreach tool for letting citizens know that the city is interested in their views and in responding to their problems. The survey responses help the city to react quickly to specific problems identified by citizens and give the city manager and council a "feel" for citizen attitudes about city services on a month-to-month basis.

Iowa City's survey is clearly more of a "communication" tool than a "measurement" tool. The accuracy of the measurements derived from surveys becomes important when the results will be used for program evaluation, long-range planning, resource allocation, and other important policy decisions.

Communities of all sizes can afford statistically reliable surveys

There are a number of technical considerations in achieving statistically reliable survey results. For example:

- Random samples of adequate size are needed for each target population of interest (e.g., at least 100 per target group).
- Quality controlled, unbiased interview techniques should be used.
- A reasonable response rate should be achieved; the 10 percent response rate often obtained by mail surveys is inadequate, but follow-up with nonrespondents can raise the response rate to acceptable levels. More costly phone and in-person interviews often result in 70 to 80 percent response rates.
- Survey questions should be pretested on people from different educational levels and ethnic groups to make sure they are clear, unambiguous, and unbiased.

These and other requirements for accuracy cost money. But communities of all sizes, from Southborough, Massachusetts (population 6000), to Dallas, Texas, have found them affordable and useful. They have conducted statistically reliable citizen surveys and used the results in local policy making.

Some survey cost considerations

The most expensive statistically reliable surveys are communitywide surveys covering a wide variety of local services. User surveys (for which the government often has a captive audience at a public facility, eliminating the cost of finding respondents) and single service citizen surveys (for which very brief questionnaires can be used) are often much less expensive. Because of the many technical considerations in survey work, many communities contract with experienced survey organizations.

Costs for a survey depend on the total sample size, mode (in person, phone, mail) of interviewing, and the amount of work needed to design and pretest the questionnaire. Survey design costs often go down once a community has done one or two, because the number of questionnaire modifications needed are usually reduced. Initial survey development costs can often be reduced by using the assistance of a university, or by using, as a point of departure for design, a survey form that has been tested in another community. Many models are available, including a widely used one developed by the Urban Institute.* Survey administration costs can be reduced by using local citizens' groups; for example, Randolph Township, New Jersey (population 18,000) has used League of Women Voters volunteers.

Dayton, Ohio and other communities have used competitive bidding to select their survey contractor to help limit survey costs. Some communities have adjusted survey frequency to keep the long-term costs of surveys down. For example, some smaller communities have found it adequate to conduct surveys every two or three years rather than annually. Dallas, Texas has a large-city variation of this approach. In even years, Dallas conducts its more expensive "large sample" survey which yields geographically segmented results used for comparing citizen needs and opinions in 20 different neighborhood districts. In odd years, at a fraction of the large sample survey costs, Dallas conducts a specialized "small sample" survey. In 1979, Dallas's small sample survey was of people running nonretail businesses.

Once the survey data are collected, they must be analyzed to be of use. Some communities make data analysis — or at least some level of compilation and sorting — part of their survey contracts. Other jurisdictions use their own staff for all or most data analysis. Data analysis costs can be reduced through university assistance or the use of student interns, as an intimate knowledge of government operations is rarely necessary for good survey analysis. The "expert judgment" of experienced government officials becomes most important when deciding what to do about the survey results.

Surveys should avoid bias, especially political bias

Because of the wide public visibility provided by citizen surveys, there can be a temptation for public officials — particularly elected officials — to take political advantage of them. Professional survey specialists will carefully construct and pretest questions to insure that respondents are not "led" to answer in a particular

---

*Several sample questionnaires are provided in *How Effective Are Your Community Services?*, the Urban Institute and the International City Management Association, Washington, D.C., 1977.

way. Sometimes, however, surveys are conducted with questions intentionally phrased in a way that will tend to favor the sponsor's position. In one community, after having two surveys professionally designed and administered, the elected officials discovered the public relations value of surveys and attempted to use subsequent surveys for political advantage. In subsequent surveys, questions have varied from district to district, depending upon the political values of the elected officials for each district. As a result, survey returns have had no statistical validity, and survey costs rose considerably higher than the previous unbiased "professional" surveys.

A local government more interested in obtaining beneficial visibility for its officials from their surveys than in obtaining reliable results should not waste its money on costly detailed surveys that give only a facade of validity. They may as well use a simple, inexpensive survey, such as Iowa City's and make no pretense as to its statistical validity.

GOOD COMMUNICATIONS CAN BE GOOD POLITICS

Regardless of whether the public receives performance reports, the ballot box gives citizens the opportunity to hold elected officials accountable for their actions. Members of the city council of Rochester, New York, feel that good communication to citizens concerning government problems and performance has helped them gain reelection even when they have had to make unpopular decisions such as to raise taxes and cut services. These service cuts have included layoffs of fire fighters, teachers, and other public employees, and closings of schools, recreation centers, and a branch library.

Rochester has had to deal with a declining regional economy and a rigid tax limitation contained in the state constitution, which can make governing a community very difficult. The city government has made many efforts to improve its operations and financial structure while being responsive to public needs. The city council members have taken it upon themselves to communicate these improvement efforts as well as the city's fiscal problems to the public. They have issued public reports on finances and operations, commissioned unbiased citizen surveys, held press conferences, and personally presented traveling slide shows all over Rochester. As a result, they have kept voter confidence despite the difficult economic conditions facing the city, and have been able to rally public support for difficult decisions. Example 5.1 at the end of this chapter describes in detail what communication efforts have been made by Rochester officials and what results have occurred.

GOOD COMMUNICATION CAN ALLOW CITIZENS TO PARTICIPATE DIRECTLY IN SERVICE IMPROVEMENT EFFORTS

An important issue highlighted in chapter 4 was *selection* of services for intensive improvement efforts, since a local government's resources for service improvement are always limited. Good communication can give citizens the opportunity to identify their most critical service problems, and thus to help direct government improvement efforts. In many cases, citizen action — or inaction — can be a key part of a service problem, and also a part of the solution. For problems such as litter, fire, and crime, citizen *prevention* efforts can reduce the need for government action. In these cases, good communication can help citizens participate directly in solving their service problems.

In its Neighborhood Services Improvement Project, supported by a demonstration grant from HUD, the City of Washington, D.C. used several complementary outreach and participation techniques to establish good two-way communication with citizens and to make the most of the city's limited resources for service improvement. Statistically reliable citizen surveys provided neighborhood-wide coverage of resident opinions. Neighborhood meetings allowed intensive interchange among more active citizens to clarify, for the city, the nature of the problems to be addressed. They also provided the city a forum to tell residents what was being done about the problems. A variety of educational efforts showed residents ways they could reduce the size of problems themselves.

As part of the project ground rules, no new operating or capital resources were added to the neighborhood services affected. The city applied only a small but capable analytic staff to the service problems the residents said were most critical. The result was not only increased efficiency and effectiveness of selected neighborhood services, but increased citizen satisfaction with these services and, perhaps most important, a measurable increase in citizens' pride in their neighborhoods. Example 5.2 describes how Washington, D.C., accomplished this.

THE NEXT STEP IN ACCOUNTABILITY: CITIZEN PARTICIPATION IN POLICY DEVELOPMENT

In our open society, every local government provides its citizens with some way to witness policy decisions that are made through open legislative sessions and to comment on proposed plans and policies through public hearings and community meetings. Many federal grant programs require local governments receiving grants to implement an acceptable citizen participation process.

Most of the procedures used by local governments to include citizen views in policy making only give citizens the opportunity to comment on budgets, plans, projects, zoning variances, or ordinances *after* they have already been drafted and proposed. Procedures that involve citizens in early stages of policy development are generally limited to long-range planning, capital project programming, or the use of specific federal grant funds. The average citizen is rarely given the opportunity to participate in developing policies affecting the day-to-day operations of local government.

Most local governments at one time or another have appointed "blue ribbon panels" of prominent citizens to investigate and to make recommendations concerning specific, often controversial issues, which may involve operational policy. While these panels may seek out broad citizen comment, the direction of the investigation is determined by the panel members, who have been appointed by city hall. The investigation is also usually limited to the specific charge determined for the panel in advance by the chief executive or local legislature.

A few communities in this country have government-sanctioned processes which support the efforts of organized groups of citizens to take the initiative in developing policy and in establishing priorities for a broad array of government operations. The success of these processes lies in the opportunity afforded citizen organizations to recommend policy options they have developed themselves in addition to commenting on policies and projects presented by government officials and special interests (e.g., developers). The citizen organizations base their recommendations on community needs and problems they have determined. When participating in regular government policy processes, these citizen groups start their involvement early enough to make a substantial difference. If participating in the budget process, for example, their involvement would start long before an executive budget is submitted for public comment and council deliberation. Governments that want to see these processes work will cooperate with the citizen organizations by providing staff support and agency interaction so the citizens' recommendations will be within the bounds of political, fiscal, and operational reality.

Communities that actively involve citizens in defining their own needs, problems, and solutions can convert the "accountability of government to the public" from an idea to a reality. Government actions can be compared directly to citizens' recommended solutions, and government performance can be viewed from the perspective of the priority needs and problems defined by citizens.

Citizens' involvement and public officials' management should be complementary

Citizen-based needs assessment and problem definition do not replace government measurement of community needs and service performance. And they certainly do not replace local officials' management of public services. Government managers will want to be sure to have the data they need in directing line operations and in making day-to-day policy decisions, regardless of whether these data are of interest to the citizen organizations. The citizen groups, on the other hand, can take advantage of data routinely collected by the government to become more knowledgeable about community conditions and government performance.

While some citizen groups want to define their own performance measures and do independent data collection, most of the data they use will probably come from government sources. It would be senseless for competing data collection efforts to develop. Citizen groups and government agencies should be aware of existing data sources and should use them to the extent possible.

From the local government's perspective, the point of the citizen involvement processes is not to take policy decisions away from public officials, but to bring policy decisions closer to the public, to help insure performance that mets public needs — performance that is accountable to the public. The idea is not to have the public *managing* the local government, but to provide the public with direct opportunities to be involved in determining policies and priorities which guide those who do manage the government.

Citizen-based planning: A proven citizen policy development process

Citizens asking their own questions, and attempting to answer them, are at the heart of a process called "citizen-based planning" which has been tested in three Massachusetts communities, with the assistance of the Massachusetts Institute of Technology and the cooperation of the local governments. The process includes citizen surveys using questionnaires developed and administered by a citizen committee.

The communities of Rockport (population 6000), Southborough (population 6000), and Arlington (population 48,000) have demonstrated that, with some professional assistance, citizens can define and measure community needs and use the results to develop useful policy recommendations. Arlington's Citizen's Involvement Committee, with over five years' experience, has progressed from making policy recommendations to negotiating priorities for services.

The Arlington experience, described in Example 5.3, has opened up the community's policy development process tremendously. Two keys to Arlington's success are solid consensus building through broad representation of the whole town (rather than special interests) on citizen steering committees and task forces, and the ability of citizens' committees to pursue actively policy issues from their own initial research all the way to the implementation of their recommendations by the town government. The town selectmen have institutionalized citizen-based planning in Arlington, confirming that citizens and local government officials can be partners rather than adversaries.

Several larger jurisdictions have been increasing accountability through neighborhood-based citizen involvement

Citizen-based policy development efforts require the development of community-wide consensus on key issues. Complete jurisdictionwide consensus is often difficult to achieve in our larger cities and urban counties. Many of these jurisdictions are collections of identifiable communities or neighborhoods. They have tended to take neighborhood-based approaches to citizen involvement, in which communitywide consensus is reached in each neighborhood by sanctioned community organizations. Many local governments have neighborhood-based citizen participation concerning community planning and development and capital projects. In a few, this participation extends to regular operating services provided in their neighborhood. In some cases, the citizen groups have been influential in the formulation of local government budgets. The key to their influence on budgets appears to be early participation in the budget development process, starting *before* departments have prepared their budget requests for submission to the central budget office.

Three jurisdictions in the 200,000 to 700,000 population range that have extensive neighborhood-based citizen participation are Portland, Oregon, the District of Columbia, and Dayton, Ohio. Portland's budget participation process is interesting in that the city did not create new organizations to represent citizens, but provided a formal method for participation by Portland's 60 or so neighborhood associations. Washington, D.C. and Dayton created special organizations to which citizens are elected to represent their neighborhoods.

Portland annually invites all neighborhood associations and civic groups to submit "need reports" for service improvements and for new or repaired facilities in their neighborhoods. Individuals are also provided with need report forms upon request; though individuals' submissions will be accepted, they are referred to a neighborhood association whenever possible. About 75 percent of the neighborhood associations submit reports — some with the assistance of one of the city government's five neighborhood offices. Each organization assesses needs in its own way. For example, some hold public meetings and others use brief mail surveys. Portland's Office of Neighborhood Associations routes the need reports to the appropriate city bureaus (service departments) several months before they begin preparing their budget submissions to the Bureau of Management and Budget. Bureaus acknowledge receipt of each need report back to the neighborhood organizations, and provide the name of a contact person in the bureau for each report. Of about 400 need reports submitted annually, over 40 percent have been funded in either the city's operating or capital budgets, or as part of the Community Development Block Grant (CDBG) program. The Bureau of Traffic Engineering has received and funded the largest number of need reports (e.g., for cross-walks, stop signs, and traffic signals). The process has inspired some neighborhood associations to raise their own funds for some items that do not make it through the budget process.

Washington, D.C.'s "home rule" charter, passed in 1974, created 36 advisory neighborhood commissions, each with about 10 unpaid commissioners elected from single-member districts and a limited budget for staff and facilities. They not only have a mandatory review and advisory role on proposed zoning variances and capital projects, but also on proposed changes to operating services affecting their neighborhood. Their open meetings serve as community forums for comments on neighborhood needs and provision of city services. Washington's Neighborhood Services Improvement Project, described in Example 5.2, shows how an advisory neighborhood commission can become an active partner with the local government in improving operating services provided to the community.

Dayton has six neighborhood "priority boards." Each has 30 to 40 members who are elected annually from election districts within each priority board's area. The Downtown Dayton Association acts as the priority board for the central business district. Dayton's priority boards were referred to earlier in this chapter as recipients of the *Program Strategies* document which includes the city manager's proposed annual budget and service objectives. The priority boards are actually involved in the development of the budget and objectives from the beginning, when they each submit a needs statement detailing the board's assessment of neighborhood conditions and priority service improvement needs. In addition, the boards facilitate citizen input to Dayton's Capital Improvement Program and federal grants such as CDBG, monitor other government units (e.g., the Board of Education and the Regional Transit Authority), and oversee resolution of citizen complaints. Face-to-face meetings between board members and public officials are an important part of the citizen participation process. To help keep neighborhood and city goals and priorities consistent, the city manager meets monthly with the priority board chairpeople. To expedite responses, each priority board meets monthly with a corresponding neighborhood "administrative council" consisting of middle management representatives of city agencies that provide neighborhood services. The city also provides on-site professional staff for each priority board. Overall, the priority boards provide two-way communication between citizens and local government and provide an effective mechanism for citizen input into policy development by the Dayton city government.

By far the most ambitious attempt in the United States at community-based citizen participation in policy development, at least with respect to sheer size, is in New York City. A 1975 city charter revision (which became effective in 1977) mandated the participation of 59 community boards in budget development and in planning and monitoring services affecting their neighborhoods. Bringing to life the various charter reforms has been one of the highest priorities of the city government, a priority backed up by funding, staffing, accessibility, and the attention of top city officials.

New York City has gone far toward involving the community boards in its budget process despite the city's fiscal constraints. Community board face-to-face consultation with high level agency decision makers early in the budget process has been one key to their success. Regular meetings of local service chiefs from city agencies which serve the community board area, with the community board's district manager, have also been an effective tool for improved service delivery. These meetings of local service chiefs are called "district service cabinets." The overall goal of the cabinet is to afford an opportunity for resolving interagency service delivery problems at the local level.

In order to effect solutions at the district service cabinet, local service chiefs must be able to exercise independent judgment and decision making. Traditionally in bureaucracies, both public and private, the sharing of power with middle and field managers has been viewed with caution and skepticism. In New York, where field managers are generally used to following instructions from the top down, the implementation of another charter mandate important to community boards, known as "management decentralization," has been a slow process. However, significant progress has been made with several large New York City agencies, most notably the Sanitation Department, in working with community boards to plan local services. With more authority given to local service chiefs, community boards, in cooperation with them, will be better able to do service planning and performance measurement on a district level. The city continues to develop district-based performance measures which are published annually in *District Resource Statements* and used in tandem with the budget consultation process. Because technical and communication skills are essential to decentralized governance, both community boards and local service chiefs are provided with on-going orientation and training sessions. The New York City experience is described in Example 5.4.

COMMUNICATION, MARKETING, PERFORMANCE, AND MEASUREMENT

In this chapter, the emphasis is on the role played by good communication between government and the public in terms of accountability. No matter how good the performance of public services or how well this performance is measured, communication with the public is needed to insure accountability. It is possible to think of this as *marketing* the local government and its services to the public. There is nothing wrong with a government marketing itself. Marketing is not only "selling," it is finding out what the market's needs are and trying to fulfill these needs. That is exactly what effectiveness measurement and responsive government are all about.

Since the chapter concentrates more on communication than measurement or actual performance, it is worth reviewing some of the ways in which communication relates to measurement and performance. At least four relationships are demonstrated in this chapter:

1. Communication can inform the public of the results of performance, as measured and documented in performance reports.
2. Performance can be measured by the results of communication, as in many citizen surveys.

3. Communication can tell a local government where to attempt to improve performance and what service to improve; it may also help achieve improvement by stimulating citizen action, as in the Washington, D.C. Neighborhood Services Improvement Project.
4. Finally, communication can help form the basis upon which performance ought to be measured. This occurs when citizen involvement helps shape public policies and goals; performance measurement against those goals is then the basis for public accountability.

EXAMPLE 5.1 COMMUNITY EDUCATION IN ROCHESTER, NEW YORK

Paul E. Haney
City Councilman

Rochester, New York, has a council-manager form of government with a politically partisan city council. Except for a brief period during the depression in the 1930s, when there were some debt repayment problems, the city's finances had always been rather conservatively handled and the city had a AAA bond rating. "Hold the line 'til '49" and "debt free by '53" had been readily accepted political slogans in the community.

One party had dominated the Rochester City Council for many years until the mid-1960s, when the other major party won a majority. In 1969, the previously dominant party was returned to office and immediately faced several critical problems:

- It owed significant political debts to the public employee unions who had been helpful in its election.
- The population of the city was changing drastically. The flight of the middle class to the suburbs was in full swing, and the economic levels of the population were dropping appreciably.
- An aging physical plant was deteriorating very rapidly. The cost of replacing it, as well as the cost of merely maintaining the city's traditional public services, was escalating rapidly.

During the following four years, the cost of city government escalated dramatically. Meanwhile, the incumbent city administration, facing greater political opposition than it had in the past, made several spending commitments without providing adequate financing. The result was a city budget that was in deficit for three years, and in the fourth year was balanced only because 18 months of federal revenue sharing funds were used in a 12-month period.

In 1973, the party out of power ran an aggressive group of candidates for the Rochester City Council. Their campaign heavily relied upon attacks on the fiscal management of the city and the inefficiency of city operations. The result was an overwhelming victory for all five "opposition" candidates, winning their party an eight to one majority on the city council that took office in January 1974. The new council majority elected one of its own as mayor and appointed a new city manager.

It did not take long for the new city council and administration to realize the city was in even worse financial trouble than had been anticipated. Expenditures in the fiscal year ending June 30, 1974 would exceed revenues by at least $3 million. Significant pay increases had previously been awarded to municipal employees and would go into effect in 1974. In addition, the new administration decided that certain annually recurring expenditures, which for the last few years had been financed with borrowed funds, should be financed out of current revenues. Financially, that decision was sound, but it added another $3 million to the city's strained operating budget. Debt service payments for similar expenditures made over the past few years would go on annually for another 8 to 10 years.

After being in office less than three months, the new city administration recognized that potentially unpopular actions, including tax increases and service level reductions, were needed to correct the city's fiscal problems. They decided to launch an extensive educational campaign that would attempt to:

- Inform the citizens of the community of the city's financial problems;
- Inform the citizens of the changes in financial and operating practices that the new administration was attempting to make, and the reasons for those changes;
- Increase significantly the public awareness of the city budget (where the monies came from and for what the monies were spent);
- Discuss alternatives with the community.

A 60-page booklet on the city's financial condition was prepared. The booklet was half graphs and tables and half written commentaries. Each set of facing pages discussed some element of the city's financial or operating situation. Each left-hand page had a chart or graph very clearly displaying the basic fact we wanted to convey on that issue. The facing page contained three or four paragraphs discussing the particular issue. The paragraphs would be as brief and as plainly written as possible. Sometimes the commentaries would only fill half the page. Clarity and brevity were considered extremely important. The issues covered the entire field of municipal finance, including sources of revenue, types of expenditures, pay scales, trends in municipal employee compensation over the prior 10 years, formulas for intergovernmental revenues, and concepts of sound financial management. We tried to stimulate understanding of issues we felt had to be addressed. Great care was taken to show how the city was saving money by altering service delivery methods to improve efficiency. A public that is generally resistant to change had to be shown that change was good, would save money, and sometimes even improve service levels.

The charts in the booklet were converted to slides. Letters were sent to every conceivable organization in the Rochester area (including suburban groups outside the city) requesting the opportunity to present a slide show about the city's finances to their membership.

The first formal presentation of the slide show, lasting about 45 minutes, was at a press conference, resulting in considerable attention given to our problems and educational efforts in the newspapers, and on radio and television news.

The second formal presentation was at a luncheon of the Rochester Chamber of Commerce. About 300 representatives of Rochester businesses gathered for lunch and the slide show. We knew their support (at least their silent acquiescence) would be needed to solve our financial problems.

From there, the "road show" (which became its nickname in the community) was taken to everyone and anyone who would listen. We asked that audiences number at least 10 but occasionally presented it to as few as five or six people. The booklet was distributed to everyone who attended the slide show, and numerous other copies were distributed to anyone who asked.

The total number of people reached by the slide show was not large. One of the great disappointments in the process was that most of the neighborhood associations did not invite us to present the slide show to their group. But in fact anyone who cared got a thorough education on Rochester's municipal operations and finance. The presentations were so widely discussed within the community that those who had not taken the opportunity to attend one or read the booklet were left in no position to take issue with the administration's statement of conditions.

The process got very wide coverage from the press, who nicknamed the chairman of the city council's finance committee (who made most of the presentations) the "City's Financial Wizard." Indeed, it readily became apparent that the substance of the presentation, while most informative, was actually less important than the visibility of the effort we made to discuss very detailed financial and operational data with the general population in an open and honest manner.

In late May of 1974, the city manager presented a city budget that called for a 24 percent increase in the city's real property tax rate. The formal public hearing on the budget was held in June. The city manager went on the local public television station for a special half-hour program, immediately preceding the hearing to explain the budget and what the city was trying to accomplish.

The station then broadcast the budget hearing, which lasted less than an hour. (Prior years' budget hearings had gone on all night.) Representatives of the Chamber of Commerce and the Citizens Tax League applauded us for the actions we were taking. Tax bills carrying a 24 percent tax increase were mailed on July 1, and there was barely a negative comment from the community.

In the next few years, another serious financial problem arose for Rochester out of the court cases beyond the city's control. In 1976, New York State courts voided the state legislature's exemptions of various local expenditures from a 2 percent property tax ceiling in the state constitution. The state legislature quickly papered over the problem by passing emergency legislation. Various citizens immediately returned to the court. While the cases were making their way through the courts, the city administration concluded that the new state legislation would probably be declared unconstitutional, and the city would face an enormous financial squeeze. This time the problem would be more difficult. The city would no longer be able to finance its operations merely by raising taxes. The property tax rate would, in fact, have to be decreased by about 20 percent. The city administration decided that in a year or so, when a court decision was anticipated, the city would have to seek alternative sources of revenue and drastically cut operating expenses. Once again, we decided to go to the people.

A new element was added to the process this time. A professional research organization was hired to do a scientific telephone poll of the residents of the City of Rochester on various financial issues. The polling was done in January and February of 1977. Citizens were asked to rate public services and to rank the relative importance of city services. They were asked to name city services on which they felt we should spend more money or less money. They were asked service delivery questions such as, "Should recreation centers be closed on Saturdays if it will save money?" They were asked their opinions on alternative revenue sources and of things the city might do to solve its financial problems. They also were asked a group of demographic questions to help us learn if citizen opinions differed by location, income, ethnic background, age, etc.

Following the telephone surveys, the "financial road show" was taken back to the community in April and May of 1977. In addition to giving our audiences a new booklet on city government finances and operations and presenting an updated slide show, we distributed questionnaires asking essentially the same questions that were asked in the telephone poll. We recognized that the questionnaire responses were not from a representative sample and should be viewed differently from the responses to the scientifically constructed telephone survey.

Our process received even greater press attention in 1977 than it had three years before. One community newspaper printed the entire booklet verbatim, filling about six tabloid pages. Another community newspaper with wide distribution ran a series of in-depth articles on major aspects of the presentation. An excerpt from our 1977 booklet is shown in Figure 5-9.

This time, in addition to the general educational value and public support for difficult governmental decisions, we also derived valid public opinion data concerning financial and operational issues. We did not, however, let public opinion prevent us from taking necessary actions. For example, the most popular public service was fire protection, and spending for fire protection had the highest community rating. When the squeeze finally occurred in the spring of 1978, and we were forced to cut about $6 million out of our city budget, we did, indeed, lay off 22 firefighters. After carefully reviewing the situation, it was our best judgment that adequate fire protection could be maintained while reducing city expenditures for this service. It produced the expected negative reaction in the community but, while the public opinion survey had not been blindly used by us, it had prepared us for the controversy that inevitably occurred. We were not shocked or frightened by the controversy, so we did not retreat from the position we had adopted.

On the other hand, we learned that some services were less highly valued than we had believed. Rochester had a very extensive public recreation program. We discovered that the community was willing to sacrifice much more of this service than we had anticipated. As a result, cuts in the recreation program and budget exceeded what otherwise would have occurred.

The Waldert decision was issued by the New York State Court of Appeals in May of 1978 after the city manager had actually presented his budget for fiscal 1978-79 to the city council. It invalidated all the laws the New York State Legislature passed in 1976 to paper over the earlier court decisions. The Waldert decision had not been anticipated until the fall of 1978, but we were nonetheless prepared for it. In a space of about 21 days, we cut about $6 million of expenditures out of the city manager's budget and created about $8 million of alternative user fees and taxes. While some other communities in New York State virtually went into chaos when the Waldert decision was announced, we calmly proceeded over a three-week period to implement the court decision because we knew where our citizens stood on various aspects of the financial problem. Only two of our fiscal actions created any public turmoil: the firefighter layoffs and the imposition of user fees which had to be paid by tax exempt organizations, as well as by holders of taxable property. Numerous religious organizations objected to the user fees. The controversy on those two issues lasted about a month and then totally dissipated.

Enormous energy has been expended over the last nine years in educating our community on the financial facts of life and on the most intimate details of the financial and operating structure of their city government. The results, however, have more than justified every ounce

Since the current City administration took office in January 1974, there has been a substantial and continual reduction in the number of authorized full-time positions. A large part of this reduction is the result of several reorganization designs that have tightened departmental operations while providing the same and in some cases an improved level of service to City residents.

In the Department of Public Works both residential and commercial refuse collection routes have been updated to consolidate and equalize the workload which resulted in a reduction of total manpower and equipment needed for refuse collection. The City's refuse disposal operation was transferred to Monroe County late in 1975 and recently the refuse and bulk collection services were consolidated - both of these changes resulted in further personnel decreases.

The City's policy of leasing services from private contractors has also reduced personnel and cut salary costs. Five of the large downtown parking facilities are now operating under such a lease agreement. This year for the first time, the spring and summer street repaving program has been carried out by private contractors.

Although our efforts to date have been successful, there is a certain minimum level of employees that are needed to maintain services at their present level. There will be continued efforts to reduce personnel wherever possible through reorganization and consolidation, but the results may not be as dramatic in the future. We are already studying the possibility of selected service reductions and additional leasing arrangements with their related cost savings as ways of continuing the pattern of expenditure control. Through this document and various other techniques, we are attempting to solicit your thoughts and opinions on service priorities so that our future planning and actions may be more responsive to your needs.

DECREASE IN FULL-TIME POSITIONS

	Number of Full Time Positions	% Decrease
January 1, 1974	4,000	
July 1, 1974	3,891	2.7
July 1, 1975	3,783	2.7
July 1, 1976	3,547	6.2
April, 1977 (estimate)	3,486	1.7
Total Decrease	514	12.8

Figure 5-9. Excerpt from Rochester, New York's Citizen Education Booklet.

of that effort. We as a community have been able to adjust service levels, alter methods of service delivery, and solve severe financial problems in a realistic and rational fashion. We have avoided the financial chaos that afflicted many of our sister cities in New York State, including the near financial collapse that affected three of the state's major cities. The second major benefit has been purely political, which is a consideration that must concern any elected public official. Our party has maintained an 8-to-1 majority on the city council ever since 1974. Whether raising property taxes 24 percent, laying off firefighters and police, or creating user fees, no member of the majority on the city council has been defeated in the three general municipal elections since this process began. Only one incumbent majority council member was defeated in a partisan primary, based on a specific district issue.

As a result of our community education efforts:

- Public confidence in the city's management process increased tremendously; without that high level of confidence we could not have withstood the resistance of employee unions to staffing cuts (particularly in the Fire Department).
- Public knowledge of the true nature of our financial problems increased greatly and turned the public's attention to the other levels of government (state and county) whose cooperation was needed to solve some of the problems.
- Our knowledge of public opinion increased significantly which prepared us for the backlash to unpopular decisions and encouraged us to take some actions we might not have otherwise taken.
- The community and its public officials achieved a shared political confidence that difficult problems could be solved.

I consider our public education to be the most important work we have done since I have been on the Rochester City Council. Without it, our fiscal situation would be much worse than it is today.

EXAMPLE 5.2 WASHINGTON, D.C.'s NEIGHBORHOOD SERVICES IMPROVEMENT PROJECT

John S. Niles
Former Project Director

A two-year effort, the Neighborhood Services Improvement Project (NSIP), was directed by staff from the District of Columbia's Executive Office of the Mayor.* The focus of the NSIP was on working within a

---

*The District of Columbia Government — not a federal agency — is the organization which provides city, county, and state level services to people who live in, work in, or visit the nation's capital. About 638,000 people live in the 64 square miles of the city.

selected neighborhood to increase the efficiency and effectiveness of service delivery affecting the physical condition of private and public property in the neighborhood. At the same time, the staff wanted to involve residents of the neighborhood directly in the activity of the project, with the goal of letting the government's constituents see firsthand what performance improvement meant to them.

The neighborhood chosen for the project encompassed 15 miles of streets and 8000 housing units in the inner city of Washington. The project staff interacted with neighborhood residents in two ways: through participation in meetings of community organizations and through data obtained in two door-to-door citizen opinion surveys conducted by Peter D. Hart Research Associates. Data from the two sources tended to be consistent. For example, both sources indicated that, of the various physical problems in the neighborhood, litter reduction was a priority. As a consequence, litter was the problem which NSIP addressed, primarily through improvements in operating procedures of cleaning crews and code inspectors, but also through an information and education program intended to reduce litter generation by residents.

The NSIP used existing community organizations as its primary link to the citizens. These organizations were an elected advisory neighborhood commission, 12 block clubs, an urban renewal advisory committee, and a civic association. Every community group operating in the project neighborhood was eventually involved in the NSIP, to increase the probability of reaching all activist citizens. The project team established close working relationships with the influential persons who were constant attendees and leaders of meetings of these groups. In this way the staff garnered support for the service delivery changes developed through the process, such as stricter code enforcement.

NSIP staff carefully structured the group process followed at community meetings to identify problems and solutions and to foster cooperation. Meetings were held monthly for four months and about 20 people attended each time. At the fifth meeting, where many issues were on the agenda besides NSIP, over 100 people attended. The size of this expanded group and its lack of familiarity with the process to date made discussion of the project plans and issues impossible; therefore, for the remainder of the project, NSIP staff participated only in smaller meetings.

At these smaller meetings, held monthly over eight months, the NSIP staff attempted to focus citizen involvement around the structured approach designed for the project: litter reduction through improved city clean-up services, through education of citizens on their responsibilities, and through stricter enforcement of city antilittering regulations. The meetings provided a continual stream of citizen perceptions, attitudes, and suggestions about the litter problem and what the city government should do. In turn, the project staff spoke to citizens about what the government was doing to improve, as well as the limits of government activity. The staff presented color slides depicting litter conditions resulting from violations of existing regulations to inform citizens of their responsibility in maintaining the community. One series of photographs showed alleys recently cleaned by city crews, and then the same alleys just a few days later, when they were again filthy. The startling contrast made clear to residents how their neighbors could negate the alley cleaning efforts of city crews through improper trash putouts and indiscriminate littering.

At first, residents were hostile to city workers, whom many citizens viewed as primarily responsible for litter. The staff continually kept the meeting attendees informed of project efforts to increase crew efficiency and effectiveness, while at the same time pinpointing the community sources of litter generation. As the streets became cleaner, hostility turned into appreciation. Toward the end of the project, a group of citizens held an awards ceremony for the cleaning crews in their neighborhood.

The NSIP staff also provided technical assistance to citizen groups in setting up action plans citizens could carry out themselves. For example, after learning that a major contribution to litter came from a few of their neighbors, some block clubs started to write letters to violators of litter ordinances. The advisory neighborhood commission developed a "cleanliness standard" to which residents were asked to adhere. Finally, the urban renewal advisory committee and block clubs sponsored several neighborhood clean-up campaigns.

In the second citizen opinion survey, carried out as the project was winding down, 28 separate questions measured the impact of NSIP. Of these questions, 20 showed a significant improvement in residents' attitude toward the cleanliness of the neighborhood and the work of city employees who clean it up. For example, fewer people thought dirty streets and alleys were a major problem, and more people thought the physical condition of the neighborhood was very important. Also, the percentage of people saying they had "a great deal of pride in their neighborhood as a place to live" jumped from 39 to 59 percent. On the other hand, the same survey carried out in a similar neighborhood where NSIP did not operate showed either no change or a deterioration in attitudes on 21 out of 28 questions.

When these opinion and attitude results are coupled with the objectively measurable changes in cleaning and inspection performance which were achieved — such as street cleaning efficiency up 42 percent and compliance time on litter code violations (effectiveness) cut in half* — the NSIP strategy of considering citizens an integral part of the service delivery system proved to be sound and workable.

---

*Compliance time is the length of time elapsed from the date of inspection to the date of abatement by the violator. Street cleaning efficiency was measured in square-yards cleaned per person-day. For a description of one method used to improve street cleaning, see Example 4.6 in chapter 4.

EXAMPLE 5.3 CITIZEN-BASED PLANNING IN
ARLINGTON, MASSACHUSETTS

William J. Grannan
Selectman, Town of
Arlington

In late 1974, after the voters of Arlington, Massachusetts, had twice rejected high school rebuilding referenda, their own selectmen felt it was important to obtain information on citizen priorities. The town of Arlington's ensuing efforts to involve citizens actively in policy making have led to a "citizen-based planning" process that has been adopted by the Board of Selectmen as a mechanism for achieving townwide consensus and negotiating service priorities. The Arlington process involves an independent citizens' steering committee which follows policy issues through four phases:

1. *Research phase:* acquisition of all available information on subjects of concern; this has included citizen-organized surveys of the community;
2. *Study phase:* analysis of research results; synthesis and ranking of issues; preparation of policy recommendations;
3. *Refinement phase:* adjustments to recommendations based on changes in circumstances and negotiation with local groups and officials;
4. *Implementation phase:* adoption by the town of policies and programs which reflect community consensus.

Arlington adopted and tailored for its own use a process first used in Rockport, Massachusetts, with the assistance of Professor Lawrence Susskind of the Massachusetts Institute of Technology (MIT). Professor Susskind and others from MIT and the University of Massachusetts assisted Arlington, especially with some of the technical issues in conducting citizen surveys.

A steering committee was formed of 11 men and women who were representative of the town's neighborhoods, age distribution, and other social, economic, and environmental concerns. To insure independence of steering committee members from the town government's regular policy makers, they were not chosen by the selectmen but by an ad hoc committee of town meeting members.* Local newspaper articles and ads inviting all interested residents to apply, as well as personal

---

*The town meeting is a New England tradition. In smaller communities all registered voters may participate in the annual town meeting which votes on budget items and other matters. In Arlington (population 49,000), 252 town meeting members are elected on a precinct basis to participate in the annual meeting.

recruiting, were used by the town meeting members to attract candidates for the committee. One important rule of thumb in selecting the steering committee was that every member had to indicate an interest in communitywide solutions to problems and not just a self-interested concern with a particular issue. The steering committee agreed to add new members in the future to maintain broad representation of community interests. The steering committee adopted a name, The Arlington Citizen's Involvement Committee (CIC), and defined as its purposes:

- To discover, define, and document the fundamental issues and priorities in Arlington;
- To provide a vehicle for interested citizens to assist in improving town policies regarding these issues;
- To interest a wider range of citizens in town affairs and to aid them in becoming more directly involved in town government;
- To provide an effective means for citizens to follow policy recommendations to an implementation stage.

With the idea of eventually conducting a citizen survey, the CIC started the first or "research" phase of its work by "brainstorming" — trying to identify as many issues or problems on people's minds as possible. To do this, they met with officials from municipal agencies, as well as private organizations and individual citizens, and held several open meetings. They sorted the issues they collected into six broad topics:

- Land use, redevelopment, and the physical environment;
- Quality and efficiency of public services;
- Community identity;
- Taxes and town finances;
- Need and responsibility for social services;
- Town government and intergovernmental relations.

The CIC prepared preliminary survey questions for each topic and revised them after a review by the town selectmen and other local officials. Some local officials strenuously objected to some questions, particularly those they perceived as asking people to evaluate their performance. Nevertheless, no questions were completely abandoned, but some were revised into more acceptable form.

A separate questionnaire, with the revised questions, was prepared for each of the six topics. Each was twice pretested with residents and revised twice more to eliminate biased and unclear phrasing. The final six questionnaires were printed, and each was mailed to 1/6 of Arlington's 15,000 households, so each household would receive one.

A numbered "double envelope" system was used to insure anonymity of respondents while still allowing the CIC to identify nonresponding households for follow-up phone calls to encourage their response. The result was a 30 percent overall response rate.

While the survey responses were being collected and analyzed, the CIC initiated a newsletter called *Feedback,* based mainly on information learned while preparing the surveys, to explain the dialogue within the community. The CIC also planned a townwide conference to present the survey results, for which it selected "task force moderators" and assistant moderators for each of the six survey topics, and held workshops for those individuals.

The conference was held in January 1976, with over 400 people attending. The survey results were presented with the aid of a multimedia display. Six communitywide task forces were organized at the conference, with an average of 30 participants each, to develop policy recommendations.

The citizen task forces met twice monthly for over eight months and developed, with supporting documentation, recommendations for townwide action. While the task forces met, local officials were already using the survey results to adjust local budgets and programs.

During this second or "study" phase for the original six topics, the CIC organized additional citizen task forces to consider local attitudes regarding two new issues: rapid transit extension into Arlington, and local secondary education concerns. The CIC expansion into new issues troubled some local officials. Some selectmen, who favored rapid transit extension as a catalyst for local redevelopment, feared their position would be undermined. Some townspeople referred to the CIC as a "shadow government" which threatened to undermine the efforts of official boards, committees, and commissions. In short, the town's reaction to the citizen-based planning process was at once enthusiastic and cynical. But the work of the CIC continued.

During the third or "refinement" phase of the citizen-based planning process, the CIC interviewed the task force participants and synthesized their recommendations into a "community action agenda" proposing 15 policy recommendations. A second townwide conference was held on April 30, 1977, with the local congressman, Speaker of the House Thomas P. "Tip" O'Neill, as keynote speaker. The CIC distributed its agenda entitled "A Call to Community Action" and showed videotape documentaries which it had prepared about Arlington.

During the fourth or "implementation" phase of the process, not only were the CIC's key recommendations adopted by the town, but the town began to use citizen-based planning more regularly to obtain citizen involvement on various issues with its boards, committees, and commissions. The reuse of school property was considered by neighborhood task forces organized to assist the Arlington Redevelopment Board, and the use of Community Development Block Grant (CDBG) funds was considered by a steering committee of town meeting members organized to assist the Department of Planning and Community Development.

Finally, the Board of Selectmen has institutionalized the citizen-based planning process. In March 1979, based on separate requests by the CIC and the Arlington Boy's Club, it decided to use CDBG funds for additional citizen surveys. The selectmen chose 30 people for an expanded CIC steering committee, which organized two task forces to draft surveys on social service priorities and on overall spending priorities. These new surveys were detailed and complicated, and administered by mail in the same manner as the earlier CIC surveys. The response rate was over 40 percent.

Armed with the survey results and additional task force information concerning the delivery of human services, the selectmen made plans to develop a detailed agenda for goal setting, establishing local priorities, and implementing a negotiation process with citizens through the CIC.

Since then, Arlington's citizen-based planning efforts have included:

- Organizing new task forces under the leadership of the Board of Selectmen;
- Reactivating the CIC's *Feedback* newsletter;
- Using cable TV as a new medium for community dialogue;
- Preparing policy documents for communitywide review;
- Conducting formal policy negotiations;
- Presenting priorities to the town meeting for ratification;
- Documenting the citizen-based planning process in Arlington.

The most exciting aspect of citizen-base planning, as it has developed in Arlington, is the active interface between local officials and citizens. Citizens have learned they can have a significant impact within the local decision-making process. Citizens have developed the capacity to provide technical assistance to their government officials and to achieve broad-based support for their policy recommendations. Some involved citizens have also realized that they too can become the elected and appointed officials who establish and implement policy.

Local officials, residents, and businesspeople need not be threatened by each other. It is not only possible, it is desirable and expedient for local officials to reach out to the community for active support in determining public policies. An understanding of roles and responsibilities, as well as realistic performance expectations, will result from a responsible citizen-based planning process.

EXAMPLE 5.4 COMMUNITY BOARD PARTICIPATION IN BUDGETING AND SERVICE DELIVERY IN NEW YORK CITY

(This Example was prepared by the New York City Mayor's Community Assistance Unit using material contributed by: Serre Murphy, former Deputy Director; Harold Nass, Deputy Director; Cathie Behrend, Coordinator, Management Decentralization; and Ronald Marco Bergmann, former Charter Implementation Associate.)

A 1975 city charter revision, which became effective in 1977, strengthened the role of New York City's 59 community boards and mandated a prominent role for them in planning and monitoring the performance of services in their neighborhoods. The charter revision was a response to a perception that city government was remote from the people. It sought to establish each community district as the basic unit for budget development, service delivery, and service planning; and to achieve this through the participation of community boards as representatives of those districts. For example, the mandate requires city agencies to consult with community boards *before* submitting their preliminary budget requests to the Mayor's Office of Management and Budget (OMB) and to consult with the boards on developing service plans for their community districts.

Each community board represents a district with between 100,000 and 250,000 residents (except for a few major business districts, which have fewer residents but a high daytime population). Up to 50 unpaid citizens, selected by borough presidents and city council members, comprise each community board.

The Koch administration's commitment to charter implementation has been demonstrated by the establishment of both the Mayor's Community Assistance Unit and OMB's Office of Community Board Relations. Both of these offices are charged with (1) aiding the 59 community boards in playing the role envisioned for them in the charter, namely as monitors of city services, as planners, and as the voice of their communities in decisions on land use and budget priorities, and (2) helping to achieve necessary changes *within* city agencies which will allow the boards to carry out their roles. Each community board has a district office budget which allows it to hire its own full-time professional district manager as well as pay for support staff, rent, supplies, and other expenses. In 1982, the operating budget for each community board district office was raised from $70,000 to $85,000.

A district service cabinet has also been established in each community board, consisting of the district manager and local service chiefs from city operating agencies. One often hears the complaint that bureaucrats never talk to each other except in a crisis. With the introduction of the district service cabinet system, there is a forum where communication can occur to help avoid crises. At cabinet meetings, representatives from the different agencies discuss, respond to, and resolve local service problems. The district service cabinet provides an excellent vehicle for interagency coordination and cooperation and for the appropriate matching of available agency resources to local needs. Eleven agencies are mandated to send a designated representative regularly to each of the cabinets. The representatives are usually the supervisors or managers responsible for local field services in each agency. Ideally, problems are to be attacked initially and primarily at the local level — moving up to higher levels only when required. In order for this local decision making to take place, the local service chief must be given increased authority as well as responsibility over his or her district operations. In the 1975 charter reform this mandate was called "management decentralization." To facilitate community-based participation in budgeting, and in service planning and monitoring, the charter revision also mandates:

- *Coterminality of agencies' service districts with community districts:* The Police and Sanitation Departments, the Human Resources Administration, and the Department of Parks and Recreation were required to conform their service boundaries so they had at least one service district for each of the city's 59 community districts. They were permitted to maintain subdistricts within a community district as long as the boundaries of the aggregate subdistricts coincided with those of the community district. The Departments of Health, Mental Health, and Housing Preservation and Development, and the Bureaus of Sewer Maintenance and of Highways were required to be coterminous with individual community districts or aggregates of community districts within a borough.

- *Agency Service Statements:* The charter requires each city agency to report annually: "Its service objectives, priorities and projected activities within each community district . . . for the new fiscal year." Moreover, agencies are required to consult with the appropriate district service cabinets and community boards in the preparation of these reports. The *District Resource Statements,* compiled by OMB to meet this charter mandate, also break down the expense budget and agency resources (including personnel, equipment, and contracts) to the district and borough level and provide local performance indicators.

- *District Based Budgets:* Agencies' budget requests and the Mayor's *Executive Budget* are required to show proposed direct expenditures by local service districts, which under coterminality, correspond to community districts or their aggregates. In addition, after the end of each fiscal year, agencies are required to report their expenditures by district, and the City Comptroller is required to maintain a system of accounts for reporting expenditures by local service districts. The district resource statement also includes this information.

Reforms this ambitious in a city the size of New York take time to implement. The charter revision set no time limit for some reform objectives and allowed up to five years for others (e.g., coterminality and district-based budgets). With the exception of the implementation of coterminality by the Police Department, which was allowed by New York City Council legislation to postpone action until January 1983, all charter deadlines have been met.

The city's progress through mid-1982 in achieving the intended citizen participation in budgeting and in service planning and monitoring is described below.

COMMUNITY BOARD PARTICIPATION IN BUDGETING

The charter gives community boards the opportunity to develop their own budget recommendations and priorities and to comment on both the city agencies' budget requests and the Mayor's Executive Budget with respect to local needs. Further, the charter requires that city agencies "consult" with community boards in the development of agency "departmental estimates" or budget requests.

In designing procedures for effecting these charter reforms, an interagency task force identified a number of additional desirable objectives:

- To develop a single, unified system whereby community boards could seek budgetary relief of local problems either through the city's capital budget, expense (operating) budget, or the Community Development Block Grant (CDBG) program. In doing so, a single timetable for boards could be established so their recommendations could be considered for both city and federal funds.
- To develop realistic expectations at the community level about projects and services the city could reasonably fund, especially in a time of severe financial shortages.
- To keep the procedures that community boards would follow in the budget process as simple as possible.

The process which the task force designed has been used in the development of the city's budgets for four fiscal years, 1980–83, and is being used for the fifth time in the development of the fiscal 1984 budgets. The six major elements of the process are:

1. *Consultation between city agencies and community boards.* During the spring and fall of each year, community boards have opportunities to consult with agency officials about budget needs and priorities and about funding of programs and projects. Consultation takes place at two levels:
   - District level: Boards meet with local service chiefs in each agency. The purpose of this district-level consultation is threefold.
     a. to provide an opportunity for local chiefs to jointly assess district needs and address general service delivery problems with community board committee members;

   b. to establish budget and service priorities based on the
      district needs assessment; and

   c. to verify information published by OMB in the *District
      Resource Statements.*

- Borough level: Building upon the district-level consultation
  process, boards in each of the city's five boroughs meet
  with top level officials in each agency. Borough-level consultation is intended to give the boards the opportunity to
  present their requests (often developed jointly with the
  local service chiefs), and the reasons for them, to the executives in the agencies who will be making the decisions about
  which items to request in their departmental estimates. During this intensive consultation period, heads of huge city agencies must meet with all 59 community boards, stripping themselves, at least temporarily, of any insulation from community leaders that their large bureaucracies provide them. At
  these sessions, community boards review current district
  needs and budget requests as well as receive current status
  reports on previous budget submissions. Agencies also convey
  to community boards what their citywide priorities and
  constraints are for the upcoming fiscal year.

Consultation has proven one of the more popular elements of the new
budget procedures, both among agencies and community boards. Board
members have expressed their pleasure at the responsiveness of many
agencies at the consultation meetings; some agencies have made on-the-
spot commitments to recommend certain projects for funding or to
address a particular service problem. Agencies have felt that consultation
served their purpose of dissuading community boards from unrealistic
requests; many boards chose not to recommend certain projects in their
formal budget submissions based upon advice or information supplied by
agencies during consultation. Agencies are also able to hear first hand
from community boards about urgent district needs which the agencies
might not have sufficiently addressed.

   2. *Public hearings.* Community boards hold public hearings at
      various times in the budget process. The boards are encouraged
      to advertise their hearings widely, using foreign language publi-
      cations, if appropriate. Under CDBG guidelines, boards must
      encourage low and moderate income individuals and groups to
      attend and testify at the hearings.

   3. *Formal budget submission.* Each board makes a formal budget
      submission. This includes:

      - A district needs assessment which serves as the foundation
        and justification for determining the board's budget priorities
        and specific requests.

      - A ranked set of requests for physical improvements which can
        be funded out of the city's capital budget or CDBG Program.

- A ranked set of requests for expense budget projects or programs.
- A ranking of the importance to the community district of selected city agencies and programs. (This is used by OMB in recommending cuts as a part of the city's "Program to Eliminate the Gap" between projected revenues and expenditures, to meet the legal mandate for a balanced city budget.)

4. *Agency evaluation of boards' budget requests.* Agencies are expected to review thoroughly all community board budget requests. The results are reflected in the *Departmental Estimates* which the city publishes in mid-January. In addition, OMB assembles agency responses to each community board request with a brief explanation of reasons decisions were made and publishes them in a *Register of Budget Requests.* Boards then comment on the agencies' decisions.

5. *OMB evaluation of boards' budget requests.* OMB reviews community board requests *prior* to the release of the Mayor's preliminary budget statement as well as the Mayor's executive budget. In a few cases, this has led to the reversal of decisions made by agencies.

6. *Testimony by boards at public hearings.* The City Council and the Board of Estimate hold public hearings on the departmental estimates and executive budget. In addition, the City Planning Commission holds hearings on the city's CDBG application. Community boards are entitled to testify at these hearings and often do so. This represents an opportunity for boards to try to advance projects which have not been approved by the agencies or OMB.

Each year a manual has been prepared for community board participation in the budget process. Figure 5-10 shows the fiscal year 1984 timetable, excerpted from that year's manual.

RESULTS OF THE BUDGET PROCESS
AFTER FOUR FULL CYCLES

How well community board participation has worked may be evaluated using two criteria: the level and extent of community board and agency involvement, and the percentage of board requests included in the city's adopted capital and expense budgets and CDBG applications.

In general, after completing four full fiscal year cycles, it appears that most of the objectives of the budget process were achieved. At first, many of the boards approached the new process with a degree of skepticism. This was understandable since city agencies had previously

FISCAL YEAR 1984 BUDGET PROCESS TIMETABLE
[Fiscal year 1984 runs from July 1, 1983 to June 30, 1984]

DATE	ACTIVITY
May 1982	Community boards and agencies receive *Manual* for participation in the budget process.
May through August 15	Community boards assess needs and prepare statements of district needs.
May through October 29	Community boards schedule and hold public hearings on their budget requests and community district needs.
June	Community boards consult with local agency service chiefs at the district level.
July	Community boards and agencies receive the FY 1983 Adopted Budget and Community District Register for the Adopted Budget.
July 16	Community boards submit borough consultation reservation form.
August 6	Community boards submit borough consultation agenda forms.
by August 15	Community boards submit statements of district needs to the Department of City Planning.
September	City agencies begin to evaluate community board statements of district needs.
September	Community boards consult with agencies at the borough level.
by October 29	Community boards adopt and submit their budget requests and priorities to the Office of Management and Budget.
November 1 through December 15	City agencies evaluate community board requests and statements of district needs, and submit departmental estimates and community development proposals to the Office of Management and Budget and Department of City Planning.
November 1 through December 15	Department of City Planning evaluates community board and agency requests for Community Development Program budget eligibility.
by January 19, 1983	Community boards and agencies receive the Community District Register for the Preliminary Budget which includes agency funding recommendations on capital, expense and community development budget requests.
January 20 through February 15	Community boards conduct public hearings on the city's Preliminary Budget Statement and the Community District Register for the Preliminary Budget.

Figure 5-10. Excerpt from New York City's Citizen
Participation Budget Manual. (continued on next page)

FISCAL YEAR 1984 BUDGET PROCESS TIMETABLE
[Fiscal year 1984 runs from July 1, 1983 to June 30, 1984]

DATE	ACTIVITY
by February 15	Community boards submit comments on the city's Preliminary Budget Statement.
February 1 through April 22	The Office of Management and Budget and the Department of City Planning evaluate community board budget requests in preparation of the executive capital and expense budgets and proposed statement for the ninth year community development program.
by February 25	Community boards and agencies testify at the City Planning Commission's public hearings on the city's capital needs and priorities and the proposed ninth year community development program.
by March 15	Community boards and agencies receive the City Planning Commission's Statement of Capital Needs and Priorities for the City of New York.
by March 25	Community boards and agencies testify at the City Council and Board of Estimate's public hearings on the City's Preliminary Budget Statement and capital needs.
by April 26	Community boards and agencies receive the FY 1984 Executive Budget, Mayor's Budget Message, and proposed ninth year community development program statement.
by May 2	Community boards receive Community District Register for the Executive Budget.
by May 25	Community boards and agencies testify at the City Council and Board of Estimate's public hearings on the Executive Budget and proposed ninth year community development program statement.
by June 3	Board of Estimate and City Council adopt expense and capital budgets and authorize the ninth year community development program statement.
by June 30	Budgets are certified by the Mayor, Comptroller, and City Clerk.
by June 30	HUD approves ninth year community development program statement.
July 1983	Community boards receive resolutions adopted by the Board of Estimate and City Council for FY 1984.

Figure 5-10 (continued) Excerpt from New York City's Citizen
Participation Budget Manual.

been relatively insensitive to community board budget recommendations. Nonetheless, during the 1982 budget consultation, almost all of the city's 59 boards took part in the process. The 59 boards submitted a total of 2937 capital budget requests and 1047 expense budget proposals.

A factor at least as important as the number of the boards' submissions is their quality. Because the budget process is actually a year-round cycle, the process is encumbered by myriad forms, directions, and deadlines. The majority of boards, however, were able to complete their tasks in a comprehensive and responsible fashion. A total of 58 boards conducted local public hearings on their budget requests. Two-thirds of the boards testified at City Planning Commission hearings and one-third testified at the joint Board of Estimate and City Council hearings on the preliminary budget. In last year's service priority rating, as in previous years, police patrol services received highest priority followed by parks maintenance, refuse collection, fire extinguishment, and sewer maintenance services. These priorities have been generally reflected in the city's funding decisions for those services.

With respect to funding, the city's overall tight fiscal condition, cutbacks in federal and state funds, mandatory spending programs, reduced tax revenues due to a national recession, and the "Program to Eliminate the Gap" continue to constrain the city's ability to fund community board budget requests. The boards' budget requests were, however, fully evaluated by the agencies and OMB in formulating the Executive Budget. As stated in the Mayor's 1983 *Budget Message,* "each proposal was evaluated in terms of cost, benefits, fiscal constraints, readiness for construction, impact on the expense budget, and feasibility. Special consideration was given to those proposals which would reduce operating expenses, stimulate the economy, increase the city's revenue base, reduce energy consumption, enhance essential services, or improve the city's infrastructure." Each community board received letters from each city agency informing it of the reasons why any priority recommendations were not included in the agency's departmental estimates.

However, even with some disappointment for individual boards, overall the community boards have been influential in the city's budget process. For example, in fiscal year 1982, 54 percent of the boards' capital budget proposals were included in the departmental estimates and 51 percent were finally included in the adopted budget. A total of 423 board-initiated capital projects were among those. Also, 59 percent of the boards' expense budget requests were in the fiscal 1982 departmental estimates. However, almost one-half of these board requests were recommended for funding within the agencies' available resources. These were to be accomplished through the redeployment of personnel and equipment, increased civilianization of uniformed forces, and the implementation of management improvements.

COMMUNITY BOARD PARTICIPATION IN LOCAL
SERVICE PLANNING AND MONITORING

While the charter mandates for community board participation in the budget process, coterminality, and geographic-based budget reporting have been effectively met, community board involvement in local service planning and monitoring is still developing. The district service cabinet system and the publication of district resource statements are now institutionalized. These give the community boards access to local service chiefs who direct field services and to information about the agency's allocation to the district of personnel and equipment. Progress has been slower, however, in achieving systematic district level planning and performance measurement.

One reason could be that local service chiefs have spent years receiving instructions from the "top down" and have had little training in management skills or experience in planning and managing service delivery within the local district. The city charter revision attempted to address this problem by mandating management decentralization. This charter mandate asks that each agency act to expand appropriately the authority level of its local service chiefs and to create necessary support systems to assist each local chief. Decentralization of management is intended to benefit the city by increasing operational effectiveness and efficiency at the district level and improving planning and communication with and by community boards.

In an effort to implement management decentralization, the Mayor's Community Assistance Unit has negotiated agreements and procedures with several city agencies which are designed to achieve this objective. Some of these procedures are:

- To clarify the role of local service chiefs to reflect their tasks and responsibilities relating to community boards;
- To increase the decision-making opportunities of the local chief where such increase will improve local service delivery;
- To maximize the participation of the local chief at the district level budget consultations with the community board and the district service cabinets;
- To improve the information flow to and from the local service chiefs and their agency's hierarchy and decision makers;
- To design and execute training programs to achieve these objectives and procedures.

A few of the specific agency initiatives resulting from management decentralization planning are:

- Rewriting local service chief job descriptions to reflect charter mandates;

- Instituting on-going training for service chiefs in preparation for budget consultation and in district service cabinet attendance;
- Involving the local service chiefs in the capital design process; traditionally, local chiefs, although responsible for managing a district, had little or no input into the design and rehabilitation of local capital projects.
- Improving or instituting complaint system mechanisms to be more responsive to community boards and local service chiefs' needs.

The most effective role of the community boards to date, in dealing with service delivery, has been in identifying day-to-day problems and working with the agency service chiefs to address them. One of the mandated responsibilities of the community boards is handling service delivery complaints of district residents. As expected by the charter, they are now a significant intake point for such citizen complaints. Community boards, through their intake process can generate important statistical data about the need for specific services, the responsiveness of agencies to those needs, and the effectiveness of present resource allocations in meeting them. Computerization is now being considered for the community board district offices to make them more effective in this respect.

Using this complaint data and their comprehensive knowledge of their districts, the board and local service chiefs plan together to make service delivery more effective. Although discussions about services occur daily throughout the year, during the district level budget consultation sessions with local service chiefs community boards can identify specific ways in which the reallocation of existing resources may meet a district service delivery need. This discussion of service planning is paired with the board's submission of budget requests.

More and more, community boards are also taking on responsibility for long-range service planning. One pilot program in Sanitation has expanded over the last few years from one participating board to ten. In this program, community boards worked with local Sanitation staff to develop a new service plan in which frequencies for street cleaning and trash removal have been adjusted to better match the actual needs of each block in the district. No new resources were added to the district. A guide was prepared, using the original pilot board in Brooklyn as a case example, to help and encourage other boards to participate in developing service plans.

Other agencies besides Sanitation have asked community boards to assist them in fulfilling their own agency service missions. Usually these board responsibilities include monitoring and surveillance of local agency operations, planning, and setting local service priorities. These tasks give the boards an opportunity to influence the way services are actually delivered. Some of the ways in which boards now advise agencies on resource allocation and program planning are, to name but a few:

- Establishing district priorities for street resurfacing work;
- Setting priorities for parks and playground rehabilitation;
- Reviewing capital designs and blueprints of planned renovations;
- Submitting to the Bureau of Forestry a list of priorities for tree pruning and tree planting sites in the board area;
- Reviewing applications for permits to use streets and parks for special events;
- Reviewing the planned demolition of buildings in the district;
- Establishing the order in which vacant lots are cleaned in the district on a rotating basis;
- Organizing volunteer street and park clean-ups.

The process of establishing local performance measures has proceeded slowly. One part of that process, the district resource statement, strives for two objectives. First, it should enable each community board to compare the local resource and service levels of operating agencies relative to other districts and boroughs and to its own district's needs. Second, it was intended that the district resource statement include agreed-upon standards by which local agency performance can be monitored both by the agency itself and by community boards.

The district resource statement represents the first compilation, under one cover, of each agency's local facilities, resources (including personnel by level), and programs. Agency expenditures are also broken down on a district basis for the previous fiscal year. In addition, operating statistics and performance measures are provided, which attempt to measure how well agencies perform with the resources they have at their disposal. Examples include:

- Measures of community conditions in community board districts, including indicators of the cleanliness of local streets and the state of repair of community park facilities;
- Measures of responsiveness, including the average length of time it takes the Bureau of Highways to respond to a complaint;
- Measures of reliability, such as how closely an agency adheres to its service schedule (e.g., the percentage of Sanitation mechanical broom routes that are completed on schedule);
- Indicators of local agency workload and volume of services provided (such as the police precinct's yearly calls for service).

Taken together, these measures, along with other easily accessible data, can assist a community board in developing an overall picture of the district's needs and priorities. Based on the use of such data, the community board can seek to effect change through its participation in the city's capital, expense, and community development budget process as well as through district-level planning.

The service planning aspect of the district resource statement is under review by OMB's Office of Community Board Relations and should be considerably enhanced in fiscal year 1984. The development of district-based performance measures against which local agency performance can be evaluated combined with training for both community boards and local service chiefs will provide a basis for meaningful consultation on service delivery.

CONCLUSION

The full scope of the New York City Charter revision and the roles of the community boards have not been explored here. Community boards have numerous other important responsibilities, such as in land use review and comprehensive planning, which are also mandated by the charter. In fact, the charter specifies that any matter relating to the welfare of the residents of a district is appropriate for the attention of its community board.

It is, however, in service delivery and budget planning that citizen participation through the community boards can have its most visible and important impact. New York City has clearly shown that processes to achieve that involvement can be successfully established and can improve the quality of life in local communities.

6
The Value of Measuring and Improving Performance

Efforts to measure and improve local government performance, communicate with the public, and improve decision making are not free. Local officials must invest their own time and the time of their staff. Their investment also may include the cost of additional staff, special training, consultants, capital equipment, or increased energy use. There is also the intangible cost of disruption of the work of an organization due to changes introduced. To make these costs worthwhile, local officials must see some *value* in the results they expect to achieve. Unfortunately, the value of a measurement and improvement effort is usually less clearcut than its costs. It is often difficult or misleading to put a dollar value on an improvement. However, even if it is not possible to determine what an improvement is worth in dollars, that improvement can still be extremely valuable to the community. This chapter examines the difficulties of identifying the value of improvements, and discusses ways to consider the value of four types of improvement:

- The value of improving decision making;
- The value of improving service effectiveness;
- The value of improving service efficiency;
- The organizational value of measurement and improvement efforts.

THE ECONOMIST VERSUS THE ENGINEER: PROBLEMS WITH PUTTING A DOLLAR VALUE ON SERVICE IMPROVEMENTS

As discussed in chapter 1, the word *productivity* can have different meanings. Since this chapter is about *value,* productivity, in its strictly *economic* sense is a useful idea to consider. In economic terms, productivity is the ratio between the value of a final product or service and the cost of the resources used to produce it. However, many economists say public sector productivity cannot be measured.

Economists have a problem with public sector productivity because they insist on putting a *dollar value* on the output and the input so they can compare and combine the productivity of apples and oranges — or of picking apples versus building cars. That's okay in the private sector, where the marketplace establishes those values. But that's why economists give up in the public sector; there's no market mechanism to determine the value of the output of government agencies. Instead there is a tax structure, with no way for people to express what they think is the dollar value of the services they receive.

Engineers, on the other hand, examine individual government services and often define productivity in terms of *efficiency,* an important form of performance measurement discussed in detail in chapter 2. For each service, they try to define specific service units for the output side of their productivity, or efficiency, ratios. Two simple efficiency ratios, expressed as unit costs, are:

- Cost per lane-mile resurfaced;
- Cost per household garbage collection made.

Engineers do not try to put a dollar value on the output of government agencies. They can't combine the productivity of street maintenance, garbage collection, transportation systems, and other services. However, they try to *improve* the productivity (efficiency) of individual services, knowing they can either save a community money by providing the same amount of services at a lower cost, or give the community more services for the same cost. But if a dollar amount cannot be assigned to the output of a public service, how can the *value* of improving it be determined? A dollar value *can* often be calculated for improving service efficiency. This "efficiency value" represents the difference in cost, necessary to provide a given quantity of service output, between more efficient and less efficient service delivery methods. This calculation can be useful to a local government. But it can also be misleading, because it will change depending on the "quantity of service" used in the calculation. The greater the quantity of service provided using the more efficient methods, the higher the "efficiency value" calculated, even if money is wasted by providing more services than a community actually needs or can afford. The calculation of "efficiency values" and their associated problems are demonstrated in the following example, "The Asphalt Paradox."

"The Asphalt Paradox" is a simplified version of an actual occurrence in one community's productivity improvement program. The problems that occur in city X do not make the calculation of efficiency values invalid. Instead, the example indicates how benefits from efficiency improvement can be achieved in different ways: by increasing service, reducing costs, or some combination of both. Local officials must make a *value judgment* concerning what forms and amounts of benefits they will attempt to achieve. The most appropriate mix of benefits for a community's needs and financial condition will not always be that mix which yields the highest "efficiency value."

EXAMPLE 6.1 THE ASPHALT PARADOX

Like many other jurisdictions, city X was in a tight fiscal squeeze. The budget officer saw the need for the city to save money and increase efficiency wherever possible. Through the chief executive, he called on all departments to make existing resources go as far as possible.

One of city X's larger public expenditures each year went for resurfacing its streets and highways, which the city did with its own work force. The city government did not want to cut this program because the streets were generally considered to be in bad shape — with lots of cracks and potholes. Poor street conditions was one of the biggest sources of citizen complaints. An industrial engineer was assigned to the resurfacing program to see if it could be made more efficient.

The engineer's initial analysis indicated:

- *The program had an operating efficiency of $17,500 per lane-mile resurfaced;* this unit cost was based on $10,000 labor cost per lane-mile plus $7500 asphalt cost per lane-mile.
- *At the current rate of efficiency per labor-hour, city X's resurfacing crews would be able to resurface 75 lane-miles in a year.*

After carefully charting out the entire resurfacing process, work sampling the resurfacing crews in action, and analyzing the results, the engineer determined it was possible, in a relatively short time, to schedule the delivery of asphalt better, vary the size of resurfacing crews to meet the needs of each job, and improve work methods. The engineer concluded such changes would increase the efficiency of the resurfacing labor force by 33 percent in the first year of implementation alone. In other words:

- The existing resurfacing work force would be able to resurface 100 lane-miles in a year.
- The unit cost of labor would be reduced to $7500 labor cost per lane-mile.
- The program's operating efficiency would improve considerably, as the total unit cost would be reduced by $2500.

The new unit cost would be *$15,000 per lane-mile resurfaced,* based on $7500 labor cost per lane-mile plus $7500 asphalt cost per lane-mile.

In seeking approval to implement the proposed resurfacing improvements, the engineer told the budget officer the improvements would have an annual "efficiency value" of $250,000 to the city, based on the benefit realized by resurfacing 100 lane-miles at a reduced unit cost. In other words, the engineer calculated:

Benefit = Reduction in cost per lane-mile times number of
lane-miles resurfaced

Benefit = $2500 × 100 = $250,000 "efficiency value"

Convinced by this argument, the budget officer supported the engineer's recommendations to the chief executive, who in turn approved them. The chief executive was pleased that they might get 100 lane-miles resurfaced by the same crews that resurfaced only 75 lane-miles last year.

The operations improvements were implemented quickly and smoothly. Labor efficiency increased as predicted, resulting in the projected $2500 reduction in unit cost. By the end of the fiscal year the resurfacing work force, without adding any staff, had resurfaced 100 lane-miles of streets and highways.

At the end of the fiscal year, the budget officer was angry at the engineer. In fact, he was livid. He had expected a $250,000 benefit. But when all the bills were added up, he decided the "improved" program had actually *cost the city budget $187,500.* Here's how that happened:

- Under the "original" program of resurfacing 75 lane-miles at a higher unit cost, *the total costs would have been:*

Labor:	$10,000 per lane-mile × 75 lane-miles	= $750,000
Asphalt:	$7,500 per lane-mile × 75 lane-miles	= $562,500
	Total Cost	$1,312,500

- Under the "improved" program of resurfacing 100 lane-miles at the lower cost, the actual total costs were:

Labor:	$7,500 per lane-mile × 100 lane-miles	= $750,000
Asphalt:	$7,500 per lane-mile × 100 lane-miles	= $750,000
	Total Cost	$1,500,000

- *The result was a net increase in city expenditures of $187,500, as follows:*

$1,500,000 – $1,312,500 = $187,500

Who was right? Was the engineer correct, who calculated a "benefit" of $250,000? Or was the budget officer correct, who calculated an added cost of $187,500? *They were both right.* It all depends on one's point of view. If city X really *needed* to have the additional 25 lane-miles resurfaced (which it did — all the streets resurfaced were in poor condition), the program really did save them $250,000 over what it would have cost to resurface 100 lane-miles using the old methods. This type of benefit is often referred to as "cost avoidance." However, the figures clearly add up to $187,500 more than city X had originally budgeted to resurface 75 lane-miles. If city X were really in a fiscal squeeze, wouldn't it be poor management to spend $187,500 more than planned on the resurfacing program, even if it was being run more efficiently?

From yet another point of view, *both the engineer and the budget officer were wrong.* They were wrong because they did not take the extra step before implementation to determine how to take their benefits from improved efficiency. By reducing costs? By increasing services delivered? By doing some of both? If, in achieving the $15,000 per lane-mile unit cost, city X had reduced its resurfacing work force by 25 percent, it would have maintained its 75 lane-mile service level and cut its budget by $187,500, as follows:

Labor: $7,500 per lane-mile X 75 lane-miles   = $562,500
Asphalt: $7,500 per lane-mile X 75 lane-miles   = $562,500
                          Total Cost $1,125,000

$1,312,500 (cost of old program) – $1,125,000 = *$187,500 savings*

Of course a 25 percent work force reduction may require politically or socially unacceptable actions, such as laying off workers. And what sounds better, anyway: $250,000 worth of increased services or $187,500 in savings? A jurisdiction could easily be tempted into taking a benefit it cannot afford.

Someone in city X must make a *value judgment* that despite the higher calculated dollar benefit of increasing services, the *greater value* to the city *at this time* is to take its productivity gains in the form of *savings.* More likely, city X's decision makers would have factored the problems associated with a large work force reduction into their value judgment and made some sort of compromise. They might have decided on increased services at *no cost* increase. For the original $1,312,500 budgeted, they could achieve the improved unit cost of $15,000 per lane-mile and increase service to 87.5 lane-miles resurfaced, if they reduced their labor costs by $103,550, or 13.8 percent. They might achieve that amount by normal attrition, without having to resort to layoffs. If attrition will not occur that fast, they might decide to implement a lesser increase in efficiency the first year and to achieve the full increase over a period of years as attrition gradually reduces the work force.

Efficiency benefits in the form of cost reductions can be difficult to achieve if they involve layoffs of public employees. Such layoffs could be considered politically or socially unacceptable, and can cause employees not to cooperate with attempted operations improvements. If a community has the foresight, three to four years before a potential fiscal crisis, to make the value judgment that it must reduce costs, it can take its labor cost reductions through attrition rather than layoffs. Then:

- Efficiency will increase *gradually;*
- The work force will be reduced *gradually;*
- There will be no big shock to the service delivery system;
- A fiscal crisis might be avoided without reducing services or creating labor problems.

As described by Financial Management Director Libby Anderson in Example 4.3 in chapter 4, the City of San Diego applied its work standards program in that fashion. Where indicated by the work standards, they started reducing staff by attrition in 1975, three years before Proposition 13 sharply limited real estate taxes in California. Of course they had not predicted tax limitations three years in advance. As Ms. Anderson described in her example, San Diego's value judgment was based on a six-year plan for the operating budget showing expenditures eventually surpassing revenues unless efficiency improved, taxes went up, or services were cut. While San Diego did not predict tax limitations, because of their work standards program they were ready for them.

SERVICE VALUE AS RESPONSIVENESS TO COMMUNITY NEEDS

The economist's "market value" cannot be determined for government services. The engineer's "efficiency value" can have perverse results, as suggested by "The Asphalt Paradox." Yet if "value judgments" are important in service improvement efforts, some useful notion of "value" is needed for local government services. Such a useful notion arises from the discussion of effectiveness measurement in chapter 2: *A service is as valuable as it is responsive to the needs and desires of the community.*

As described in chapter 2, and in several of the examples throughout this book, community needs and desires for local services can be measured, as can local government responsiveness to those needs and desires, all as forms of effectiveness measurement. Thus, measures of effectiveness can be helpful to public officials who must make value judgments concerning service improvements.

One strong citizen "desire" always seems to be the desire to pay no more taxes than necessary. From another viewpoint, this can be seen as the "need" to limit the burden of the costs of government on its citizens. Thus, cost and efficiency measurement are also important in making value judgments concerning service improvements. It is important, however, never to consider efficiency measurement in a vacuum, as the engineer did in "The Asphalt Paradox."

Since the community's needs and desires always exist in an environment of limited resources, basic policy decisions on the allocation of resources always involve value judgments concerning government responsiveness, whether or not service "improvements" are concerned and whether or not these value judgments are made consciously. These decisions involve:

- The allocation of resources among different services;
- The allocation of services and assistance among:
  - Different geographic areas;
  - Different client groups (e.g., elderly, handicapped, children, indigent);
  - Different facilities requiring service (e.g., parks, public buildings, housing, streets, sewers);
  - Other service targets.

In essence, these are all value judgments concerning the allocation of resources to meet competing needs and desires. Measures of effectiveness, efficiency, and cost can thus be useful for making these most basic of all public policy decisions. Just as helpful is some sort of systematic process for building information on community needs and desires into the resource allocation process, so public officials have a better understanding of the value judgments they are making. The data collection and decision-making process can be simple or elaborate and they can take a variety of forms, as described in many of the examples throughout this book, most notably those on Savannah (chapter 2), Dallas, Iowa City, and Dayton (chapter 3), and Rochester, Arlington, and New York City (chapter 5).

The value of improving policy decisions

The value of using performance measurement to improve policy decisions will rarely be obvious to public officials in terms of clear "good versus bad" judgments, definite savings, or benefits they would not otherwise have achieved. To a large extent, public officials notice this value in the form of increased confidence in the decisions they make. The value becomes clearer when large reallocations of resources are made due to an examination of performance data. Such redirection of resources represents an increase in the value received for public tax dollars, because they are shifted to meet community needs more closely.

The value of improving performance: improved effectiveness and improved efficiency

When a service has measurably improved, it is generally easy to feel that some increase in public "value" has been achieved. But it is often impossible to assign a *dollar* value to the improvement. Nonetheless, such improvements can be extremely valuable to the community.

If a service improvement concentrates on increasing service *effectiveness*, rather than efficiency, it is particularly difficult to establish a connection between the improvement made and a dollar value to the community. "Cost-benefit analyses" are sometimes made in which the cost of improvement is weighed against some dollar value of the benefits received by the community as a result of the improvement. For example, the number of accidents avoided as a result of street improvements might be estimated. The "benefit" would then be the estimated cost of medical and repair bills and of lawsuits from those accidents, if they actually had happened. Of course, no one can really tell how many accidents did not happen or what they did not cost, but if extensive "before and after" accident data are collected, one might be able to make a convincing case that a specific dollar value could be assigned to the street improvement. Usually, it is much more difficult to assign a dollar value to an improvement in service effectiveness. What is the dollar value of cleaner streets and sidewalks? Probably the most important result from Washington, D.C.'s Neighborhood Services Improvement Project (chapter 5) was a significant increase in citizens' "pride in their neighborhood," as measured by citizen surveys. But because it has no clear dollar value, is neighborhood pride unimportant? Much like improved policy decisions, the value in improved service effectiveness must be seen as an increase in the responsiveness to citizens' needs and desires. When a service is made more effective, the resources used for that service, and the public dollars that supply those resources, become more valuable because they are meeting community needs better. Often such improvements in service effectiveness are more valuable to a community than other improvements for which clear dollar values can be calculated.

When there is a measurable increase in service *efficiency*, and that increase is verifiable through careful performance measurement and cost accounting, it is often possible to calculate a dollar value for a service improvement. However, as shown in "The Asphalt Paradox," "efficiency value" taken out of context can be misleading and cause local officials to make poor judgments concerning service changes. Like city X, they may choose to take a higher valued "benefit" they cannot afford. Or, they may improve efficiency at the cost of effectiveness. Service quality may suffer as a result of crews working faster, but with no quality controls. Responsiveness may suffer if geographic distribution of services is based solely on the most efficient way to deliver them, without concern for the distribution of need. It is reasonable for public officials to calculate a dollar value for an increase in efficiency, so long as they understand the limited meaning of that "efficiency value," and consider it in its context of the impact on service effectiveness and the impact on the budget.

Local governments should not necessarily take their efficiency improvement benefits in a way that will cut a service's budget or hold it even. To a growing jurisdiction (say a city that recently annexed a few square miles with additional residents and infrastructure), the "cost avoidance" benefits described in "The Asphalt Paradox" represent *real savings,* even though the budget goes up, as the jurisdiction has to increase services to meet the demands of growth. Even a jurisdiction that is not growing can still make a valid judgment to increase a service if there is a real need or desire in the community for that increase, preferably supported by effectiveness measures or some process that documents community priorities. The jurisdiction can make up for that increase by reducing costs in *other* services through increased efficiency or actual service reductions. The important thing is for the community's officials to recognize the need for a value judgment and to make that judgment consciously rather than let it be made by default, as in "The Asphalt Paradox."

THE ORGANIZATIONAL VALUE
OF PERFORMANCE MEASUREMENT

The learning process involved in establishing a performance measurement program can result in important organizational benefits for a jurisdiction. This can occur at the legislative and chief executive levels as well as within operating departments. Organizational benefits can result from the processes of selecting measures, defining or reexamining public purposes and program goals, or analyzing decision processes. They can also result from the experience of actually using performance measures to help make decisions, and from implementing performance improvement projects.

Several of the examples in this book indicate growth in the capacity of organizations or individuals that have accompanied measurement and improvement efforts. As described in chapter 4, Charlotte's operating departments have developed analytic capabilities to balance those in the Budget and Evaluation Office. Phoenix and San Francisco (chapter 4) are also emphasizing developing staff capabilities in operating departments. By involving employees in problem identification and solution, San Diego's organization development staff (also chapter 4) helps improve employee understanding and ability as well as organizational performance.

The organizational benefits of measurement essentially involve officials learning to think about public programs in new ways. A worker who has changed his or her work methods with the assistance of a consultant or management team is more likely to keep employing the new methods properly after the consultant leaves, if the worker is convinced they are helping him or her do the job better. New facts learned from measurement, or a new perspective gained from participating in the measurement process, may cause a manager to see his or her program in a different light, leading to a much more creative approach to managing it in the future — well beyond the scope of a particular improvement project. In the best case, the manager's new perspective is picked up by others, so a creative approach to using measurement and improving performance lasts within the organization even after the manager leaves.

The organizational benefits of performance measurement and improvement are not guaranteed. To be sure to achieve them, a jurisdiction must pay some attention to developing its human resources when implementing a measurement or improvement program. But these benefits are well worth the extra effort needed, even though their full value will never be measurable in dollars. Organization benefits are potentially the most valuable that a jurisdiction can gain from performance measurement because of their lasting effect on the organization.

SUMMARY OF THE DIFFERENT "VALUES" OF IMPROVEMENT

The value of performance measurement and improvement efforts is not always clearcut. But it is real. Different kinds of improvement produce different kinds of benefits, yielding different forms of value to the public. Figure 6-1 summarizes the four types of improvement discussed in this chapter, the forms of benefit produced, and the forms of value received.

Type of Improvement Achieved	Form of Benefit Produced	Form of Value Received
IMPROVED POLICY DECISIONS	Reallocation of resources to more closely meet community needs.	Shifted resources increase in value to public, as needs are better met by public tax dollars. Not expressible as a hard dollar figure.
IMPROVED SERVICE PERFORMANCE		
Improved Effectiveness	Services made more responsive to community needs.	Services increase in value to the public, as needs are better met by public tax dollars. Not expressible as a hard dollar figure.
Improved Efficiency	Increased amount of services delivered per dollar spent. Also expressible as decreased cost per unit of service delivered.	A dollar value of increased efficiency may be calculated, representing actual savings, cost avoidance, or both. This "efficiency value" can be misleading, particularly if it is in the form of cost avoidance. But it is a valid calculation.
IMPROVED ORGANIZATIONS	Managers and employees see their programs and jobs in a new light, becoming more creative as well as more efficient and effective (human development benefits).	Public organizations increase in value to the public, as their ability to change and improve is enhanced. Not expressible as a hard dollar figure.

Figure 6-1. Forms of value associated with performance
measurement and improvement efforts.

7
Creating Change:
Some Pointers and Pitfalls

Public officials thinking of starting or enhancing a performance measurement and improvement program, or considering efforts to improve decision making, communication, or accountability, must be concerned with implementation of such efforts. They also should consider how they will sustain and develop their measurement programs over the years. The principles and examples presented in the previous chapters can provide these officials with ideas for using measurement and improvement techniques in their own communities. Many of those principles and examples suggest some pointers for implementing, managing, and developing measurement programs, as well as some pitfalls to try to avoid along the way. In this chapter, those pointers and pitfalls are discussed in greater detail.

CREATE A CLIMATE FOR CHANGE

As discussed in chapter 4, implicit in any approach to improvement is the necessity of *change*. But change is rarely readily accepted in organizations. Officials interested in improvement must seek or create favorable conditions for change in their community. Creating a climate for change involves assessing local conditions for changes that are needed and feasible, building an awareness of the need for change, and gaining the support of the people who must implement and cooperate with the change.

Assess the local situation

The wide variety of measurement and improvement approaches used by different communities, as indicated in the many examples in chapters 2, 3, 4, and 5, reflects a wide variety of measurement needs and interests existing in local governments throughout the country. As described in chapters 3 and 4, performance measurement and improvement approaches develop differently in different communities, depending on the conditions and problems in a community, the interests of its elected officials and managers, the abilities of the staff, and the resources available for improvements. No one approach or combination of approaches is "correct." Selection of an approach depends on the local situation. Local officials should embark on attempts to create change with their eyes open and assess all aspects of their local "situation" that may affect the success of each new approach considered.

Local development and economic conditions can affect the type of measurement approach that is needed and feasible. In a growing community, in which development gives the local government more streets to maintain, more garbage to collect, and more people to serve in many ways, there is no question that the total cost of local government will rise. Consequently, there is a need to control the growth of government costs, resulting in a natural emphasis on efficiency measurement and improvement.

In a growing community, efficiency improvement can be relatively painless in human terms. When work force reductions are indicated for one activity, there will be other activities for which additional workers are needed to meet growing demands on community services. Thus, reductions can often be accomplished quickly through transfers and normal attrition. In such an environment, large efficiency gains can be quickly achieved. Since both services and tax base are expanding, efficiency gains can often be achieved in the form of "cost avoidance," representing real community benefits and no labor reductions. It is not surprising that San Diego and Phoenix, both in growing economic regions, emphasized efficiency when they started their improvement programs.

Local governments in stable or declining economic regions may have a great need for improving efficiency but may find this difficult to accomplish. Cost avoidance is often inappropriate in such settings, causing some efficiency gains to be smaller. Labor reductions by means other than attrition may be politically unacceptable, causing efficiency savings to be achieved slowly. The greatest need of such governments may be to make sure their shrinking resources are being aimed effectively at priority community needs. These governments may find it more useful to move quickly into effectiveness measurement, to help direct basic resource allocation decisions.

A community's political environment can affect the measurement emphasis taken. Dayton, Ohio can only increase its tax rates or pass new taxes once every five years, and then only by approval of the voters in a citywide referendum. Dayton's emphasis on effectiveness measurement (chapter 3) grew out of the city government's need to justify its tax packages to the voters. Effectiveness measures provide a picture of needs throughout Dayton, which the city government presents to its citizens through the "program strategies" process. Citizen participation in Dayton's budget process through their priority boards (chapter 5) enhances the program strategies approach by increasing citizen identification with the programs that new tax packages will support.

The bureaucratic and management environment in a community can also influence the feasibility of measurement and improvement approaches. As described in chapter 5, the City of New York has found implementing mandated neighborhood service planning and performance monitoring to be a slow process, as field service managers have spent years following instructions from the top down. They have no experience planning performance in their own districts. Not surprisingly, New York more quickly developed its thorough centralized performance monitoring system which results in the public *Mayor's Management Reports*. As described in chapter 5, community board participation in New York's budget process has worked well. One of the keys to that success has been the participation of the top level (central) decision makers of city agencies.

Local governments with a background of successful management or technological innovation generally will have staff who are more willing to accept new measurement and improvement techniques. Thus, once one measurement approach has succeeded in a community, a second or third approach is often easier to implement. This accounts for the evolution of multiple measurement approaches in such communities as Dayton (chapter 3), and Charlotte and Phoenix (chapter 4).

Many other factors of the local situation can contribute to the need and feasibility of measurement and improvement approaches, such as the strength and sophistication of public employee unions. Cultural or sociological factors can even play a role. In a "working class" community in which people are used to the application of industrial engineering in the local factories, efficiency measurement may be more readily accepted in the local government. This may have contributed to the successful efficiency measurement and improvement efforts in Milwaukee, Wisconsin and Genesee County, Michigan, even though they are not located in growing economic regions.

The general conditions discussed above barely begin to describe some of the factors local government officials must assess in their own situation. If they are to be successful in creating a climate for change, these officials must be very specific when assessing community needs, organizational strengths and weaknesses, managerial and political styles, and resources available to implement change. Perhaps most of all, local officials must assess the *people* within their own organizations to determine what will motivate them to support or to resist change.

Build support for change

Essential to a good climate for change is the support of people whose cooperation is needed to achieve change. For almost any measurement approach to succeed, the cooperation of at least two or three levels of management is required (e.g., top management, operational department managers, operations supervisors). For some approaches, cooperation must extend from elected officials down to line employees. Gaining the support of people from these different groups is sometimes referred to as "building a coalition for change."

People must be made aware of the need for change, as well as the advantages change will bring them. In the best case, someone will see a compelling reason to change (e.g., "I will lose the next election if I do not do something differently"). Generally, people who cooperate with change do so because they see some advantage for themselves, their organization, or the community. People who see a threat to themselves, or to ways of work or life they are comfortable with, will often be resistant to change. The advantages must be emphasized and the threats minimized.

It is important to emphasize to both elected officials and top managers that performance measurement can help them make decisions and improve performance. The ability to make services more responsive to community needs should interest elected officials and can be a good argument to support the use of effectiveness measurement and techniques involving communication with the public. The ability to improve service operations should interest managers and can support the use of a variety of efficiency and effectiveness measurement techniques. An argument that should appeal to all busy officials is that performance measurement allows them to make better use of their time, by helping them identify important issues.

While stressing the contributions of measurement techniques, it is equally important to insure that officials recognize that these techniques are simply tools which can only augment their own decision-making roles. The point is not to take decisions away from officials, but to sharpen their decision-making abilities.

The support for change among public employees, who more often follow others' decisions than make their own, can be obtained by giving them a voice in the change process. They are more likely to support improvements if they feel problems they have identified will be solved. Several examples in chapter 4 involve employee participation in performance improvement.

The participation of all levels of officials in selecting measurement and improvement approaches is helpful in building a coalition for change. Such a collaboration helps insure that the interests of all key officials and groups of people are represented in the approaches selected. Chapter 3 describes how a collaborative approach to selecting performance measures helps insure that the measures will actually be used by the people receiving performance reports.

To be successful, a coalition for change needs an acknowledged leader to give a new performance measurement and improvement program an identity and to move it forward with authority. When critical actions are needed to get a program started or keep it progressing, the leader must be willing and able to see to it that those actions are taken. The leader need not necessarily be an autocrat who has the final decision on everything concerning the new program. Rather, a respected, visible official is needed whom others can look to for guidance, confidence, and support. If that person also has a position of high authority, so much the better. It is impossible to say who should be the leader of any move for change in a community. For example, it could be the chief executive or a prominent deputy, a budget director or assistant, or a respected department head. Generally, the acknowledged leader will emerge from among the early supporters of change. It is important for someone who wants change to recognize the need for leadership and to provide it. Of course, the person who sees the need for leadership may not be prominent enough among other officials to provide it. In such a case, that person should encourage a more prominent official to take the lead. The acknowledged leader need not be a performance measurement expert, so long as adequate support staff is available to provide the needed expertise. The leader is not needed to conduct analytic studies, but to turn studies and ideas into actions. Without leadership, a "coalition for change" will at best be a group of people who never get past discussing what the local government "ought to do."

Most people will be hesitant to attempt a change unless they are confident of success. One of the best ways to build that confidence is by example. If there are one or two able managers who are not so hesitant — who are willing to risk change in their organizations first — work with them to measure and improve the performance of their organizations. Give them special attention and assistance to insure success. Their example can be held up to others in the government. They should be encouraged to talk to other local officials about their experiences. There may even be some way to reward them and their organizations. With luck, their examples will build the confidence, and reduce the hesitancy, of other officials to attempt change.

HAVE A PLAN, BUT BE AN OPPORTUNIST

It is difficult to force people to use measurement for decision making and performance improvement. As described in chapters 3 and 4, measurement uses tend to evolve in a community. Their evolution generally requires assistance, however, in the form of careful planning, adequate resources, and a healthy dose of opportunism.

A good plan to implement a new measurement and improvement program in a local government should include these four components:

- A training and development strategy;
- An information systems strategy;
- A project management strategy;
- Plenty of time for installation *and* refinement of the program.

A *training and development strategy* should include not only building and training a central staff to manage a new measurement program, but also developing staff capacity in the operating departments that will participate in the program. In the Charlotte example in chapter 4, a balance in analytic capabilities between the budget office and the departments is cited as a key factor in their success. San Diego and Phoenix (chapter 4) also realized that developing departmental staff capabilities will help departments solve problems and implement improvements on their own, after central staff analysts or consultants leave. If their staff capabilities are so developed, departments' confidence and ability to achieve performance improvements will increase. Thus, departments are more likely to agree to targets that challenge them to improve their performance. As described in chapter 4, San Francisco has also paid attention to developing departmental staff capabilities, as evidenced by the series of handbooks specially developed by the mayor's office to assist departmental staff with performance measurement and analysis. If citizens are an important part of a measurement and improvement strategy, their education and training is also important, as noted in the Rochester, New York, Washington, D.C., Arlington, Massachusetts, and New York City examples in chapter 5.

A training and development strategy should also include a plan for growth of a measurement program. This plan should provide for both quantitative growth, such as adding new departments and covering more employees, and qualitative growth, such as developing new uses for performance data, linking performance measurement to other government systems (e.g., budgeting, accounting), and developing complementary uses of different measurement and improvement approaches. A good plan will keep a government from overextending itself by calling for increasing the measurement staff to accommodate new approaches or the addition of new departments. This is especially important for approaches involving follow-up (e.g., updating work standards).

An *information systems strategy* does *not* necessarily refer to use of a computer system. Most local governments store and process their performance data manually. What is important is that attention be paid to developing consistent procedures for accurate and timely collection, storage, and reporting of performance data. All forms of measurement and improvement discussed in this book can be done with manual information systems. Unless computer systems already exist in a community that can readily accommodate performance measurement in a useful way, it may be wise to start with manual approaches and invest in computerizing them after the measurement techniques have proven their usefulness. An information systems strategy should include assigning clear responsibilities for collecting and reporting data, developing ways to verify information reported, and designing and producing performance reports that are useful to the people who receive them. The strategy should include steps for the involvement of all key participants (e.g., collectors and users of data) in the selection of performance measures, the development of imaginative and understandable data display formats, and the refinement of measures and reports. Refinements should be encouraged to accommodate difficulties that arise and new uses of performance information. Just as important as the addition of new measures that performance report users find helpful is the deletion of measures that are not useful. Briefer reports are generally easier to understand, and they represent simpler data collection and reporting burdens.

A *project management strategy* refers to the clear definition of tasks and schedules for implementing a new program, as well as the roles and responsibilities of all participants. Methods for monitoring completion of tasks and progress against schedules are also important. Optimally, one person has overall responsibility for managing a measurement program and has the necessary authority over program participants to back up that responsibility. Such authority usually requires support from top management of a local government. That support is necessary but often no better than tentative at the start of a program. A chief executive's or council's solid support must be earned. A chief executive does not like to have to make difficult decisions because of an untried program (e.g., forcing a department to submit to a study or cut its budget). So a good project management approach will emphasize cooperation rather than confrontation. A good project management approach will attempt to implement training and development, build a coalition for change, and demonstrate early success and usefulness to top management *before* difficult decisions are needed. It is then more likely that top management support will be forthcoming when it is needed. "Lack of top management support" is no excuse for failure unless an honest attempt was made to earn that support, without putting management in an unreasonable position.

Plenty of *time* should be allowed in a plan to implement a measurement program, not just for installation of new systems and approaches, but also for their refinement and development until they prove undeniably useful. In a large jurisdiction, it may take as long as five years before most departments are reporting information that officials actually use for decision making or performance improvement. If management drops its attention from a measurement program before substantial use is achieved, the effort is likely to be wasted.

A good plan for a measurement and improvement program should be opportunistic. It should build on existing strengths in a government, such as a department that already collects and uses performance information or a computerized cost-accounting system that can facilitate efficiency measurement. A measurement program can be designed around recognized needs to help garner support. For example, in Iowa City (chapter 3) and Charlotte (chapter 4), the need to improve the budget process provided the impetus to start performance measurement programs. When managers and council begin to count on receiving performance information to help make budget decisions, the measurement program has been effectively institutionalized. Many of the communities featured in this book have linked performance measurement with their budget process. Performance measurement can also be linked to a community's long-range revenue and expenditure forecasting. As described in chapter 4, it was a long-range forecast that provided the impetus for San Diego's work measurement program. Performance measurement and communicating with citizens can also be linked for good results, as many communities featured in this book have done in some form. As in Rochester (chapter 5), it can be good politics. As in Washington, D.C. (chapter 5), the citizens may pitch in and help solve service problems. To the extent possible, opportunities to achieve complementary uses of different measurement approaches should be built into a plan — though these opportunities are often hard to predict in advance.

Plans are made to be broken, especially plans for developing performance measurement and improvement efforts in a local government. Opportunism demands it. This is not to say plans should be ignored or that they are not worth making. A plan provides guidance in selecting from the endless options available in developing a measurement and improvement program. But as people begin to get used to working with measurement and as new people and agencies are brought into the program, unanticipated measurement approaches and uses will become apparent. In general, when people suggest promising new approaches, it is wise to consider them — and try them if they seem feasible — to encourage creativity among all participants in a measurement effort. Opportunities to use existing measurement systems in new ways, as with the Dallas street inventory system (chapter 3), should not be missed. Opportunities should also be seized to combine different measures or measurement approaches in new ways, as San Diego and Phoenix have done with their industrial engineering and organization development programs (chapter 4). With careful attention, new approaches that prove successful can be tied into existing programs by opportunistic managers, as was done in Dayton (chapter 3) and Charlotte (chapter 4). As Phoenix (chapter 4) learned, flexibility and change with changing community and management needs is a key to long-term success. Even the Dallas City Auditor, whose performance auditing program relies heavily on systematic planning (chapter 4), allows staff time for unscheduled work to meet unanticipated auditing needs and occasionally goes back to the city council for approval to change the audit plan while it is being implemented.

BUILD AND MAINTAIN CREDIBILITY

A carefully cultivated climate for change will be wasted if a measurement program does not establish its credibility to all key participants. As noted above for chief executives, the support of key participants, be they elected officials, managers, supervisors, or employees, is likely only to be tentative at first. They will not want to lend too much of their time, energy, authority, or cooperation to the program before they are convinced it will help them in some way. Once a program's credibility is established, it must be maintained through continued usefulness and beneficial results. Building and maintaining the credibility of a performance measurement and improvement program involve:

- Building an awareness of the value of measurement and improvement;
- Building the capabilities of people and their organizations;
- Building communication and accountability links with the public;
- Emphasizing the *uses* of performance measures rather than the measures themselves;
- Increasing participation and communication among *people* in the measurement program over time.

Building an awareness of the value of measurement and improvement

As discussed in chapter 6, the *value* of performance measurement and improvement often is not easy to understand. But public officials must be convinced of a measurement program's value for them to continue to fund its costs over a sustained period. Often the head of a measurement program will select early projects that are expected to result in highly visible improvements to give other officials a sense that the program is worthwhile. The City of San Diego carefully selected its Equipment Division as its first work measurement project because of the opportunity for large efficiency improvements, the support of the division's management, the opportunities for staff training and development, and other criteria listed in Example 4.3. Sometimes improvement of a revenue producing activity (e.g., collecting permit fees or parking fines) is a good early project because officials can easily understand the value of increased income.

The value of increased effectiveness is often less clearcut because of the difficulty of assigning a dollar amount. But some effectiveness improvements can be persuasive by their visibility, such as noticeably cleaner streets. Once officials gain confidence in a measurement approach because of verified dollar benefits or visible increases in effectiveness, they will be better prepared to understand and accept the less tangible but equally important benefits of improved decision making and organizational development.

When performance measures are included in the budget process, it is important for people to feel that the measures actually make a difference in the way funding decisions are made. Adequate staff support in preparing budget requests and analyzing funding options with respect to performance measures can help make that difference. If department heads feel measures help justify their budget requests and if elected officials and top managers feel measures give them more confidence in their budget decisions, they are likely to be convinced of the value of performance measurement.

Build the capabilities of people and their organizations

Once the managers of a local government agree to participate in a performance measurement and improvement program, the measurement staff sent in to work with their organizations must demonstrate confidence and ability and must leave the managers feeling that their organizations have been improved by the effort. Sloppy staff work can easily destroy the credibility of a measurement effort to a participating organization. Able measurement staff will then have a doubly difficult time achieving results in that organization. It is best to leave a good impression the first time in an organization. Partly for that reason, San Diego emphasized measurement staff training from the start of its work measurement program (chapter 4) and now provides training in both industrial engineering and organization development techniques to staff in their interdisciplinary Organization Effectiveness Program (OEP). Some learning on the job is inevitable for anyone entering a new situation. San Diego, however, wants to be sure its OEP staff are well enough prepared *before* they visit an operating department so their on-the-job learning curve is short. They do not want departmental managers to feel the improvement staff are being trained at the department's expense.

Just as important as training of measurement staff is training and development of people in the organization being studied. Credibility of performance improvement efforts can be lost if people come to believe that improvements tend to be short lived. Organizations must have the ability to sustain performance improvements after a measurement analyst or other special staff leaves. No measurement effort can replace good supervision and management, or the ability of employees to do their jobs properly. That is why training and skill building within operating departments are stressed in several examples in chapter 4. In the best case, departmental staff will not only be able to sustain the improvements arising from a special measurement study, but will be able to add new improvements of their own. That is why San Diego has stressed team building and training of departmental staff to identify and solve problems after the organization development and measurement specialists leave. Charlotte, San Francisco, and Phoenix have also stressed building improvement capabilities within operating departments.

**Build strong communication and accountability
links with the public**

Public knowledge of and confidence in a performance measurement and improvement program can enhance the credibility of the program to local officials. As discussed in chapter 5, communication is the link between performance and accountability. Once a community has "gone public" with its measurement and improvement efforts, there can be more pressure on managers to cooperate in order to live up to the public image of improved management and public account-ability. This is less true when a program is first announced than when various successes have helped to build public confidence in improvement efforts. If public officials feel a program is popular with the public, they will be particularly inclined to cooperate with it and keep it going.

Some communities have taken a systematic approach to communicating with citizens to learn their problems, perceptions, and priorities, as exemplified by Dayton, Englewood (chapter 4) and several of the communities featured in chapter 5. As indicated in the Dayton (chapter 3) and Rochester (chapter 5) examples, public perception should not be the only criterion on which individual decisions are based. Occasionally actions must be taken that are contrary to "popular" public opinion. But to maintain credibility with the public when surveys and citizen participation are used, by and large the local government ought to be able to demonstrate responsiveness to citizens' problems and priorities. The credibility of citizen participation approaches will be damaged if citizens feel all important decisions were made before they had a chance to express their opinions and contribute their ideas. In the communities discussed in chapter 5 that stress citizen participation in the budget process, the common success factor is *early* citizen involvement, *before* departments prepare budget requests. In Dayton and New York, regularly scheduled face-to-face meetings between citizens and public decision makers have also contributed to the credibility and success of these programs.

Emphasize the uses of performance measures rather than the measures themselves

Performance measures are not exclusively researchers' tools. They are meant to be *used* by local officials to make services more responsive to community needs, desires, and ability to pay. Public officials will be more likely to cooperate with a measurement program, and the credibility of the program will be strengthened, if the officials feel they can use the performance measures to do their jobs better.

One barrier to the use of measurement by public officials is their image of the performance improvement analyst. Many officials see the analyst as a bright but naive person who measures and analyzes difficult problems only to come up with solutions that do not account for political realities or day-to-day managerial problems. Analysts often contribute to that impression by making long, detailed presentations and reports to managers and elected officials. The busy officials often lose interest before the analysts come to the point.

It is essential for analysts to learn how to communicate with high level officials to gain their trust and support. Instead of waiting until the end of a study to communicate with the managers who will make the key implementation decisions, the analyst should keep them briefed on the progress of the study and build their preferences into the direction the study takes. It is often difficult to get the attention of busy senior managers, but it is possible if reports and meetings are kept short and to the point. The analyst should use these briefings to get feedback concerning political and operational limitations of potential solutions. Where possible, the analyst should present managers clear, direct questions to respond to, along with easily understood data (supported by brief, clear verbal or written narrative) on both sides of the questions. Such use of prepared data can ease managers into using performance measures to help make decisions. When officials see their responses reflected in recommendations, they are more likely to accept them. They also may learn something about performance measurement and come to use it and support its use in the government.

Whether in an analyst's presentation or a regular performance report, too much detail will cause busy public officials to lose interest. They cannot be expected to plough through reams of data to find the most relevant information. Managers will also resent unreasonable data collection burdens on their organizations, especially if the measures reported appear useless. As discussed in chapter 3, careful selection of measures, so performance reports will be understandable and useful, is needed to increase the likelihood that public officials will actually read and act on the reports. Graphics and narrative used to highlight important results will save officials the time and effort it would take to analyze the data themselves. As discussed in chapter 4, Charlotte keeps its reports understandable through "exception reporting" — concentrating on problems and special achievements in the performance reports used to monitor its MBO program. Phoenix learned that reports can become both too detailed and irrelevant in managers' opinions. As described in chapter 4, departmental managers lost interest in periodic reports that showed few changes in efficiency based on work standards, after initial improvements had been implemented. With more work standards than analysts to keep up with them, many of the standards became obsolete as methods and procedures changed. Also, department directors felt the goals and objectives reports used in the budget process were too detailed to be useful. As a result, Phoenix switched to performance reports emphasizing a smaller number of key trends in each department.

As Phoenix learned, a measurement program's credibility can be eroded even after it has been operating for many years. To rebuild and maintain credibility, a measurement program must become and remain useful to all participants. When the needs of those participants change, so should the measurement program.

**Increase participation and communication among people
in the measurement program**

Performance measurement and improvement programs often start small (e.g., one or two pilot departments or studies, a single measurement approach) to limit the risk of change and concentrate on cases where good results can be expected. Once some early success is achieved, performance improvement staff should reach out to increase the participation of local officials in measurement and improvement efforts. The more people who participate and find it useful, the greater its stature and credibility.

Communication among measurement program participants should also be encouraged. As discussed in chapter 3, communication among the users of performance reports, data collectors, and the people running the measurement program will help insure selection of useful, practical, and valid performance measures. The Dallas City Auditor uses a systematic planning process (chapter 4), involving verbal and written communication with the city council and city management, to insure selection of high priority, useful performance audits that fill important information needs. Communication also gives people in different agencies a chance to share ideas and measurement techniques.

The main reason to extend performance measurement participation to more people and increase communication among participants is to raise the awareness of performance measurement and improvement at all levels in government organizations and to transfer "ownership" of measurement and improvement efforts from a small group of people to all public employees, managers, and elected officials. A performance measurement program will be most productive, and its credibility will no longer be in doubt, when most people in a government feel that improving efficiency and effectiveness is *everyone's* business.

SOME SUGGESTIONS ON USING CONSULTANTS

Consultants can be helpful to a community in starting out or revising a performance measurement program, and in doing a one-time study or improvement project. Whatever the purpose, there are four general rules for using consultants:

1. The work must be clearly defined from the start, even before a consultant is chosen

To serve a local government better, the consultant should know from the start what kind of a final product is desired. If the government officials in charge understand what they want, it can help them choose the right consultant for the job. If some initial analysis by the consultant is needed to determine the nature of the final product, reviews should be held at key stages in the project to make sure the consultant heads in a direction acceptable to the jurisdiction. At the very least, a clear description of the problem as the government sees it should be provided from the start. It is wasteful to pay a consultant to take time to figure out what the government already knows. Lack of a clear problem or work definition can also lead a consultant to provide what he or she has already done for someone else, even if it does not quite fit the government's needs. It is easier for the consultant to solve the wrong problem (i.e., that of a former client) rather than the right one that is not defined by the current client.

2. Care must be taken to select the right people for a specific job

Written proposals by consultants in response to a written statement of what is desired (often referred to as a "request for proposal," or an RFP) can provide a good idea of who understands the problem. Consulting firms must not only have an understanding, they must provide people with the competence to do a given job. Make sure a firm provides resumes of proposed staff to do the job and specifies how much time the key staff — especially the project leader — will spend on the project. Look for two kinds of experience from the key personnel: past projects of a similar nature and general experience working with local government. Written proposals and resumes will probably only narrow the choice rather than decide it. Face-to-face discussions with the top contenders will narrow the choice further. Once two or three firms are under serious consideration for a contract, request government references for the key staff specified for the job. Other government officials who have previously used these staff can provide the best assessment of their competence. When a final choice is made, have the amount of time to be worked by the project leader and other key personnel written into the contract to be sure the government gets the people it wants.

3. At best, a local government gets what it pays for

An RFP should require competitors to state their charges so local officials may use price as *one* criterion for selecting a contractor. For management consulting contracts, price should never be the only criterion. Local officials often find that the most interesting proposals, in which they have the most confidence, are not from the low bidders. To keep price from prejudicing officials' judgment of proposal quality, some governments require consultants to submit separate "management" and "cost" proposals. They evaluate the management proposals without looking at price to select a few consulting firms they feel are well qualified to do the job. Only then do they examine the cost proposals of those consultants considered "well qualified," so they will not be tempted to hire an unqualified low bidder.

When evaluating proposed costs, make sure there is enough money allocated to pay for all the consultant time needed to do a job properly, taking into account any government staff assistance to be provided. Otherwise the project may not be worth doing at all. If one firm considerably underbids others, study its proposal and question the principal staff carefully to make sure that the firm will provide enough experienced staff time to do the job properly and that what is proposed really fits the jurisdiction's needs. Occasionally a firm will attempt to "buy" a project by underbidding to the point of taking a loss on it. If this appears to be the case, try to determine the firm's motives. The firm may be trying to break into the local government sector, a new region of the country, or a new type of work for the first time. If that is the case, what the jurisdiction gains in lower costs, it may lose in lack of experience.

4. The consultants eventually go away, but the government must live with what they leave behind

Make sure there are government staff who keep abreast of what the consultants are doing, and that someone at the decision-making level occasionally reviews consultants' progress to be sure the results will be useful to the jurisdiction. This is especially important for systems which will be operated by government staff after the consultants leave, such as performance measurement and reporting system. Local officials must be sure not only that a consultant designs and implements a system that meets their needs, but that they will be left with a system their staff can operate and update. Many local governments, including those in Phoenix and San Diego, have found it useful to build staff training into consultants' contracts. Their consultants not only do system design and implementation of initial performance improvement projects, but also work closely with government staff throughout, training them in performance measurement and improvement in the process. A performance measurement and improvement contract that includes staff training may pay for itself many times over. The local government not only gets some initial gains from the consultant project but is left with a staff that can multiply those gains many times in the years to come.

THIRTY WAYS TO SABOTAGE PERFORMANCE MEASUREMENT AND IMPROVEMENT PROGRAMS

The following is a list of pitfalls to avoid, or "things *not* to do," when planning and implementing measurement and improvement programs. Some of these pitfalls can keep measurement and improvement programs from getting anywhere, while most are more likely to slow them down or reduce their effectiveness.

DON'T

- Assume that performance measurement and reporting *by itself* will solve the jurisdiction's problems and improve service performance;
- Ask a chief executive to choose between an unproven measurement program and a powerful department head, or to support unreasonable departmental data collection requirements;

DON'T

- Oversell measurement and improvement programs to local officials or the public, promising more than can safely be delivered;
- Publicize performance improvement efforts widely to the community *before* any improvements have actually been achieved;
- Assume regular performance reports *by themselves* will turn people into better supervisors, managers, and policy makers, without any training in using measures to improve performance and decisions;
- Assume performance measures can replace a manager's judgment, or the skills of a good supervisor in getting efficient, quality work from employees;
- Expect that operational improvements implemented in a department will be maintained without properly training departmental staff in the new methods and monitoring their performance after implementation;
- Ignore the human side of performance improvement — the needs of the people actually doing the work involved in providing services;
- Forget about trying to build the capacity and motivation of staff within operating agencies to identify and solve their own problems, and measure and improve their own performance;
- Use employee surveys and other outreach techniques to give the impression management "cares" about employee problems, without doing anything to solve those problems;
- Ignore effectiveness measures that cannot be directly controlled by government action (these are generally indicators of community conditions);
- Fail to measure or account for important aspects of each service measured;
- Ignore citizen perceptions and satisfaction, especially if "more objective" data provide contradictory results;
- Measure efficiency to the exclusion of work quality or effectiveness, especially if managers or employees are offered incentives for increased efficiency;
- Assume work standards derived from "historical" records or by "expert judgment," without systematic analysis and testing, represent the true potential of efficient workers using the best methods for their jobs;
- Assume "engineered" work standards will always be valid, despite changes in work methods or new equipment that might be introduced;
- Allow surveys that provide citizen priorities for service improvements, funding, or cutbacks, to dictate resource allocation decisions without considering other information on needs and the capacity to fulfill them;
- Allow bias to creep into citizen or user survey questions so the government gets the answer it wants;
- Try to make citizens feel good by offering lots of involvement in budget preparation and other policy making processes, but only after all the important decisions are made;
- Attempt to measure and report on everything that moves and some things that do not, so long as they are measurable;

DON'T

- Report all performance data collected to all important public officials, without giving supporting narrative or using formats that highlight important problems or achievements;
- Select performance measures to collect and report without bothering to consult the people who have to collect the data and the people who are expected to use the data;
- Ignore the questions, "Why are we measuring this, where have we been, where are we going, and how are the measurement and improvement needs of the government and the community changing?"
- Forget about making a plan for implementing measurement and improvement efforts and developing these efforts over the years;
- Stick entirely to a measurement and improvement plan through the years without adjusting for the natural evolution of management and political styles in the community, or taking advantage of opportunities that arise to try new measurement and improvement approaches;
- Treat each measurement and improvement approach separately, without trying to get them to complement each other for increased decision making and performance improvement power;
- Try to achieve the highest possible "efficiency value" of service improvements, without regard for whether the community needs or can afford the resulting service increases;
- Take efficiency gains only in the form of savings, even if there is a good justification to include some "cost avoidance";
- Ignore the benefits of improved service effectiveness, improved decision making, and organizational development because they cannot be measured in "hard" dollar values;
- Concentrate all initiative for performance measurement and improvement in a small, centralized group of experts, without trying to get people throughout the government to feel that improving effectiveness and efficiency is *everyone's* business.

TWO FINAL REMINDERS

Two important points must be reemphasized here. These points cannot be repeated too often, as local officials who may attempt to use some of the ideas in this book must never lose sight of their ultimate purpose.

Too often officials using performance measurement forget that these techniques are a *means* to help local government do its job better, not ends in themselves. Repeated again as final reminders, these ideas are:

- *Measurement by itself will not improve local government performance. PEOPLE make DECISIONS to take ACTIONS to improve performance.* Measurement helps people make better decisions and take better actions. Measurement then lets them know the consequences of their actions, how good their decisions were, and how well those decisions were executed.
- *Local government services should be RESPONSIVE to the needs and desires of the community.* All of the approaches discussed in this book are aimed at helping local officials make services more responsive to community needs and desires. Efficiency measurement and improvement respond to the need to keep down the burden of government costs while providing adequate services. Effectiveness measurement and improved communication help local officials see an expansive picture of needs and desires, so they can make decisions and improvements that make local government more responsive to the community.

Appendix
A Resource Guide of
Experienced Organizations

This Resource Guide is intended to help readers obtain further information on local government performance measurement and improvement. Addresses and phone numbers are provided for organizations with experience in performance measurement and improvement.

The listings include government, academic, research, public interest, and other organizations. A brief description is provided for each. Some of the organizations are simply sources of publications, others provide information clearinghouse and bibliographic search services, and still others have actual experience in research, development, and implementation of performance measurement and improvement approaches. The more experienced organizations can often provide useful advice, materials, and referrals. Some can also provide technical assistance.

Council On Municipal Performance (COMP)
84 Fifth Avenue
New York, N.Y. 10011
(212) 243–6603

COMP has years of research experience in many aspects of local government financial management and service delivery, including performance measurement. COMP produces publications and newsletters, holds conferences, and helps market internationally used research and measurement tools. COMP has worked with local governments in New York State to help develop performance measures for a variety of services, and has done numerous comparative performance evaluations of services in American cities.

Division of Government Capacity Building, Office of Policy Development and Research, U.S. Department of Housing and Urban Development
U.S. Department of HUD, 8th Floor
451 7th Street, S.W.
Washington, D.C. 20410
(202) 755–4370

This Division has sponsored the development and demonstration of a wide range of performance measurement, decision making, and productivity improvement procedures, and has sponsored workshops and publications on these topics.

Performance measurement materials and information have been made available through the Division's Capacity Sharing Program, Hartley Fitts, Program Manager and Division Director.

International City Management Association (ICMA)
1120 G Street, N.W.
Washington, D.C. 20005
(202) 626-4600

ICMA has contributed to the literature, research, and practice of performance measurement in local government since before its publication of *Measuring Municipal Activities* by Clarence Ridley and Herbert Simon in 1938. ICMA continues to develop performance measurement materials, provides information through its Management Information Service, and manages a variety of training and technical assistance programs. ICMA often includes performance measurement and productivity improvement in its national conferences, and in regional and state workshops.

Municipal Finance Officers Association (MFOA)
Government Finance Research Center (GFRC)
1750 K Street, N.W., Suite 650
Washington, D.C. 20006
(202) 466-2473

As the research arm of MFOA, the GFRC includes performance measurement and productivity improvement as part of its research and information efforts. These topics are covered in the GFRC's periodical *Resources in Review* which reviews publications and training materials, announces conferences and workshops, and reports on recent developments in local financial management. The GFRC occasionally organizes MFOA training or workshops in performance measurement or productivity improvement.

Municipal Finance Officers Association (MFOA)
180 North Michigan Avenue, Suite 800
Chicago, Ill. 60601
(312) 977-9700

Most MFOA publications, including the periodical *Governmental Finance,* are published from MFOA's headquarters in Chicago. MFOA often includes performance measurement or productivity improvement sessions in its national conferences.

National Association of Counties (NACo)
440 First Street, N.W., 8th Floor
Washington, D.C. 20001
(202) 393-6226

NACo maintains a central reference service, including material on performance measurement and improvement, and has organized training and workshops for local officials on performance measurement and productivity improvement.

National Center for Public Productivity
John Jay College
445 West 59th Street
New York, N.Y. 10019
(212) 489-5030

The Center produces publications and bibliographies dealing with performance measurement and productivity improvement, and operates the National Clearinghouse for Public Productivity, which maintains a bibliographic data base and distributes selected items. The Center also conducts research and training, holds conferences, and publishes the quarterly *Public Productivity Review*.

National League of Cities (NLC)
1301 Pennsylvania Avenue, N.W.
Washington, D.C. 20004
(202) 626-3000

NLC maintains a reference service for local officials, covering local services and their management. Training in performance measurement and improvement is often provided through state municipal leagues.

Public Technology, Incorporated (PTI)
1301 Pennsylvania Avenue, N.W.
Washington, D.C. 20004
(202) 626-2400

PTI has developed descriptive materials and presented workshops on performance measurement and improvement. PTI has also developed computer models for location of public facilities (e.g., fire stations, parks) that have been used in numerous communities, as well as other management and technological approaches to local problems. PTI can provide staff to assist local governments in implementing management and technological improvements.

The RAND Corporation
1700 Main Street
Santa Monica, Calif. 90406
(213) 393-0411

RAND has developed several computer models for location and deployment of fire, police, and ambulance services that have been used by numerous communities. RAND has documented the models, several case studies of their use, and the analytic methodology involved.

Research Triangle Institute (RTI)
P.O. Box 12194
Research Triangle Park, N.C. 27709
(919) 541-6000

RTI has years of research and development experience in local government performance measurement, and has worked with local governments in North Carolina on developing performance measures for a variety of local services.

U.S. Conference of Mayors (USCM)
1620 Eye Street, N.W.
Washington, D.C. 20006
(202) 293-7330

USCM maintains a reference service in local management improvement and provides training for elected local chief executives.

U.S. General Accounting Office (GAO)
Accounting and Financial Management Division
441 G Street, N.W.
Washington, D.C. 20548
(202) 275-5200

The GAO has been an important force in the development and use of performance auditing in government, and has issued guidelines for its use. The GAO also helped develop total performance measurement.

Urban Institute
2100 M Street, N.W.
Washington, D.C. 20037
(202) 223-1950

Through its State and Local Government Research Program, the Urban Institute has been a leader in research and development of state and local government performance measurement and improvement approaches. It has produced numerous practical publications on performance measurement and related topics, and helped local governments develop citizen survey, trained observer, and other measurement techniques. Staff are available on a limited basis for suggestions to governments on their attempts to improve their measurement capabilities.

Workshop on Political Theory and Policy Analysis
Indiana University
814 East Third
Bloomington, Ind. 47405
(812) 335-0441

The Workshop has conducted research and development of ways to measure and evaluate local services, including physical measurement of street lighting and street surface conditions, citizen surveys, and police performance evaluation. The Workshop has published numerous papers and reports on these topics, and worked with local governments in various parts of the country to test and evaluate measurement techniques.

Organizations with expertise in citizen involvement approaches

Civic Action Institute
P.O. Box 39208
Washington, D.C. 20016
(301) 279-6717

The Civic Action Institute has studied and documented the roles of citizens and neighborhood organizations in numerous local governments, including citizen involvement in budgeting and policy making.

Massachusetts Institute of Technology (MIT)
Department of Urban Studies and Planning
77 Massachusetts Avenue
Cambridge, Mass. 02139
(617) 253-2022

MIT's Department of Urban Studies and Planning has been instrumental in the development of the "citizen-based planning" process, and its implementation in several communities (including Arlington, Mass. — see chapter 5).

The Nova Institute
853 Broadway
New York, N.Y. 10003
(212) 533-2530

The Nova Institute helped the City of New York develop and implement its participatory budgeting process involving the city's 59 community boards, developed the initial budget manual for community board participation, and has helped some community boards participate in neighborhood service planning.

Special sources for government sponsored publications

HUD USER
P.O. Box 280
Germantown, Md. 20874
(301) 251-5154

HUD USER maintains full bibliographic citations and annotations for all publications sponsored by HUD's Office of Policy Development and Research (PD&R). Many of these publications can be obtained for a fee by writing or phoning HUD USER. If a publication is not available from HUD USER, ordering information for other sources will often be provided. HUD USER also provides free bibliographic listings on certain topics upon request, or for a fee will do specialized searches of its data base.

U.S. Government Printing Office (GPO)
Superintendent of Documents
U.S. Government Printing Office
Washington, D.C. 20402
(202) 783-3238

Numerous federally sponsored documents on local government management improvement are available for purchase from the U.S. Government Printing Office. Request documents by full title or GPO stock number. Orders must be prepaid or charged to a GPO account. Mastercard and VISA charges are accepted and can be used for phone orders.

National Technical Information Service (NTIS)
5285 Port Royal Road
Springfield, Va. 22161
(703) 487-4600 (general information)

Many federally sponsored documents are available through NTIS as well as the funding agency, contractor, or grantee who prepared the report. After the original source or GPO runs out of stock, copies of federally sponsored reports will often be available for purchase from NTIS. An NTIS order number is needed for each document ordered. To learn the order number for a document, phone (703) 487-4780 (up to three titles accepted by recording; a card will be sent out in about a day with order numbers and prices) or write to the Identification Department at the above address. Once order numbers are known, order by mail at the above address or by phone at (703) 487-4650. Orders must be prepaid or charged to an NTIS account. Mastercard, VISA, and American Express charges are accepted, and may be used for phone orders.

Bibliography

This bibliography is in three parts:

- Part 1, which is fully annotated, lists articles and publications that provide general coverage of performance measurement and improvement (including effectiveness or efficiency measurement in general, and decision making, management, and productivity improvement) as well as more specific publications that cover several measurement and improvement approaches.
- Part 2 lists publications and computer models that concentrate on specific measurement and improvement approaches. Part 2 is divided into seven topics that roughly follow the order of presentation of measurement and improvement approaches in this book.
- Part 3 lists collections of case studies, training materials, bibliographies, and other resource guides on the topics covered in this book.

A word on obtaining publications

Those citations followed by an asterisk (*) are publications which have been available from organizations whose addresses and phone numbers are listed in the appendix. Check with publishers for prices and availability, which are subject to change.

Many of the publications listed below were originally published by government agencies, and as such they are not always easy to find. These are sometimes available at research libraries, and sometimes at the sponsoring agency. There are several clearinghouses, which are repositories of federal publications, from whom copies may be purchased. These clearinghouses often have publications available many years after they are no longer available from the original sponsoring agency or the Government Printing Office. Three clearinghouse organizations are listed in the appendix: HUD USER for HUD publications, the National Technical Information Service (NTIS) for many federal agencies (including HUD), and the National Center for Public Productivity (at John Jay College, New York City) for selected publications from the U.S. Office of Personnel Management and the National Center for Productivity and Quality of Working Life. The relevant program of the U.S. Office of Personnel Management (Washington, D.C.) was ended in 1982, and the entire National Center for Productivity and Quality of Working Life (Washington, D.C.) was ended in the late 1970s. For citations listing either of these organizations, either NTIS or the National Center for Public Productivity (New York) is a more likely source for the publication than the sponsoring agency.

HUD USER and NTIS order numbers are shown for some publications listed below. If no such numbers are lised, a federal publication may still be available from HUD USER or NTIS. See Appendix for the addresses and phone numbers of the three clearinghouse organizations discussed above, for determining whether specific titles are available.

Part 1. General publications on performance measurement and improvement

"A Council Member Looks at Performance Measurement" by Carol deProsse. In *Resources in Review,* Vol. 1, No. 4, May/June 1979, pp. 4-5. Government Finance Research Center, Municipal Finance Officers Association, Washington, D.C.*

These excerpts from a presentation by a city councilmember from Iowa City, Iowa, refer to the continual give and take between elected council and appointed administrators in a realistic performance measurement and budgeting process, and the need for a performance measurement system to allow the council to have political flexibility in its decision making.

"Attributes of Performance Measures" by Gerald Hurst, In *Public Productivity Review,* Vol. 4, No. 1, March 1980, pp. 43-49. National Center for Public Productivity, John Jay College, New York, N.Y.*

Though it does not take a government perspective, this article is an interesting theoretical discussion of the desirable characteristics of performance measures, and the trade-offs among these characteristics that arise in selecting performance measures.

Efficiency Measurement for Local Government Services: Some Initial Suggestions, by Harry P. Hatry, Sumner N. Clarren, Therese Van Houten, Jane P. Woodward, and Pasqual A. DonVito, 1979. Urban Institute, Washington, D.C. (204 pp.)*

This text discusses approaches to measuring the efficiency of local services, with specific suggestions for water supply, apprehension of criminals, central purchasing, and group residential care for children. Attention is paid to the problems of accurate cost estimation, and of accounting for quality of output and difficulty of incoming workload.

Factors Related to Local Government Use of Performance Measurement, by John R. Hall, Jr., 1978. Division of Government Capacity Building, Office of Policy Development and Research, U.S. Department of Housing and Urban Development, Washington, D.C. HUD USER # HUD0000468; NTIS # PB-300-241 (46 pp.)*

This document discusses a number of apparent success and failure factors in the establishment and use of performance measurement in local governments. It is based on interviews with personnel from a number of local governments, and studies of local operating budgets.

How Effective Are Your Community Services? Procedures for Monitoring the Effectiveness of Municipal Services, by Harry P. Hatry, Louis H. Blair, Donald M. Fisk, John M. Greiner, John R. Hall, Jr. and Philip S. Schaenman, 1977. The Urban Institute and the International City Management Association, Washington, D.C. (318 pp.)*

This guidebook contains the most comprehensive compilation of existing effectiveness measures and measurement techniques, covering nine local services: solid waste collection, solid waste disposal, recreation, library, crime control, fire protection, general transportation and public mass transit, water supply, and handling citizen complaints and requests. Specific procedures such as citizen surveys and trained observer techniques are discussed in detail. Illustrative questionnaires and implementation suggestions are included, as well as chapters on efficiency measurement, and on using effectiveness measurement.

Improving Productivity and Decision-Making through the Use of Effectiveness Measures: Interim Working Procedures Manual I, 1979 (92 pp.). Division of Government Capacity Building, Office of Policy Development and Research, U.S. Department of Housing and Urban Development, Washington, D.C. HUD USER # HUD0000647; NTIS # PB-80-136-476.*

The "Working Procedures Manual" documents procedures, suitable for use in a large urban jurisdiction, for matching effectiveness measures with operational decisions in three services (fire, library, street maintenance). It is based on the early experience of the City of Dallas under a HUD demonstration grant. A volume based on the further experience of Dallas and the experience of San Francisco as part of the same grant, as well as other experiences, is being prepared by Public Technology, Inc. of Washington, D.C. under the title *Guide to Implementing Performance Measurement in Large Jurisdictions.*

Improving Productivity of Neighborhood Services: A Washington, D.C. Case Study (2 volumes: "Executive Summary and Assessment," 1979 [21 pp.] and the complete case study, 1978 [192 pp.]) Division of Government Capacity Building, Office of Policy Development and Research, U.S. Department of Housing and Urban Development, Washington, D.C. HUD USER and NTIS Nos: Summary: HUD0000635 and PB-80-136-450; Case Study: HUD0000402 and PB-300-193.*

These publications document Washington, D.C.'s "Neighborhood Services Improvement Project." The project combined industrial engineering, organization development, employee incentive, and citizen participation techniques to significantly improve neighborhood cleanliness in a test district (a problem identified by district residents). Technical procedures used, the coordination of multiple city agencies and neighborhood organizations, and improvements in service efficiency and effectiveness are well documented in the case study. Citizen survey questionnaires used are included.

Managers Guide for Improving Productivity, 1980. U.S. Office of Personnel Management, Washington, D.C. (24 pp.)

This is a "how-to" guide which outlines five steps managers can take to improve productivity.

Managing Local Government for Improved Performance: A Practical Approach by Brian W. Rapp and Frank M. Pattitucci, 1977. Westview Press, Boulder, Col. (422 pp.).

This book provides a comprehensive analysis of the management process in local government and offers guidelines for developing management plans and improving municipal performance. Based largely on the authors' experiences as city manager and finance director of Flint, Michigan, the book includes many brief case examples from Flint to illustrate systemic, political, and incidental problems faced by local managers.

Managing with Performance Measures in Local Government: A Dialogue, edited by Paul Epstein and Gene Ritzenthaler, 1979. Division of Government Capacity Building, Office of Policy Development and Research, U.S. Department of Housing and Urban Development, Washington, D.C. HUD USER # HUD0001172 and NTIS # PB-80-179-666 (24 pp.).*

This is an edited transcript of a discussion among an elected commissioner and the appointed controller of Genessee County, Michigan (pop. 450,000), the city manager and public works director of Sherman, Texas (population 30,000) and the consultant retained by Sherman to help implement a performance measurement system. The panelists briefly describe their measurement approaches and discuss how they each use performance measurement, the benefits they've achieved, why their communities implemented measurement systems, the costs of implementation, and lessons they've learned along the way.

Measures Project Technical Reports Package. Eleven reports (1975-78) available separately or as a package from the Workshop in Political Theory and Policy Analysis, Indiana University, Bloomington, Ind. (216 pp.)*

These are research papers on developing physical measurements of services — particularly street lighting and street surface conditions (roughness) — and relating the physical indicators to citizen perceptions.

Measuring the Effectiveness of Basic Municipal Services: Initial Report, 1974, The Urban Institute and the International City Management Association, Washington, D.C. (118 pp.)*

This report provides an overview of effectiveness measurement and needed procedures.

Measuring Urban Services: A Multi-Mode Approach, by Elinor Ostrom and Roger B. Parks, 1975. Workshop in Political Theory and Policy Analysis, Indiana University, Bloomington, Ind. (129 pp.)*

This is a user-oriented presentation for measuring the output and effectiveness of public agencies, with special focus on street surface and street lighting conditions. Included are citizen survey instruments and designs for special equipment to use in making physical measurements.

Monitoring the Outcome of Social Services, 1977, 6 volumes available individually or as a set. Urban Institute, Washington, D.C.*

While targeted at the five *state* responsibilities under Federal Title XX legislation, these reports may interest local governments with similar service responsibilities, particularly counties. Performance measures are suggested for economic development and employment and training programs, mental health treatment programs, chronic disease control programs, and prison and parole services. Suggestions for data collection and performance monitoring procedures are also included.

Performance Measurement: A Guide for Local Elected Officials, 1980. The Urban Institute, the National League of Cities, and the National Association of Counties, Washington, D.C. (31 pp.)*

This brief guide is aimed at helping local elected officials understand performance measurement and how it can help them make budget decisions, resolve program, policy, and accountability issues, and answer media questions. It explains how performance measurement can guide local officials to take actions that achieve service improvements.

Performance Measurement and Cost Accounting for Smaller Local Governments, 1979. Rhode Island Department of Community Affairs, Providence, R.I. (99 pp.)

This handbook was designed to aid smaller jurisdictions in measuring performance without introducing complex technology or increasing staff. One chapter is devoted to a manual approach for accumulating direct costs to use in calculating efficiency of service activities. Sample forms and worksheets, with step-by-step instructions are included for direct cost accounting.

Performance Measurement Principles and Techniques: An Overview for Local Governments by Harry P. Hatry, 1981. Available from the State and Local Government Research Program, the Urban Institute, Washington, D.C.

This paper provides a procedural overview of local government performance measurement, covering four main topics: criteria for selecting performance measures, types of performance measures, data collection procedures, and how targets can be established. Workload difficulty and equity measurement are also briefly discussed.

Productivity Improvement Handbook for State and Local Government edited by George J. Washnis, 1980. Wiley-Interscience, Somerset, N.J. (1500 pp.)

This is a desktop reference on the tools, techniques, and systems for improving the effectiveness and efficiency of state and local services. Several chapters are devoted to general improvement approaches such as industrial engineering, the application of technology, and organization development. About 30 chapters are devoted to improving specific operating functions and services of state and local government. Many of the functional chapters include performance measurement techniques for the service involved. Over 200 project briefs are included which describe successful applications of performance improvement techniques in state and local governments.

So Mr. Mayor, You Want to Improve Productivity, by John S. Thomas, 1974. National Center for Productivity and Quality of Working Life, Washington, D.C.

This is a brief guide for the local chief executive interested in establishing a performance improvement program. It describes an approach to obtaining and organizing the analytic resources needed to realize the full potential of a performance improvement program, and discusses union participation and public understanding.

The Phoenix Productivity Program, 1979. The City of Phoenix, Ariz. (32 pp.)

This report describes the history of performance improvement efforts in Phoenix and the wide variety of improvement approaches they have put into practice over the years, including organization development and incentive approaches, industrial engineering, and management by objectives. Most of the report is devoted to "productivity briefs" on specific improvements that have been implemented.

Using Productivity Measurement: A Manager's Guide to More Effective Services, Management Information Services Special Report, No. 4, May 1979. International City Management Association, Washington, D.C. (175 pp.) *

This guidebook contains an introduction to performance measurement, and technical details that focus on measuring the effectiveness of solid waste collection and recreation.

Part 2. Publications on specific measurement and improvement approaches

Trained observer techniques for measuring community conditions:

Comparing Citizen and Observer Perceptions of Police-Citizen Encounters, by Roger B. Parks, 1981. Workshop in Political Theory and Policy Analysis, Indiana University, Bloomington, Ind. (22 pp.) *

How Clean is Our City? A Guide for Measuring the Effectiveness of Solid Waste Collection Activities, by Louis H. Blair and Alfred I. Schwartz, 1972. Urban Institute, Washington, D.C. (67 pp.) *

Improving Performance in Honolulu's Park and Street Maintenance, Division of Government Capacity Building, Office of Policy Development and Research, U.S. Department of Housing and Urban Development, Washington, D.C. NTIS # PB-300-201.*

Performance targeting and monitoring: MBO and budget related approaches:

Linkages: Improving Financial Management in Local Government, by Frederick O'R. Hayes, David A. Gossman, Jerry E. Mechling, John S. Thomas, and Steven J. Rosenbloom, 1982, Urban Institute, Washington, D.C.* Discusses relationships among budgeting, accounting, auditing, and performance measurement.

Local Government Program Budgeting: Theory and Practice by Werner Z. Hirsch et al, 1974. Praeger Publishers, New York, N.Y.

"Management by Objectives in Local Government: A System of Organizational Leadership" by Thomas K. Connellan, *Management Information Service Report,* Vol. 7, No. 2A, February, 1975. International City Management Association, Washington, D.C.*

Performance Measurement Manual (for using the city government's performance monitoring and reporting system), 1978. The City of Portland, Oregon.

Zero Base Budgeting in the Public Sector, by Peter C. Sarant, 1978. Addison-Wesley Publishing Company, Reading, Mass.

Industrial engineering and operations research approaches:

Improving Municipal Productivity: Work Measurement for Better Management, 1975. National Center for Productivity and Quality of Working Life, Washington, D.C.

Improving Productivity Using Work Measurement (2 volumes: "A Management Report" and "A Technical Guide"), 1977. Public Technology, Inc., Washington, D.C.*

"Work Measurement in Local Government," by Patrick Manion, *Management Information Service Report,* Vol. 6, No. 10, October, 1974. International City Management Association, Washington, D.C.*

Work Schedule Design Handbook: Methods for Assigning Employee Work Shifts and Days Off, 1978, 2 volumes: "Summary and Introduction" (23 pp.) and the complete handbook (368 pp.) by the Institute for Public Policy Analysis. Division of Government Capacity Building, Office of Policy Development and Research, U.S. Department of Housing and Urban Development, Washington, D.C. HUD USER and NTIS Nos.: Summary: HUD0000427 and PB-300-210; Handbook: HUD0000428 and PB-300-193.*

Computer models and related publications:

Equipment Management Information System, computer programs and user documentation for vehicle and heavy equipment fleet management. Public Technology, Inc., Washington, D.C.*

Fire Resource Management Package, computer programs and procedures manual, including the *Fire Station Location Package* (computer programs and 4 volumes: "Chief Executive's Report," "Fire Chief's Report," "Project

Leader's Guide," and "Project Operations Guide"), and the *Strategic Fire Planning System* (programs and user documentation). Public Technology, Inc., Washington, D.C.*

Parking Meter Control System, computer programs and user documentation. Public Technology, Inc., Washington, D.C.*

"Public Facilities Location Model" available in two versions: *Ambulance Services Location Package* and *Leisure Service Location Package* (each package uses the same computer program and each has its own version of a "Management Report" and a "Project Operations Guide"). Public Technology, Inc., Washington, D.C.*

RAND Emergency Service Deployment Models: Five Models for location of fire, police, and ambulance/paramedic stations, and for deployment of police patrol cars and paramedic rescue units. Numerous publications describe these models, including:

- *The Deployment of Emergency Services: A Guide to Selected Methods and Models* by Warren Walker (discusses all RAND models), 1975. RAND Corporation, Santa Monica, Calif.*

- *Deployment Methodology for Fire Departments,* 1975. RAND Corporation, Santa Monica, Calif.*

- *Improving Station Locations and Dispatching Practices in Fire Departments – A Guide for Fire Chiefs and Local Government Executives,* 1978. Division of Government Capacity Building, Office of Policy Development and Research, U.S. Department of Housing and Urban Development, and the U.S. Government Printing Office, Washington, D.C.*

- *Patrol Allocation Methodology for Police Departments,* 1975. RAND Corporation, Santa Monica, Calif.*

Organization development, incentives, and other motivational approaches:

Employee Incentives to Improve State and Local Government Productivity, 1975. National Center for Productivity and Quality of Working Life, Washington, D.C. NTIS # PB-293-474.*

Human Factors in Productivity Improvement Project (based on a City of San Diego Project), 3 volumes: "A Case Study," 1978, "Assessment Report," 1979, and "Teambuilding Workshop Modules," 1979. Division of Government Capacity Building, Office of Policy Development and Research, U.S. Department of Housing and Urban Development, Washington, D.C. HUD USER and NTIS Nos.: "A Case Study": HUD0000457 and PB-300-232; "Assessment": HUD0000456 and PB-300-231; "Teambuilding": HUD0000458 and PB-300-233.*

Improving Productivity and the Quality of Work Life, by Thomas G. Cummings and Edmund S. Molley, 1977. Praeger Publishers, New York, N.Y. (305 pp.)

Labor-Management Committees in the Public Sector: Experiences of Eight Committees, 1975. National Center for Productivity and Quality of Working Life, Washington, D.C. (70 pp.)

Monetary Incentives and Work Standards: Impacts and Implications for Management and Labor, by Greiner, Dahl, Hatry, and Millar, 1977. Urban Institute, Washington, D.C.*

Motivating Managers: Guide to Performance Targeting and Performance Based Pay in State and Local Governments, 1982. Public Technology, Inc., Washington, D.C.*

Productivity and Motivation: A Review of State and Local Government Initiatives, by Greiner, Hatry, Koss, Millar, and Woodward, 1981. Urban Institute, Washington, D.C. (488 pp.) *

Total Performance Management Project ("Trijurisdictional Project": 5 volumes, including a "Case Study" from each local government and an "Executive Summary" for the entire project), 1980. Cities of Long Beach, Manhattan Beach, and San Diego, Calif., and the U.S. Office of Personnel Management, Washington, D.C.

Total Performance Management: Some Pointers for Action, National Center for Productivity and Quality of Working Life, 1978. NTIS # PB-300-249 (49 pp.)*

Program evaluation and performance auditing:

"Performance Audits in Local Government — Benefits, Problems, and Challenges," by Herbert A. O'Keefe, Jr., *Management Information Service Report,* Vol. 8, Special Report, April, 1976. International City Management Association, Washington, D.C.*

Practical Program Evaluation for State and Local Governments (second edition), by Harry P. Hatry, Richard E. Winnie, and Donald M. Fisk, 1981. Urban Institute, Washington, D.C. (123 pp.)*

Program Analysis for State and Local Governments, by Harry P. Hatry, Louis H. Blair, Donald M. Fisk, and Wayne A. Kimmel, 1976. Urban Institute, Washington, D.C. (155 pp.)*

Program Evaluation and Analysis (2 volumes: "A Management Report" and "A Technical Guide"), 1977. Public Technology, Inc., and the Division of Government Capacity Building, Office of Policy Development and Research, U.S. Department of Housing and Urban Development, Washington, D.C. HUD USER and NTIS Nos.: Management Report: HUD00000008 and PB-300-007; Technical Guide: HUD00000009 and PB-300-008.*

"The Case for the Internal Auditor in Local Government: The Eyes and Ears of Public Officials and the People," by Robert M. Atkisson and Edward P. Chait, in *Governmental Finance,* Vol. 7, No. 3, November 1978. Municipal Finance Officers Association, Chicago, Ill.*

Using Auditing to Improve Efficiency and Economy. Audit Standard Series, No. 7, 1975. The U.S. General Accounting Office and the U.S. Government Printing Office, Washington, D.C.*

Citizen surveys and public marketing:

701 Planning and Management – Dallas, Texas: City Profile Survey. International City Management Association, Washington, D.C.*

An Introduction to Sample Surveys for Government Managers by Carol H. Weiss and Harry P. Hatry, 1971. Urban Institute, Washington, D.C. (48 pp.)*

Comparing Citizen and Observer Perceptions of Police-Citizen Encounters by Roger B. Parks, 1981. Workshop in Political Theory and Policy Analysis, Indiana University, Bloomington, Indiana (22 pp.)*

"Marketing and Local Government Service Delivery," by James R. Cleaveland, in *Public Management,* May 1980, pp. 12–14. International City Management Association, Washington, D.C.*

Obtaining Citizen Feedback: The Application of Citizen Surveys to Local Governments by Kenneth Webb and Harry P. Hatry, 1973. Urban Institute, Washington, D.C. (105 pp.)*

Surveying Citizens for Police Performance Assessments, by Roger B. Parks, 1981. Workshop in Political Theory and Policy Analysis, Indiana University, Bloomington, Ind. and the U.S. Government Printing Office, Washington, D.C. (165 pp.)*

Using Citizen Surveys to Evaluate Policing, by Gordon P. Whitaker, Elinor Ostrom, and Roger B. Parks. Workshop in Political Theory and Policy Analysis, Indiana University, Bloomington, Ind. (14 pp.)*

Citizen involvement in service improvement and policy making:

Citizen Involvement in the Design, Assessment, and Delivery of Public Services, by Lawrence E. Susskind, 1976. Department of Urban Studies and Planning, Massachusetts Institute of Technology, Cambridge, Mass.*

Citizen Involvement in the Local Planning Process: A Handbook for Municipal Officials and Citizen Involvement Groups, by Lawrence E. Susskind, 1976. Department of Urban Studies and Planning, Massachusetts Institute of Technology, Cambridge, Mass.*

Citizens and the Local Budget Process: Working Papers on Community Development, 1980. Available from the Civic Action Institute, Washington, D.C.*

Guide to the District Resource Statement: New York City's New Approach to Community Level Budget and Service Information, 1980. The City of New York (66 pp.)

Innovative Citizen Roles in Local Budget-Making, 1981. Civic Action Institute, Washington, D.C.*

Manual for Public Participation in the Fiscal Year 1982 Budget Process, 1980. The City of New York (113 pp.). This manual is updated annually. Manuals for later fiscal years may also be available.

Sanitation: A Guide to Community Board Participation in Planning the Delivery of Services, 1979. The City of New York (103 pp.)

Part 3. Collections of case studies, training materials, bibliographies, and other resource guides

A Casebook in Public Budgeting and Financial Management, edited by Carol W. Lewis and Grayson A. Walker III, 1984. Prentice-Hall, Englewood Cliffs, N.J.

Current Approaches to Financial Management: A Directory of Practices, 1979. International City Management Association, Washington, D.C. (80 pp.)* These 44 minicase studies include six on performance measurement and several more on budgeting systems involving performance measurement.

Effectiveness Measures: Literature and Practice Review, 1979. Division of Government Capacity Building, Office of Policy Development and Research, U.S. Department of Housing and Urban Development, Washington, D.C. HUD USER # HUD0001225; NTIS # PB-80-179-716.*

Improving Governmental Productivity, Selected Case Studies, 1977. National Center for Productivity and Quality of Working Life, Washington, D.C. (84 pp.)

Performance Measurement and Improvement of Local Services: Proceedings of National Workshops, 1980. Public Technology, Inc., and the Division of Government Capacity Building, U.S. Department of Housing and Urban Development, Washington, D.C. HUD USER # HUD0050758; NTIS # PB-81-128-548.* Includes presentations by six jurisdictions, workshop findings, expert resource contact list, and bibliography.

The PRACTICAL IDEAS Series (five booklets, 20–40 pages each, describing 18 HUD-funded projects involving productivity improvement approaches used in over 200 state and local governments, including descriptions and ordering information for more than 85 training manuals, case studies, handbooks, research reports, and computer programs), 1979. Division of Government Capacity Building, Office of Policy Development and Research, U.S. Department of Housing and Urban Development, Washington, D.C. The titles of these booklets are:

- *Practical Ideas for the Government That Has Everything — Including Productivity Problems*, HUD USER # HUD0000801; NTIS # PB-80-122-013.*
- *Practical Ideas for Small Governments Facing Big Problems*, HUD USER # HUD0000785; NTIS # PB-80-122-005.*
- *Practical Ideas for Governments Facing Planning and Scheduling Problems*, HUD USER # HUD0000782; NTIS # PB-80-121-973.*
- *Practical Ideas on Ways for Governments to Work Together*, HUD USER # HUD0000784; NTIS # PB-80-121-999.*
- *Summary of Productivity Improvement Projects*, HUD USER # HUD 0000783; NTIS # PB-80-121-981.*

Productivity and Program Evaluation in the Public Sector: An Annotated Bibliography, by Charles R. Wise, 1978. Available from MITC Publications, Indiana University School of Public and Environmental Affairs, Bloomington, Ind.

Productivity in Local Government, by Frederick O'R. Hayes, 1977. Lexington Books, Lexington, Mass. Case studies of productivity programs in eight jurisdictions, with an overall analysis.

Sources and Resources for Public Financial Administration, an annotated bibliography and resource guide compiled by Donald Levitan, 1983. Government Research Publications, Newton Center, Massachusetts.

Trainer's Resource Service Catalog of Resources, Vol. 4: Training in Productivity Improvement, the National Training and Development Service, 1980. Academy for State and Local Government, Washington, D.C. (77 pp.) Lists programs, courses, publications, audio-visual materials.

Tried and Tested: Case Studies in Municipal Innovation, edited by Fred S. Knight and Michael D. Rancer, 1978. International City Management Association, Washington, D.C. (190 pp.)*

Urban Management Curricula on *Policy Program Analyses and Techniques* (series of modules for local managers and public administration students and teachers, available separately or as a group, including: *Management-by-Objectives* and *Performance/Program Budgeting*) by the National Training and Development Service, 1978. Academy for State and Local Government, Washington, D.C.

Workforce Effectiveness: Personnel Bibliography Series No. 118, 1980. U.S. Office of Personnel Management and the U.S. Government Printing Office, Washington, D.C.*

Index

Work (continued)
  methods or procedures, 23–25, 59, 61,
    199, 203
  observation techniques, 90–93
  performance targets, 60
  quality, 22, 24, 63, 90, 99–101, 203
  sampling, 86, 90–93, 114
  sampling, periodic, 121
  scheduling, 90, 101, 114, 121
  simplification, 89

  standards, 23–25, 59, 60, 85–94, 96, 97,
    98, 121, 183, 193, 199
  standards, engineered, 24, 54, 118, 203
  standards, historical, 23, 203
  structure, 61
Workload, 3, 38, 76, 85, 97, 176
  difficulty, 22–23

Zero base budgeting, 123